Marooned on Moloka'i

Coconuts, Dreams and Death

Kalikiano Kalei

Aeolian Flights Press

SACRAMENTO, CALIFORNIA

Kalikiano Kalei/Aeolian Flights Press
5960 S. Land Park Drive, #256
Sacramento, CA 95822-3313 USA
webs.lanset.com/aeolusaero

Publisher's Note: This is a work of fiction. Names, characters, places, and incidents are a product of the author's imagination. Locales and public names are sometimes used for atmospheric purposes. Any resemblance to actual people, living or dead, or to businesses, companies, events, institutions, or locales is completely coincidental.

Book Layout © 2017 BookDesignTemplates.com

Marooned on Moloka'i/ Kalikiano Kalei. -- 1st ed.
ISBN 978-0-692-94448-6

Dedicated to Carlo and the good ship VANDA, wherever they may presently be!

"Life is the farce which everyone must perform".

—Arthur Rimbaud

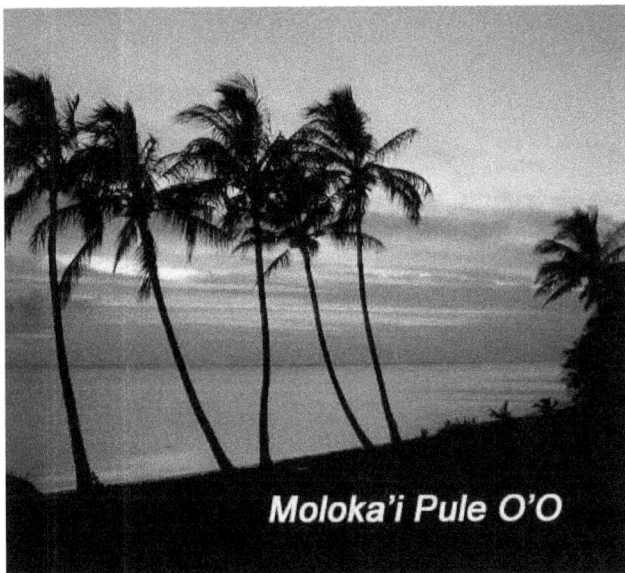

Moloka'i Pule O'O

Being the log of a 30 day stay on the island of Moloka'i, known to the ancient Hawaiians as '*Moloka'i the Island of Powerful Prayers*' ('*Moloka'i Pule O'O*'), owing to its much respected (and also feared) kahuna sorcerers. *Lanikaula* in particular, on the east end of the island who trained *Kahuna Anaana* (priests who were reported to be able to 'pray people to death', such was their spiritual *mana*), to this day is respected by the locals. Today, official Hawaiian State PR would have us believe that the island is '*The Friendly Island*'...but woe to the *haole malihini* (mainland outsider) who disregards the old customs and legends that permeate the island in his naïve enthusiasms to '*live the Hawaiian Dream*' there...

Foreplay: a prologue of sorts
(with sincere apologies to *Mark Twain* and the *Hawaiian kanaka maoli*)

History records that the first use of a journal in the Hawaiian Islands occurred when Captain James Cook and the officers of HMS Resolution set down on paper their impressions of the 'discovery' of the 'Sandwich Islands' and their native inhabitants in 1778, after temporarily misplacing the ship's compass and stumbling across the islands by accident (the actual credit for 'first western discovery' seems to go to the Spanish in 1555, who were too busy buckling their swashes to make a big deal of it). Of course, it remained for the 'infidel' Christian Protestants (they weren't pagan, you see) who followed on Cook's coat-tails to set the wheels of literacy in motion among the Sandwich Islanders, after first taking the spoken Hawaiian language and developing a Romanised alphabet suited to that language's unique syllables and sounds.

Next, the Christian invaders remodeled the islands after their own unique interpretation of a liberal Scots Presbyterian's concept of paradise. The rest is all land speculation, greedy profiteering, and real estate development.

If you've been to the islands as a visitor, chances are great that you've seen the obligatory tourist hula, sat through the fire-dancing at the showcase *lu'au* (most of it is actually Tahitian), wondered if those coconut-half bras the dancing gals all wore were as irritating to certain tender parts of the upper female body as they looked, and if you ever wasted any time wondering what a Scotsman wears under his kilt...*forget it!*...ponder instead what a hula girl wears under her Ti-leaf skirt.

Our brief hysterical recap of the islands concluded, now you are presented with a unique opportunity: to experience a very special part of what is regarded as 'older Hawaii' through the glazed eyes of a genuine, card-carrying, currently-*Malihini*-but-soon-to-be-*Kama'aina*-*Molokaiian*.

If parts of this journal seem occasionally to plough precipitously to port, shear shockingly to starboard, list dangerously in heavy seas of completely unrelated trivialities, wallow willfully, and blunder unbeckoned onto dangerously shallow (minded) shoals of surreptitious sublimation, tangential trivia, effervescent effluvia, lugubriously lurid laments, etc., relax…there's doubtless more allegorical turbidity ahead.

Press enthusiastically forward with me, inspired initially by Cook's voyages of discovery and later by Twain's 1866 voyages of whimsical observation, to venture into the remotest recesses of the author's mind, where no other man assuredly has ever gone before (or ever wants to go again, parallels to the voyages of the Starship *USSS Starpoop's* exploits not withstanding).

Actually, the chances of anyone reading this through tome all the way to the end are remote to slim (more likely: death from boredom half-way), and hopefully well after my own death from a severe case of being *"too full of it"*.

A LOG OF 30 DAYS ON 'MOLOKA'I PULE O'O

April 11th, 2005 (Monday)

Flight out from mainland on Hawaiian airlines (9th, the day before) was smooth and uneventful. Arrived in Honolulu after an unremarkable flight on Boeing 767-570 (latest & greatest version) and caught the local (*Island Air*) connection (DeHavilland Dash-8 twin turbo) flight from the Honolulu Inter-Island terminal to Ho'olehua Airport on Moloka'i. Budget Rent-a-Car was waiting for me with a bright (screaming) yellow, late model Chevy Cavalier—so much for my idea of remaining low-profile (non-touristy). Normally I like bright yellow as a color, but this time did not want to advertise myself as a newly arrived *haole* (Royal Hawaiian Ali'i yellow being a royal color or not!).

While waiting in line for my car, I had a momentary contact with a *haole kama'aina* (an older white-haired Caucasian man, in this case resident on the island for 20 years). He was leaving on the plane I had just arrived in for the return flight to Honolulu and had to turn in his rental quickly; since the plane was already warming up, he asked me if he could go ahead of me in the line. When I told him we had just bought some property on the island and planned to build a house, the response accompanying his stark look of pity had a brief but chilling impact: *"Good luck in finding someone to build it!"* Uh-oh!

Cicada was waiting for me at the airport, so I followed her in my car to the place where she had made arrangements for me to stay, a room in the Ranch Camp (a small subdivision of Kaunakakai, formerly plantation housing) house owned by her friend, Mrs. Inocencia Baitan. The 'room' turned out to be a large detached room measuring about 10 x 15, with a separate but

9

adjacent shower and toilet. The amenities included a two-element hotplate, microwave and fridge, along with a toaster, portable fan and vertical heater.

The bed (a large double) was quite comfortable (firm'ish) and there was a roomy closet as well. Louvered windows on two sides assured a good Trades breeze to keep things cool. After meeting Mrs. Baitan, aged 65, and her husband Selix (90 years old and looking only 70!), Cicada and I went to look at my new property, which lies directly next to hers.

Regardless of what I was expecting, the first sight of the property was a bit of a shock, since it is basically a recently cleared strip of land sloping down to the *Kaloko'eli Fishpond*, measuring 50 feet across at the Kamehameha V roadhead and extending 160 feet back towards the shore. Cicada said she had whacked the weeds recently and sprayed 'Round-up' weed killer on the plot. The sea side end of the property (*Makai*) ends in a thick tangle of Mangroves (an imported tree, not native to the islands, and now a nuisance growth in many shore areas on Molokai) and the property has a sloping plane that drops off a bit more sharply at the fishpond end.

Mindful of the two types of indigenous, man-eating termites that infest Molokai, my plan for building a house suddenly loomed in my mind as infinitely costly and complex—concrete pilings would be absolutely mandatory for the home's ground floor.

At any rate, Cicada pulled out two chairs and we sat in the shade, chugging no-caffeine *Sprite* and 'taking story' (chatting about nothing in particular and everything in general). I gave her some background on myself and Suki, and she told me about herself and Ferdie (her husband). Turns out Cicada is a Molokai native, having been born on the island (she's about 59), and a teacher by profession. Her mother was a resident from the early

30s and passed away in 1950, leaving some property in the K'kai area to her survivors.

Cicada told me that she had inherited two parcels of land, her brother one also, and her nephew another (the one Suki and I bought). The brother married a Hong Kong woman whom Cicada apparently doesn't get along with, so she informed me she doesn't speak to her brother and his wife much these days. Apparently, the mother's property was contested by her brother, so that created a lot of intra-sib bad feelings (from what I infer). Interestingly, *brother* runs the island's only gun shop and his wife (the Hong Kong *'dragon lady'*) operates one of three ladies' beauty salons on the island.

After a while, having enjoyed the cool tropical trade winds blowing the coconut palm tops for about an hour, we drove down to the K'kai downtown area and I bought some groceries from *'The Friendly Market'* and a loaf of bread from the *Kanemitsu Bakery* (just a few basic things like 2 pounds of Molokai Espresso coffee beans, Instant Quaker Oats, some Spam, a sack of rice, some utensils, a gallon of water, and a few sacks of dried fruit...*really*) for $91.00.

Then, after a loop to K'kai wharf to see the Maui Ferry arrive (*The Molokai Princess*), we stopped at the relatively new *'Paddler's Inn'*, a pub and restaurant owned by the former operators of the Molokai Hotel (which is now operated by an off-island hotel chain). Having mentioned island architect Daniel Crispin to Cicada (she informed me he is now about 70 and semi-retired), she told me about another younger architect she knows, who has an office next the Paddler's Inn (this may prove fortunate, since my single email contact with Crispin revealed he is presently otherwise engaged and has no time for new projects).

The dinner at Paddler's was good (I had the steak special, that included sides of beans, macaroni salad, a scoop of rice (the typical 'local' usually consumes TWO scoops of rice with his meals) and a salad for a total of about $20.00) and afterwards Cicada dropped me off at my new room. Just before bed, I called Suki in Sacramento up on my cell phone, which functioned moderately well although the signal seemed to ebb & flow like the tide; at least I know it worked!

My expectations of complete island peace were considerably off base by a wide margin, as I quickly learned when I went to bed that all the Ranch Camp neighbors keep chickens. Fine enough, except that this means absolute legions of loud, horny roosters crowing all night long. Sure enough, this raucous cock-a-doodle-dooing kept pace with the passage of each hour, basically nullifying the soothing effects of the *Actifed* I usually take at bedtime.

Still, I managed to get in enough sleep to satisfy my requirements and stayed in the sack until about 0630 hours in the morning. Getting up, an act synonymous with drinking some java, I put a pot of it on, read a chapter in my book about the history of Hawaiian coffee, and was about to start writing this page in my journal when the closest neighbor decided to take what sounded like a 200 HP weed whacker on steroids and clear out his entire back yard—using the entire the family labor pool. This was exactly the sort of insane ambient noise that I had fled from back in Sacramento and yet here I was in paradise, learning that there is no real escape from the depredacious downside of technology today—no matter *where* you are.

So, despite the background of the weed whackers, grass mowers, and non-stop day & night rooster crowing, I finally managed to commit these opening observations to paper. As I write this, I am well reminded of the recent legal case in California where a fellow went amok and killed his neighbor over a long-standing dispute about the other fellow's free-ranging chickens and roosters. Must have had a severe sensitivity to noise like me and finally snapped, after being continually frustrated in his multi-year efforts to have the neighbors' roosters & chickens banned as a zoning violation (city residence versus country use zone). We shall see how well I end up handling the roosters—in reality I have no choice in the matter. The room is only $300 for the whole month of April, after all.

Since it's now about noon, I think I'll take off in the rental car, grab some ice cream at the local creamery downtown and maybe do some reconnoitering & area recon in my *Screaming Yellow (Chevy) Zonker*. Tomorrow I'll try to hook-up a broad-band inter-face connection at the K'kai community center and up/download to the internet.

Weather is beautiful: daytime is mild (mid-70s, but high humidity) and sunny, with light winds and occasional clouds. Nighttimes are cool, in the low-to-mid 60s, but with gentle breezes to keep things fresh. Pretty much this way most of the year here, except in the winter, when there are occasional storms and strong trade winds.

Later in the afternoon I went up H-way 470 to the *Paia Au State Park*—about 5.5 miles from the convergence with H-way 450—to *Ka Ule o Nanahoa* (the famous phallic rock formation). It was raining very lightly and the top of the park was encased in cloud. On the whole, the overall mood was grey and mysterious as the heavy cloud settled on everything—dripping on trees, rocks, and undergrowth. Overhead the trades rocked the tree tops and murmured through their foliage, adding substantially to the somber effect already established.

I hiked the short 500 or so yards through the trees to the phal-lic rock and found myself bemused for second time by its graphic shape and reputation as a focus of fertility for the ancient Hawai-ians. About 100 yards further down the trail, and somewhat lesser known to the outside world, is another large rock that has the appearance of a vagina or vulva. Legend has it that both these rocks could work powerful effects on those who spent a night on them and many tales tell of hitherto barren women who became pregnant shortly after visiting the phallic rock.

Standing there next to these massive earthly totems and lis-tening to the silence (broken only by the soft fall of rain and the indistinct murmur of wind in the trees), was about as spiritual an experience as I have had in a long time. I could easily see how the ancients could believe the rocks held great *mana* (spiritual power). There was no one else up there except me at the time, so the experience was particularly profound. Strangely, it was an experience of considerable peacefulness and calm resolve, but you could definitely sense great mystery in the thick tangle of nearby undergrowth. The locals all believe great forces of spir-itual power inhabit these woods.

Interestingly, visitors leave offerings on the rocks, typically a coin or token wrapped in Ti-leaves. It takes a bit of imagination to visualize this high perch of land as it originally was (totally nude and devoid of tree growth, since in the past decades great groves of trees have sprouted up to shroud the site in foliage. Add the sea fog that filters in and among them and the effect is positively enchanting (as in sorcery)…especially when the Trades are blowing.

Afterwards, a drive home and a dinner of SPAM and rice (SPAM is, of course, an island delicacy and favorite, but NOT to me. Yuk!), then to bed.

April 12th, 2005 (Tuesday)

Lazy Monday. Got up at about 0630 (thanks to *foul fowl* alarm clocks), had some of the delicious *Kanemitsu* apple bread loaf I bought yesterday and made coffee. Then it was up and at 'em, trying to orient myself in K'kai. No joy trying to scare up Rand Salsado (the local computer guy), so I dropped in at the drug store (*Moloka'i Drugs*, a long time island institution) and got a few things (some books, a coffee cup, and sunscreen lotion). Severe stomach upset last evening (the usual upset & gas pain, & loose gut I occasionally suffer from), but seemed to be OK on rising. Then bought a few groceries at *'Friendly Market'*, found out that there is a one-month long Kaunakakai USPS mailbox wait-list (*"Would you like to get on it, sir?"*).

Next stop was the Molokai Visitors' Bureau for some information, which was helpful, and I also managed to find Guido Montero, the architect Cicada had suggested I look up. Turns out that Guido is not a certified architect, but merely an architectural draftsman (oh well). We sat down and discussed the possibilities of drafting a home plan for my planned dwelling and he produced a nice plantation style plan, one thousand square feet, rectangular in size, and built upon pilings. Also found out that the property is in a flood area (gulp!), requiring a special clearance from Maui County, but since it would be built up above the ground, Guido said he didn't think that would necessarily be a problem. He also said he had some friends in the Maui County Public Works Department, so that would undoubtedly help the process along, if need be. He also suggested getting the water line and meter in right away (as soon as the escrow closed), since he confided that word had it that the meter installation would go up from $6000 to about $9000 at the end of the month. The water line will cost about $2000 and with the $6000 for the meter, that's $8000 in addition to the $84,000 purchase price, with no provision for a home structure! The design he produced looked great (pretty much exactly the simple, basic dwelling I was visualizing in my mind's eye, amazingly enough) and when asked about costs for building it, he mentioned about $150 per ft squared, which is $150,000 for *'good quality work'*. Suki's going to love that! Everything in the way of construction materials must be brought to the island by barge, of course.

At any rate, we agreed that as soon as escrow closed, I would contact him and we would start getting the ducks in a line for the water line & meter permit process, since that at least should be completed before I leave the island (ideally).

Next, tried to contact 'Pete' at *Molokai Bicycle*, but again no joy. I left a message for a call-back on his cell phone VM, but nothing so far. Then I managed to find Rand at *MoBettah.net* and asked about a USB cable to use to download my camera images to my laptop, but no luck there. And since there's nothing resembling a computer store on Molokai, that idea is probably still-born. Jack at MoBettah.net is the real computer guru, but he's out for the day. I need to contact him tomorrow to ask him about my incomplete internet connection at the Kaunakakai Elementary School Computer Resources Building.

Which leads to the next item: after finding absolutely no internet help at Sturgess' coffee house (they have WiFi), I managed to contact the school, where I was told they could connect me to the internet via an Ethernet connection.

Sure enough, from 3 to 5 and from 6 to 8 PM daily, their internet access is available for the public to use. I managed to configure my laptop for internet access well enough, but found for some frustrating reason that while I could download email, I couldn't send anything out! I hope it's something as simple as my server's time-out setting (at *Lanset*, which I suspect it may well be…with any luck, that is). Frustrating enough to find, but more so since I was just getting a grip on things when we were chased out for dinner (from 5 to 6 PM). I'll not return to the school this evening, since I'm not at my best in the evening anyway. Will wait until tomorrow and maybe try to contact Rand Salsada again. If no luck there, then it's back to the school at 3PM Tuesday to struggle through the process some more. Never seemed to have an easy and natural touch with computers in the past and the present situation seems to conform to the norm perfectly (at least I'm consistent!).

The last event of the day was a trip to the old *Molokai Coffee Plantation*, which is now under new (off-island) ownership (again). However, at least they have the old coffee shop and gift shop open again. I had a double espresso and chatted with the help for a few minutes. I also learned that my real estate broker (Cheryl Apaia) was located right next to the Kahulua Post Office—in a beauty shop! Drove the two blocks and found that she owns and operates the beauty-shop, but also runs her real estate business from there as a side-line. Much surprised to find that Cheryl is an older, blonde Caucasian; she apparently married a native (they prefer to be called 'locals') Hawaiian. At any rate, we talked for about half an hour about this and that, including the cause of her husband's death (dissecting aorta) five years ago, the fact that she had to return an 8-week old Maltese Terrier today to its owner (too high a maintenance cost, she said), and a bit about the ancient legendary Hawaiian *'Night Marchers'* (ghosts of long-dead Hawaiian royalty and their ghostly retainers who reappear *en masse* on certain days of the lunar moon). Cheryl's quite a character; psychic and very much into astrology—both conventional and Hawaiian.

After I left Cheryl (we discussed the sale of the property and agreed to close escrow earlier than the 25th, freeing up more time to take care of the water line and meter installation), I returned to my room at the Baitans in Ranch Camp. And now it is nearly 7 PM and too dark to continue pecking away at the computer. All for today, after a hunk of cold turkey SPAM for dinner (yum... *NOT!*), and the stomach already rumbling ominously. *Ulp!*

April 13, 2005 (Wednesday)

Awakened at 6 AM to a chorus of barking dogs, wild bird song, and the ever-present rooster crowing; not actually awakened, really, but rather permitted to return to consciousness by that part of my awareness that is learning to blank out the above incessant noise that is a constant and continuous background in this section of Ranch Camp.

Last thoughts at bedtime last night were strong feelings of insecurity over what I have willingly fallen into: a hasty acquisition of some property (a money hole) on Molokai that promises to be an endless string of expensive necessities. The land is itself $84,000, with another $8,000 for waterline hookup and installation of a water metering device. This is attended by a quarterly tax due on property of about $675. The next step is the building of a house, which in the simplest 1000 ft sq form suggested by Guido Montero will cost about $150 per square foot to build (if it is done now—if done 5 years hence, who knows how much more?). We had to scramble to raise the money for the property (home equity loan of $53,000, plus Suki's cashed-in Fed Savings Bonds, sale of my beloved Porsches, and a few other things). With only about 5-7 more years of work for the State of California left before retirement, one can't help but wonder about "how?" And that doesn't factor in the cost of fairly regular flights to and from the states to take care of details, take care of the property, etc., etc. Thoughts of what probably flashes through the minds of people in quicksand that is rapidly rising over their heads stream through my mind. Must try to put these thoughts aside and take a positive approach. It's almost too late for any alternative plan of action.

Today's agenda includes attempting to contact either Rand Salsada or Jack at MoBettah.net to see if my email is working properly. Then another attempt to link up via the local school's Ethernet internet connection later this afternoon.

Wednesday seems to be *"the day"* when everyone in K'kai chooses to be active. The new *Molokai Island Times* newspaper (funded by anti-virus guru John MacByte and operated by his cousin, thinly disguised as an advocacy front for MacByte, so I am told by some) is published on this day and *Pete's Molokai Bicycles* is also open in the afternoon from 3 to 6PM. Speaking of MacByte's paper, I was told by Cheryl Apaia that MacByte's publicly announced intention of using his several thousand acres of Molokai East End property to build homes for himself and his family wasn't quite the *whole* story. According to Cheryl, MacByte is into what she called *"Kama Sutra Yoga"* (I discern she was referring to *Tantric Yoga*); one doesn't really need much imagination to visualise what this is, even if the descriptive term she used is inaccurate. The appearance of several beautiful young women to speak at public debates on his behalf during the recently very contentious public furor over sale of some of his extensive property on Molokai's East End (identified only as 'close friends') would thus appear to be explained.

After all, power is the ultimate aphrodisiac, and money such as MacByte has certainly buys him one hell of a whopping package of 'power'. Other rumored affinities consist of drugs, etc. Sex, drugs, and rock & roll. What else is new? Apparently (from what Cheryl tells me) MacByte has a very strong opinion of himself and confidence in his attitudes (*natch!*—so would I, if I had gobs of money). Cheryl told me of a local friend who apparently went on a sailing cruise with him that saw a lot of substance use/abuse throughout the trip.

One big problem has occurred with regard to email connections here. I can download email, but not send out through the school's Ethernet connection. Rand Salsada of 'Salsada and Sons' computer repair here on Molokai just called via cell-phone to explain my problem. He said that since the school has internet connection, but no email server, my regular pop3 email won't function. What I need to do is go to the Lanset website and log in there to access my mail that way—at the server site, apparently (since I was able to send and receive that way through the Porsche website). Makes sense! Another problem to overcome in this sojourn to Molokai! Hopefully I can take care of the difficulties this afternoon at the school before being chased out at 5PM (as yesterday).

Lots of clouds today. Overhead formations of clouds are spontaneously created from the surrounding waters by the thermal interference caused by the island land masses that counterbalance the cooler depths. This is what brings water to the islands, so it's all part of the natural life support system that nourishes these otherwise isolated coral and volcanic mountain tops.

My early morning cups of java are the perfect excuse to peruse a few chapters in whatever I am currently reading. At present, I am wading through Stewart Lee Allen's fascinating *"The Devil's Cup"* (*"A History of the World According to Coffee"*). His thesis is that the real rise of human rationalism is/was due to the discovery and widespread adoption of coffee. Using a writing style that is as fresh and invigorating as a triple espresso, he describes a personal journey of discovery he made to follow the history of coffee from its early antecedents in Africa to its transmission to (by the Turks) and adoption by Europe. A fascinating read and filled with a lot of carefully researched factoids and documentation. Great thing to divert the mind from more immediate and pressing problems associated with my present visit to Molokai. Also bought several new books on Molokai history from the local stores (Molokai Drugs carries a few good ones, as there are no real book stores in town—hence an idea for a small business in this community of K'kai that doesn't yet exist!).

More random thoughts: Molokai needs to embrace a more careful awareness of proper water use and conservation, if Selix's watering of his back yard is any indication. Ironically, although one constantly hears about how Molokai is a relaxed community, with even more of a distinct "slow-mo" attitude than the other Hawaiian Islands have, you wouldn't know this judging from the proliferation of local pick-up trucks on steroids (complete with those ridiculous elevated suspension lifts that are so popular with all dimbulbs these days on the mainland). These things seem to disregard the speed laws and local custom by a considerable margin, in my observations at least. They are usually noisy, seemingly over-juiced, and speed along at considerably 'over-limit' speeds. Usually driven by locals, of course. So, despite the cost of gas (at this time about $3.03 a gallon), everyone seems blissfully mindless of the need to conserve gas AND hew to the prevalent traditional 'relaxed' lifestyle that gets so much lip-service hereabouts.

It's extremely ironic to see a large number of the locals speeding obliviously along, while many of us more mindful 'newbies' strive vainly to keep the speeds down to the posted limits. This is not, I hope, symptomatic of the present wave of fast-paced (mainland-type) change that we have been led to believe the traditional inhabitants of Molokai so much live in dread of. In that regard, someone today told me that the local penchant for jacked-up 4WD trucks is actually due to frequent winter flooding on the island and not 'white trash styling'.

Just listening to the neighbors last evening before sleep, I was unfavorably impressed by the sounds of cars 'laying strips', apparently fueled by some end-of-the-day beers one block over from here. This is nominally objectionable activity (at least by my standards) that one commonly finds on a daily basis back in Sacramento; how sad to find it also an apparent fixture here on "The Friendly Isle". Seems as if many of the less astute resident locals (in Ranch Camp, at least) all enjoy the same unhealthy lifestyle accoutrements mainlanders do: cars, alcohol, high-tech toys, loud pop-music (i.e. 'rap'), etc. With that discovery, a lot of my fond preconceptions are immediately swept away like the waters of local Molokai flash-floods (our new property is located on flood prone ground, I recall).

Wind outside rising up. Love it. Time to get on with the day's tasks and quests. I guess next stop is the Molokai Island Times to see if they have an Olympus camera downloading cable that I can borrow to get my digital images onto my laptop hard-disc. Then maybe a trip to Mauna Loa to visit the editors of Molokai's original newspaper, *The Dispatch*. After a quick shower, that is, since Selix seems to have finished lavishly watering his backyard (it's almost 10AM). *Mo lattahs, brah.* Strains of 'Barney', that ubiquitous friendly purple dinosaur on Public Television float in the background (*"I love you, you love me!"* etc.), further evidence that here on Molokai even the traditional Hawaiian pre-school educational customs have fallen in step with modern televised mainland schlock. Yow! Pity. So much for the myth of *'the most traditional of the Hawaiian Islands'*, methinks.

Later this morning I went into town to take care of a couple of things, one of the first of which was a visit to the Molokai Island Times (MacByte) after Molokai's computer guru Rand Salsada suggested I see if they had a compatible USB cable to use in downloading my camera images to my laptop. As luck would have it, I ran into John MacByte's cousin there (Daniel Whittaker), the 'money' behind the newspaper, who is co-owner and also primary financial backer (he's a limey), Seemed to be a nice chap, actually, and we had a good conversation for a while, but they were using late model Olympus digital cameras ($$$) that come with the newer USB-2 connector, so no joy there. Then Brandon, the erstwhile editor-in-chief, walked in; Brandon is the former editor of the *Molokai Advertiser News*, radical NRA gun nut (*"The Molokai Militia"*) George Peabody's paper that is published on the East End of the island. Mentioned the possibility of doing some brief freelance stuff for him and he seemed to welcome the idea. Brandon Putzer is young, only in his mid-20s. Has a strange sort of affect. Hard to read.

After that it was back to the apartment to do some writing and during that activity, Cheryl Apaia called to say the escrow papers were ready to pick up for signing. Took care of that with a quick trip up to her office in Halaupu'u. Then, having found out that there are no PO boxes available in either Kaunakakai or Halaupu'u (one to two-month waiting list), I dropped by the *Ho'olehua Post Office* (the one that sells real coconuts that can be mailed back to the mainland as postcards) and was able to find one available there for $68 per year. My official Molokai mail address is now 'John Q Smith, PO Box 536, Ho'olehua, HI 96728'. Has a nice, convoluted, tongue-twisting Hawaiian ring to it, I think. The Ho'olehua Postmaster is Chinese-Hawaiian and named Gerald Chang. He knew Cicada Lee (of course), since interpersonal ties are strong and evident everywhere here in the islands.

Last thing done was to drop by the school again at 3PM for another go at getting the email problem sorted out. This time I successfully got through to my server's web-based email page and was able to access my email. However, just after this minor moment of victory occurred, the door to the classroom swung wide open and in trooped a hoard of noisy 'keiki' (kids). In short order near chaos had established itself as it became apparent that a beginner's ukulele class was convening in my computer resources room. I had serious trouble focusing as 25 young ukulele students spent the next 15 minutes tuning their instruments while being harangued in Hawaiian by their instructor. I was about to hang it up after having barely managed to access a few of my collected email messages, when they all broke out in a Hawaiian song that I have to admit brought a smile to my face. It suddenly became not just bearable, but whimsical to the extreme as I whacked away at my keyboard against a background of ukulele chords and lyrics about a surfer's bad luck with the waves. What a moment! Finally got a few messages answered, not the least of which was a sort of initial progress report to my wife, who by now probably thought I had dropped off the edge of the world. Lots of wind today, as the trades raked the island, accompanied by many clouds (but still nice) .

Tomorrow, I sign the escrow papers, using my 'power of attorney' instrument to sign for Suki and myself. Then, I have to send them in (to Honolulu) and finally email the wire address of the escrow company to which she needs to wire the money ($84,000). Pete's 'Molokai Bicycle' is also open tomorrow, so I'll drop by there and see about renting a bike for the month ($175 for 30 days). Then I'll plan to take part of the day to drive east on Highway 450 (Kam V Highway along the coast) to spend some time at one of Molokai's beautiful and deserted beaches. I owe it to my shamefully pasty white legs to get some sunburn on them before the locals get so disgusted by the sight of them that they run me out of the town!

And now it's 7 PM and I have to end this—no more light to see well enough by. The only other interesting thing that happened today is the fact that a local wasp decided to perch on the rental car's gear-shift as I grabbed it and he stung the righteous shit out of me when I placed my palm directly on top of him. Clearly no sense of humor (or sympathy for what to him must simply be just another dumb Haole tourist). Enough! To bed, and more endless choruses of Rooster music, all night long...

April 14th, 2005 (Thursday)

Rose from sleep to a strange mix of horrific barking from the local dog I have named 'Ralph', and more strangled falsetto songs of educational TV's purple Dinosaur 'Barney' (from the neighbors' TV), with the ubiquitous rooster crowing providing a strong and constant back-beat (in Hawaiian: "Olowalu ka moa"— "roosters all crowing", or "much talk"). Ralph has a ferocious bark (Alsatian? Mastiff?) that would make anyone think twice about invading his turf, and last evening the thought occurred to me that perhaps that explains one reason why there seem to be so many dogs in the Ranch Camp area. Ice, or crystal methamphetamine, is near epidemic on the island. Due to the fact that so many families have intermarried on Molokai, a great number of them are related, thereby making it difficult to roust out drug users (no one wants to turn in family members amidst a culture where the o'hana, or family, is a sacred and time-honored traditional concept). Thus, despite the signs here and there stating 'ICE PILAU' ('ICE use stinks') and 'A'OLE ICE' ('No ICE') in front of homes, there could be a user house just about anywhere you cared to look.

After getting up and reading a chapter of Stewart's fascinating book on coffee (while drinking the first of several espressos made from Molokai Coffee Plantation beans), I popped out for a quick dump and shower. The shower and toilet are located adjacent, but via another door in the breezeway that separates the room I am staying in from the main house. In so doing, I ran into Inocencia and Selix, who were sitting in the breezeway chatting briefly before Inocencia left for work at the Molokai Ranch (although retired and 65, she puts in a few hours each day to make some extra money, so as to be able to afford the inter-island air-fare required to visit her kids on the other islands).

We started chatting for a few minutes and that led to a bit more protracted sit-down conversation, since we haven't really had much interaction since I arrived and that's not polite in the islands (where taking time to 'talk story' is considered one of the chief social courtesies). In the course of the next few minutes, I began to grasp a bit more of the interesting story I am now a part of (as a guest living briefly in the Baitan's let room).

It emerged that not only is Cicada Lee a close friend of present Hawaiian Governor Linda Lingle, she was also her gubnatorial campaign manager! [Always the Richard Harvey *"Rest of the story"* experience, it would seem, to dog me at every step of my journey in life!] Not only this, but Governor Linda Lingle used to stay with the Baitans in the very same room I am presently occupying (she was also their houseguest for about 10 years). Inocencia told me that Lingle first came to Hawaii from the mainland (California) in about 1976 and from that time forward became increasingly involved in Hawaiian politics (as a progressive Democrat). She first started out as a Maui County Council person, then ran for Major of Honolulu, and finally went on to run (successfully) for Governor of the state. *Whoda thunkit?*

This past March 26th Inocencia's husband Selix turned 90 and despite the fact that Lingle is now circulating among the upper levels of Hawaiian society as the state's Governor, she flew over to Molokai to personally help celebrate Selix's birthday. That's a good example of how closely-knit Hawaiian ties are (and remain), once forged. Inocencia also told me that of her three children, one is a lawyer, another is an official in the Hawaiian State Housing Bureau, and her youngest daughter is Governor Lingle's personal secretary! Again, *Whoda thunk it*? There's definitely a strong and revealing insight into Hawaiian affairs to be found in this small but potent peek into 'ordinary' island life here.

Come to think of it, when Cicada and I sat down under the trees to chat on the first day I arrived here, I reflected briefly that she seemed to be asking some pretty directed questions about my background and past history. Now that I know what I do about Cicada and her connections (more and more, all the time), it would seem that Cicada undoubtedly has the normal pedagogic tendency to analyse and store potentially useful information, since she is a school teacher by profession; everything I was telling her was probably being mentally entered into a ledger headed 'John Smith' in her mind. Nothing is ever as uncomplicated as it may seem, as I am always being reminded. The culture of Hawaii and the sub cultural networking ties of Molokai are an excellent example of this truism at work, so it would appear.

Today's agenda includes signing the property escrow (why am I always inadvertently spelling that word "*escrew*", I wonder?) final (closure) documents and mailing them off to Maui. Then, I need to pick up a copy of the latest Molokai Island Times issue and try to figure out how to download the articles I have written for Brandon, its editor, without having a printer attached to my laptop. Finally, it's off to the Molokai Elementary School again at 3PM for another internet link-up (this time with the benefit of my handy-dandy Bose noise-canceling active earphones).

The island of Molokai is so small that despite the fact that the Ho'olehua Airport is nearly 5 miles away, you can invariably hear

27

the twin-engine DeHavilland Dash-8 turboprops departing and arriving. STOL aircraft are very interesting as application-specific aeronautical designs and the Dash-8 is no exception. Seems like a whole lot of arrivals and departures, though.

Perhaps I can make it to the east end today; dying to spend a few hours on one of those stunningly beautiful and unfrequented beaches that face Maui across the 8.5 mile wide *Pailolo* Channel. Not as if I haven't plenty of time for this and everything else! Munching thoughtfully on dried Banana chips as I write these words, hoping they don't upset my stomach any more than it already is. Tried dried Taro chips yesterday, after finding them at 'The Friendly Market'. Really quite good—much like potato chips, except just a hint of some of the exotic flavor of the Taro root in them. Lightly purplish color flecks in their otherwise whitish appearance.

Taro (native word: *Kalo*) is actually an interesting food (like everything else native in Hawaii) and was the traditional base food for Hawaiians (much like the potato was for the Irish). Most people are unaware that the lowly (but nutritionally very useful) potato came from Hawaii long before the Irish discovered that it met their own needs quite well.

One thing I have been doing in my odd moments here is reading up on the Hawaiian language (really a distinct dialect of its Polynesian mother tongue and with only 13 letters), and most recently on Hawaiian names. I find that my own first name more or less translates to *'Kalikiopela'*, with the short form being rendered *'Kalika'*. Since Hawaiian culture has been so firmly made over in the Christian model, the name Christopher is well known in its Hawaiianised form, since it means 'Christ-bearer' (coming originally from Greek roots). Therefore, a more distinctly Hawaiian transliteration of 'Christopher' would be *'Imi Loa'*, which means 'seeker' or 'distant traveler', and is also used to mean 'one with deep knowledge'. [I find I prefer 'Kalikiano' (Christian) to 'Kalikiopela' (Christopher), a supreme irony given that I am a firm, life-long 'non-believer'!]

Attempting to do a similar breakdown of Suki's name (and aided by several scholarly Hawaiian language references), I come up with nothing equivalent; her other name (Suki), translates to 'Alina', which can be a translation carrying a bit of risk to it. Reason being that if one is not careful here, the name can be embarrassingly misconstrued; according to Pukui and Elbert's *'HAWAIIAN DICTIONARY'*, the prefix "Ai" can and does mean "intercourse" or "sex", in one application, and the suffix "lina" can be understood as "sticky, juicy, gummy, gelatinous" within another. Suki's Hawaiian name of 'Ailina' therefore could be understood as "sticky sex". Part of me finds that vastly amusing, of course! Suki would probably be mortified to hear about this, of course. As with any attempt to translate from one language into another (that may have vast phonetic or linguistic differences), one must always be extremely careful before assuming anything to be a given. Best practice is to always have the translation checked over by a native first! I am going to submit my Molokai Island Times articles under the pseudonym of *"Uncle Kalika"* (Uncle Chris), since the term "Uncle" or "Auntie" is a permitted local assumptive honorific under such circumstances for anyone over the age of 50.

Just returned from a trip into town to mail the property purchase documents to the escrow office across the channel. I dropped into the local Molokai visitors' bureau (a sleepy little office with a relaxed but pleasant Haole woman at the desk) to inquire where I could get my copy of the notarized power of attorney Suki that had given me reproduced and found she was happy to do that for me gratis, which was nice. We had a conversation meanwhile over the latest issue of the Molokai Island

Times, which had come out today. It seems that a recent study by the Hawaiian Department of Education has just found that of all the schools in the Hawaiian Islands, Molokai's are some of the worst in terms of math & English literacy—absolutely bottom of the bucket.

The person I was talking to (Marienne) said that one of the reasons for this was the terrible way the high school students treat the teachers at their school. She went on to say that many of the teachers in Hawaii come over from the mainland, thinking they are going to be able to teach in a sort of paradise. Then comes the shock of meeting abject disrespect of the worst kind from the very students they are supposed to be reaching (so said Marienne, giving me a few specific examples to mull over). Result is that the new hires either shortly thereafter leave the islands, or they settle in to a sort of apathetic staying action wherein they draw their pay but no longer try to teach effectively. Combine this with the blatant effects of pop-culture that kids absorb in today's youth music, violence, the overtly sexual nature of videos and electronic gaming, then add a dose of old fashioned Hawaiian laziness (perhaps that is too pejorative a word here—better to use *'relaxed'*) and it is no great mystery what is happening on Molokai.

Marienne and I both agree that something in paradise is getting *pilau* (rotten) quickly, and I glimpse the fact that am now starting to see the whole picture beginning to emerge here on Molokai more clearly—warts, beauty marks, treasure, garbage, the good, bad and ugly all unsparingly merged together. I am told by Marienne that local parents are quite concerned, very unhappy about all these findings, but I also agree with her observation that parental concern stops just short of taking charge of their children and exerting more forceful (positive) direction over their lives. After all, it should not be the primary job of teachers to help children grow to responsible adulthood. School instructors are only one (albeit disproportionately important) part of the process, with parents (ideally) being principally responsible for most of the basic foundation of the growth and maturing processes.

I suppose I am glad, knowing this, that the computer resource laboratory I am using each day is at the local elementary school, where the kids are not yet old enough or big enough to have fully optimized their disrespectful rejection of adults. I am also reminded that this was one of the main reasons why my mother, who remained a grammar school teacher all of her professional life, chose to remain at that level of instruction, rather than aspire to higher academic venues. At least kids are not yet completely ruined in those pre-pubescent years and there is still some innocent happiness and youthful openness left in them. They are, in short, still 'reachable' at that point. It is at and after the onset of puberty that most of these terrible changes seem to take hold, sewing the eventual seeds of cynicism, bias, hatred, feigned sophistication, "styling", rebellion and all of the other acquired adverse effects of fully blossoming adulthood.

Outside the window of my room the trades are howling across the treetops and there are many clouds today. Even the birds are holding fast on the landing aprons, rather than taking flight. April…a month of changes from winter to spring…strikes a fitting parallel as to what is happening to this island paradise in present times.

While in town, I dropped by the Molokai Island Times and downloaded my two articles for Brandon (the young paper's editor). I had to do this by tapping into their ethernet broadband connection and sending him an email with the two articles as attachments, since I don't have a printer and it's just as easy to transmit them electronically. Their paper came out today and

31

again, I was impressed with the quality of the content. Young Brandon Putzer (he must be in his mid-20s) just doesn't initially strike me as the type who would be an effective, let alone knowledgeable chief editor of a newspaper at his age—he looks more like a kid just in from taking an afternoon surfing than a journalist. But who am I...a hack writer... to try to stereotype a journalist, any journalist, for that matter?

As I walk about, taking care of things on my daily list, I am constantly checking out others...observing their affect, manner of dressing, actions, and interactions, in an effort to gain some sort of understanding of the community. It isn't at all easy, given the wide range of people about. There are of course the locals, easily identified by their skin color and characteristic Hawaiian faces. Then there are the *Malihini* (long-time residents, not of Hawaiian origin) who are usually Caucasian in appearance. Next comes the *Kama'aina*, or native born but not necessarily indigenous Hawaiian people.

At the bottom of the stack come the *Haoles* (recently arrived mainlanders, usually tourists) who characteristically look a lot like me, quite often with white pasty skin, beards, and a palpable earnestness about them (eager to fit in) and sincere looks. It is hard to figure out what the 'mean' ends up as being, given the radical dispersion of all these traits and affects. One thing is for certain and that is that the local 'truth' varies as much with the person pronouncing it as by any other standard of measurement. With a State of Hawaii Public Relations fabricated rep as *"The Friendly Isle"* among all the islands, Molokai has now become without a doubt the *"We'll-wait-till-you-show-your-true-colors-before-we-welcome-you island"*. Locals somewhat selfishly resist all change (full well knowing that without some sort of economic base, the island hasn't any real long-term chance at all), while recent outsiders equally selfishly insist on modernizing and updating *everything*—often with little or no regard for the past customs or the traditional sensitivities of the local people. It is a battle constantly being waged and one in which there are no real winners or losers...yet. Meanwhile, the fight goes on *sub rosa*.

Mega anti-virus software guru John MacByte's sale of property on Molokai was the most recent provocation of the old guard resistance to change. Local Island activist Winston Rider (half Caucasian and half Hawaiian—*'Hapa Haole'*) led the charge of the anti-change coalition when MacByte elected to sell his 1008 acre chunk of the island through an Alabama-based real estate brokerage, thereby raising all sorts of hell amongst the locals. Main reason was due to the fact that shortly after MacByte first relocated to Molokai, he donated handsomely to the local schools—primarily computers and electronic communications equipment (his money was probably behind the same Molokai Elementary School Community Computer Learning Resource Center I am now using each afternoon to link up with the internet to send and receive email). This and other similar generous donations to the community weal prompted a very favorable initial reaction to him...until he recently put about half of his land up for sale to the highest bidder.

Long-story-short, the auction came off as scheduled, despite a substantial protest, and MacByte made about 3.5+ millions from his original investment of about $1 MM. The battle lines had already been drawn, however, and the main contention seems to have been that the auction firm he chose to sell the property through had advertised it as being *'suitable for development'* and implied opportunity for speculators to subdivide the parcel for private residences. MacByte defended his decision to sell on the basis that he just wanted a place to build private vacation residences for himself and his family (see previous information about MacByte's 'Kama Sutra Yoga' interests), but it seems the 'family' alluded to consisted of gorgeous young ladies who were willingly attracted by MacByte's money & notoriety (and why not, since that's the real way of the world everywhere; no one has a franchise on paradise, but everyone wants a chunk of it, of course).

Before the MacByte brouhaha, there was a local furor (mid to late 90s) over the possibility of cruise ships visiting Molokai, but the hard-line resistance forming against that was based on the sentiment that cruise ships would be dumping their effluent tanks locally and that that would grossly pollute Molokai off-shore waters. In that instance, the 'no-changes' resistance won and cruise ships thereupon *did not* further include Molokai as a stopover on their itineraries.

Of course, the issue at the heart of everything is change. Locals, of whom at least 50% on Molokai are at least partly of native Hawaiian blood, do not want to see old timey Molokai become another Oahu, or Maui. This is understandable, since foreign development and capital has been busily ripping Hawaii apart to extract potential profits since the Sandwich Islands were first discovered. On the other side of the spectrum is the fact that Hawaii (especially Molokai'i) has no really substantial economic base to thrive upon, other than a few small industries (many of which have long since come to an end, such as pineapple cultivation and sugar cane production), hence tourism and visitor-related industries are an attractive alternative that is hard to resist.

The problem with tourism is that the process is poorly (it at all) regulated, with the result that wealthy visitors (many of them Japanese) have overrun the other islands, reaped fortunes, exploited whatever economic opportunities previously existed, and in general ruined almost all vestiges of the original, traditional Hawaiian culture. Much of this 'road to ruin' came through the door concurrent with the arrival of the Christian missionaries of the early-to-mid-1800s, who admirably managed to convert the free-living, pagan Hawaiians from their innocently care-free and traditional existence to the same sort of guilt-based, capitalistic entrepreneurial ethics that have today ruined any higher mainstream American aspirations that may have previously existed on the mainland.

Sadly, today's Hawaiians are all good little God-fearing Christians (many of them are Mormon, regrettably enough) who are as ashamed of their natural bodies and liberal inclinations as the most blue-blooded mainlander Yankee Protestant.

At best, it's a tough issue, with no clear-cut 'superior' approach plainly evident. Clearly, some change is going to be inevitable, but the trick is to control that change as much as possible to make sure it doesn't steamroll traditional Molokai in the doing. The locals, unfortunately, want to have the cake and eat it too. They want to limit change, but at the same time they don't want to take much personal responsibility for controlling the process of change. They also suffer mightily from the natural (traditional) island tendency to want to take it easy and not break a sweat making a living, which means that native Hawaiians are not the most productive, energetic and industrious people the world has ever seen. This last quality is a decided detriment to any sort of beneficial effort to inspire changes for the better of the community.

The people (John MacByte's cousin) behind the new newspaper (The Molokai Island Times) are keenly aware of all this and know that some changes are going to be necessary (if painful to effect), sooner or later. Tourism is going to have to be expanded, like it or not, since there just doesn't seem to be any really valid or promising alternative to tourist dollars at the moment...no matter how you cut the pie. *Molokai Ranch* is almost constantly battling this very issue, since they want to develop their properties more than they are at present (including reopening the now closed 'Kaluakoi Resort Hotel', a former Sheraton Hilton property, on the northwest end of the island), but again the bugaboo of change—how much, how fast, and to what extent?—is at the core of the contention.

Didn't get to the bicycle shop today, since it is only open from 3 to 6 on Wednesdays and briefly on Saturdays (how VERY *island*!), and I need to use that afternoon time to link up my email with correspondents. Oh well. I'm starting to wonder if renting a bicycle for the whole month is really worthwhile, since the island is really not yet what I would call 'bicycle friendly' (that is, cars are still the favorite means of transport of the locals, who all seem to just love their jacked-up 4WD pick-up trucks with big engines). There are no bike paths, certainly, and the small roadway shoulders that do exist are very narrow and island drivers are not trained to watch out for human powered vehicles on the few highways that span the island. It may be a bit premature to start promoting bicycle use, not least of the reasons for this being that drunk driving is a far bigger problem here than elsewhere (there are parallels to the continental Native American problems with use of alcohol, delicately put).

Ah well, time for dinner and then to bed. It's 6PM and the sun is setting. Life for me here is definitely 'up at sunrise and to bed at sunset', a life habit that has long been cited as promoting health. Perhaps that is a good thing, though, since I get lots of sleep (only in theory, however, due to the problem with Roosters). Thank God for noise-cancelling earphones!

April 15, 2005 (Friday)

Since I finished Stewart's most amusing book about the storied path of coffee's historic journey to the west (from its origins in East Africa—Somalia/Ethiopia) last evening, I am starting to read about Hawaii's modern history. In particular, history of the Hawaiian Monarchy's transition during the missionary period, up through the annexation of Hawaii by the United States in 1898. This will entail a visit to the Molokai library, since there are no references of sufficient scope or detail available to buy anywhere on the island. This highlights, in my opinion, the need for a good bookstore on Molokai, since that is one community asset that has yet to be addressed in meeting the needs of the people. The problem here is that I lack any sort of capital with which to open such a store and I haven't the faintest idea of how to go about raising any (unless through a grant, possibly?). There was, actually, a local book store at one time, but it was one of those 'Christian book stores' that are obsessed with saving you for Jesus, so it quickly folded. It's a safe bet they'd NEVER carry any of my books, LoL!

The story of Haoles and locals interacting here on Molokai has parallels in the historical context of Hawaii having been overrun by Christian missionaries, who wittingly or unwittingly played their part in 'preparing' the islanders for the sort of economic rape and ravaging that followed by private (capitalistic) enterprise. Reading some of the stories of how the last of the Hawaiian monarchs were exploited by powerful interests in the USA and eventually deposed makes the blood run cold, as the details of this deception and betrayal become clearer.

Identifiable and central elements in that process that immediately stand out include the inherent friendly traditional disposition of the Hawaiian people and the role the Christian missionaries played in co-opting and cultivating that quality and harmonizing it with precepts of Christian kindness and egalitarianism. The classic legend of the great white God (*Lono-Makua*), who appears among the native people (in so doing perhaps fulfilling one of their ancient prophesies, promising to benefit the natives), only to prove to be another mere mortal (perhaps only more techno-logically advanced) who exploits and ultimately betrays that simple native faith, is a very ancient one here. A familiar story certainly, and not one that deals with any uniquely new or star-tlingly different concepts over succeeding generations.

A basic aspect of that cross-cultural conflict is still playing out here on Moloka'i, as the locals view the unwanted profusion of new Haoles with a combination of mistrust, suspicion, envy, and awareness of unhappy recent events (such as the MacByte af-fair). As previous mentioned, Molokai used to be known (more or less, and like it or not) as *"The Friendly Isle"*, but that cachet has since become a victim of the times and now the operative attitude is one of wary watchfulness. Newcomers are no longer automat-ically welcomed with open arms and a friendly smile; now they are generally viewed with neutrally until the nature of their pres-ence and interest in Moloka'i becomes more apparent.

This naturally leads to another awareness and that is that it is hard to stereotype the population here. That is, it's not a simple matter to lump all the locals (or even *Malihinis*) into a single cat-egory of thoughtfulness or attitude—even as merely a simple and convenient filtering process through which to better understand local mind-sets, etc. Meeting some of the locals as I have (very few, really) is a process that has to date been fairly superficial, with not much in-depth interpersonal communication upon which to draw meaningful conclusions. Judging from what I have seen (or more correctly 'heard') in the Ranch Camp neighborhood I am staying in, most local people (at least here) are in that average group of people who are simply living their lives instinctively as the flow of days continues. There are no deep thoughts apparent (emphasis, emphasis), no great questions about where Moloka'i is going, and certainly no very deep intellectualizations (in the classic European manner) about these somewhat cerebral subjects.

Families have children, young adult males have their hopped-up cars (or trucks) and boats, older adult males drink; God only knows what adult local women (wives) do, except take care of the keiki (kids) and gossip ('talk story'). Families are almost all uniformly Christian (thank you, missionaries!) and there probably aren't more than a handful of atheists or 'serious agnostics' on the whole island. Meanwhile, the devastating problem of drug use continues to weigh heavily on Moloka'i's small social milieu, with the most worrisome effects of this substance-abuse plague being most felt in the local high school.

Something that I became aware of while still back on the mainland is the indigenous self-determination movement to secede from union with the United States as a state and reestablish either a Hawaiian Republic or the ancient Hawaiian Monarchy. This idea has been simmering for a number of years now, with most recent efforts clustering around the late 90s.

While many would doubtless shrug and dismiss Hawaiian secession as trivial and meaningless fantasy, the idea has some very serious proponents and backers on the islands. All political complexities aside, the central question in this would be economic. Since Hawaii has very little in the way of an indigenous economic support-base, the question of how to provide economic wherewithal for such a grand and far-reaching undertaking would be both perplexing and challenging. Aside from small local businesses and tourism, the only other powerful economic activities are all foreign (i.e. mainland or internationally based) supported. Still, considering the shameful suppression of the traditional native culture by Christian religion from the 1700s onwards and the endless exploitation of the native population by American capitalism from about 1850 to the present, such an idea of self-determination does have a certain attractive populist nature to it.

In thinking through some of these problems, I am frequently reminded of a parallel that can be found in Saudi Arabia. Up until the discovery of oil in the Kingdom (1932), the Saudis were merely another tribal grouping of desert nomads who occupied the greater Arabian Peninsula. The discovery of oil changed all of this almost overnight, as oil money started to seep up through the ground and into the hands of the formerly dirt-poor Arabs. In a matter of a few years, that money was being put to work, supporting the Al Saud Monarchy, and before too many decades had passed the Saudis were literally in charge of the greatest cash reserves in the world. The result of all this sudden wealth, among other things, was confusion over the actual status of the Saudis in terms of their identity and inherent self-esteem. On the one hand, they were the world's richest people, with all the power and status that immense wealth automatically confers; on the other, they were still in many ways quite ignorant, backward, and rudely tribal people, unversed in the cultural niceties and sophisticated ways of the western world.

This dual nature led to a sort of role and status confusion, as well as I was able to read it. That is, while their money proclaimed them *Very Important People,* in contrast to the least educated western expatriate hired from abroad to work for them even the most-wealthy Saudi was still pathetically ignorant and rough by comparison. This characteristic and inherent insecurity felt by the Saudis, who were often acutely mindful of these ironies, was quite palpable—at least to me while I worked there (80s/90s). One never knew, in one's daily dealings, whether one was interacting with *Ahmed Al Qhatani* the unsophisticated and uneducated son of desert *Bedu,* or *HRH Ahmed Al Qhatani* the powerful *Saudi Assistant Minister of the Interior.* I exaggerate here for the sake of clarity, but the basic quandary was always present in one's daily interactions in Saudi Arabia.

So too, do many of the Moloka'i 'locals' reflect this polar duality of insecure awareness of their present status. On one hand, they are economically poor and minimally educated people, descended from the original native Hawaiian inhabitants. Many of them rely on state support and subsidies to thrive. Substance abuse (alcohol and harder drugs, in that order) issues are a recurrent and serious concern among them, and there are few or no healthy locally-owned businesses they may point to as communal foundations of economic support.

On the other hand, they are mindful of the ironic fact that this is still their traditional native homeland and that the Haoles are only carpetbagger-intruders from the outside, upon whose regular economic infusions of economic wealth they must necessarily rely. Once again, the polar duality of mindfulness settles in to create a sense of mild social identity schizophrenia that I vaguely sense among some whom I have met and talked to (at least superficially). Again, the parallels between the status quo here and that I found in Saudi Arabia are not all that far removed from one another. It is a fascinating (although not altogether happy) subject to reflect further upon.

Meanwhile, as I type these words on my Dell Inspiron 4000 laptop computer (running MS/XP OS, with an 850 MHz Pentium III chip, and 512 MB of RAM), I am being treated to a non-stop chorus of little kid chatter, parental corrections, and more strains of purple dinosaur songs (Barney) in the background. It invariably strikes me as curious (and a little painful) how small kids can consistently hit such high frequencies with their shrieks that are typically at or above the adult threshold of pain (depending on proximity of *shrieker* to *shriekee*, of course). Even with the incurrence of routine high-frequency hearing drop-outs that are part of the aging process, such painful high notes still make me cringe momentarily. At least Ralph-the-dog (no outbreaks of rabidly vicious barking) is quiet for the moment and the roosters have temporarily retired their horny cackling to the somewhat cooler confines of their sun-shelter, next door.

Another curious thing, aside from the profusion of huge Moloka'i bumblebees that are constantly blundering into the window, is the fairly regular tap-tap-tapping of large rain drops that fall from the frequent large clouds that blow over the island onto the tin roof of my room. Of course, the heat is such that they evaporate as soon as they hit anything, so there's no puddling anywhere on the ground...just their strangely beguiling *tap-tap-tapping* on a hot tin roof that they produce in their passing.

Well, time I got up and out to do something. It's now about 11 AM and I haven't even taken my daily shower or washed the dishes yet. I find I am tending to eat sugary sweet stuff instead of taking the trouble to eat real meals here. Although dinner is typically rice with SPAM over it, and breakfast of instant Quaker Oats with dried cranberries (with soy milk), I have bought several packages of cookies from 'The Friendly Market' and seem to reflexively gobble few of these for lunch (or whenever the hunger pangs strike). With no bicycle to exercise on, as back at home, and no *'OWFLEX'* torture rack to work out on, I am definitely falling prey to the super-relaxed ambience that the tropical climate confers upon all who live here for any length of time. [This last fact undoubtedly helps explain several local phenomena: 1) the high level of obesity that is a major problem on the island, and 2) the disproportionate, extraordinarily high levels of tooth decay local kids have that require serious dental attention on Moloka'i.]

Finally got off at just before 12 AM and drove the 17 some odd miles to *Maunaloa*, the old former plantation town on the west end of the island that is now owned by Moloka'i Ranch. There really isn't much to Maunaloa, but what there is has been carefully planned and constructed by Moloka'i Ranch to resemble a modernized plantation community. One place well known to anyone familiar with the island is the *"Big Wind Kite Factory"*, operated for many years (several decades) by Jim and Debbie Sincher, a Caucasian couple who have been islanders for a long time (*kama'aina*).

The place is quite interesting, actually, and not just your 'average tourist trap', as one might expect. It is filled with many imported art objects from the Far East (most from Tibet and Nepal), although many carved items are from other parts of the Far East. I enjoyed meeting and talking with Jim about various things for a while and then started to look about. It didn't take me long to find the large number of books he has on premises dealing with Hawaiian culture, history, and society. Also, a fair number of books on or about Moloka'i that one wouldn't otherwise find anywhere. Didn't take me long to gather up about two dozen, ranging from a 3rd edition University of Hawaii *'Atlas of the Hawaiian Islands'* through several different histories of Hawaii, both modern and ancient, and many more on a range of related subjects. Thus burdened, I finally managed to stagger out of the store with a bill for about $395 and two heavy bags full of books. About status quo, by my usual habits. Every time I buy books I am reminded anew of that old saying, *"A truly educated person never graduates."* How true, and how true also that the learning materials costs for such a student's education are a continual, life-long concern.

This morning I read through a few of the books and found that one I had particularly fancied, a small and beautifully simple Hawaiian flavored paean to women titled *"Wahine"*, had somehow been misplaced and didn't make it through the final check-out tally. I shall have to return to retrieve it, since I wanted to give it to Suki on my return, but that's not a major concern, since it's a pleasant and short drive to reach Maunaloa on Highway 460 out of K'kai. Pity, though, that the one book I really wanted most somehow got lost in the shuffle. I also had my eyes on a nice two-headed drum hanging in the shop (price $500) that had a mellow sound to it, but thought better of my impulse in view of the great costs we are facing with our new property.

This reminds me that I spotted a huge *Hula Pahu* (Hula drum) at the Moloka'i Plantation Coffee gift shop up in Kaluapu'u. What really caught my attention was the fact that the carver was Vince Lorenz of Kaunakakai, whom Cicada had pointed out to me as being one of the acknowledged local pahu craftsmen. The drum is huge for a pahu, probably measuring at least 20 inches at the drum-head in diameter, but appears to be beautifully done and also has genuine shark skin for a drum-head (although use of shark skin is traditional for pahu drum-heads, its present scarcity makes ordinary cow-hide a more commonly used material for such things). The price tag on the pahu in question is $1250, which is a stiff chunk of change by any reckoning, but it sits up there beckoning to me in a manner I can't easily explain to those who don't know me well (hell, let's not kid ourselves...I can't even explain it to those who DO know me well). We'll see if I finally succumb to that sore temptation before I leave the island (spoiler alert: I did), but considering the fact that I am operating on a strictly limited budget over here, it really isn't a realistic option at all. There's also the concern of getting it back home, since the baggage limitations of my flight would make it extraordinarily tough to take with me; having it shipped home via post office would require extensive protective packaging, so even if I had a spare $1250, I'd still face some perplexing considerations.

The rest of the afternoon passed uneventfully, as I returned to K'kai and grabbed my computer for the usual afternoon internet link-up at the local school to download my day's email (from 3PM to 5PM). A quick trip to 'The Friendly Market' for some canned SPAM (Turkey) and a dash to the local drug store for some indigestion meds ended up my day. I read some of my new reading material before bed, with the sweet *lullaby from hell* of the neighbors' roosters drifting in through the window, mixed occasionally with outbursts of Ralph's ferocious barking.

Many of the books I brought back from Jim's store in Maunaloa dealt with arcane aspects of Hawaiian (and Moloka'iian) culture, history, and ancient civilization. Fascinating reading, all of it. I am reminded that probably 98% of all the so-called Hawaiian 'locals' (native Hawaiians of Hawaiian blood) have been so completely socialized into that homogenous mishmash of Western culture that is uniquely American, that they have lost almost all understanding of not just their own cultural history, but awareness of traditional Hawaiian attitudes, outlooks, wisdom, and knowledge of ancient practices, customs, and practices. It's sad, but true, and probably a condition not unlike that found in any other part of the world today as American culture spreads out in the world like some great stupefying soporific virus that erases reflectivity and intelligent analysis of the 'lived life'.

A parallel exists to my earlier interests in Asian culture, back in the 70s & 80s. At the time I initially discovered the various rich cultural traditions of the Far East, I made the mistake of thinking that all Asian-Americans were highly connected to their past history and ancient culture. What a shock it was to find that most Asian-Americans, instead of appreciating the interest of a *Honky* who was keen on their culture, felt that such unusually strong interest in another culture (such as their own) was a sort of freakish disappropriation of their culture and bordering on the downright weird. Pity. Locals who find out about my intense interest in their affairs undoubtedly feel somewhat the same, no doubt. Of course, to the local teenagers, people like me are just plain strange anyway, since we are about as far from their concept of what's currently 'cool' (e.g. rap, hip-hop, grunge, body-piercing, tattooing, etc.) as one could possibly be, and those of us with pasty-white skin are clearly marked as culturally uncool Haole pariahs anyway.

Today is 'Earth Day' in Moloka'i and there is a celebration being held in downtown Kaunakakai to mark the occasion during the AM hours. I'll wander down for a look after I finish this, but will probably also drive back to Maunaloa beforehand to retrieve that beautiful book I mentioned earlier that was somehow misplaced.

Called up Cicada yesterday to talk with her about Vince Lorenz and see if she could arrange an introduction for me, but she wasn't in. Her (husband) answered and seemed pretty casual to me about taking down my cell number for a call-back. Didn't hear from Cicada all day, so I wonder if he forgot to mention my call to her. I'll wait till Saturday and then call her again. Don't want to be too intrusive, in recognition of all that she has done to ease things for me on my visit so far.

One last thing: during my talk with Jim at the Kite factory in Maunaloa, we discussed Winston Rider, the local ('Hapa') left-of-center radical activist. Winston has been at the forefront of most of the organized resistance to development efforts for some time here and has also been responsible for many of the local fish pond restorative efforts. It would be interesting to meet him and chat with him for a while, but I've been unsuccessful to date in connecting with him. Perhaps I'll drop by MoBettah.net and ask Rand or Jack if they know what his email address is. He lives on the East End (predictably), since the East End is the sort of 'Left Bank' gathering ground for free spirits on the island of Moloka'i.

Drove back up to Maunaloa at noon, stopping to gather some red soil samples of volcanic origin. I had forgotten to pick up one of the very books I had been so fond of at the Kite Factory (*"Wahine"*). Predictably, I also 'found' at least 10 other books I hadn't earlier acquired, so 'The Kite Factory' was doubtless VERY happy to see me again ($150 this time). Since the offices of 'The (Moloka'i) Dispatch' are directly across from the kite store, I walked over to check out the office. Having been told by co-owner Mary (via email) that they didn't keep regular office hours, I didn't really expect to find anyone there. However, as I gazed through the front door, an elderly gentleman whom I had not noted leaving 'The General Store' (next building over) walked up asking me there was anything I needed. This turned out to be Editor Gary Edmonds himself, who just happened to have dropped by at the same time I had.

Showing the signs of his recent struggle with lymphoma (which he had mentioned in an earlier email exchange), I was impressed by his attitude of determination to recover from his recent chemotherapy and continue his work. We had a nice conversation for about 20 minutes, covering a number of subjects, including drugs in the schools, the recent determination that Moloka'i schools ranked lowest of all those in the islands, the circumstances attending John MacByte's recently concluded auction of a large parcel of his Moloka'i property (1008 acres), the new Moloka'i Island Times newspaper started by MacByte's English-national cousin (Daniel Whittaker), and a few other timely topics. Gary revealed that MacByte's cousin (Daniel) has spent a lot of time in prison (he didn't elaborate) and that "co-owner" Brandon Putzer (who is also "Editor-in-Chief", according to the paper's masthead) is a Chico State graduate with an undergrad degree in journalism. As per the last revelation, I was rather bemused by this fact, since when reading through Putzer's 'editorial' in the last issue, it was quickly apparent that journalism degree or not, Putzer tends to make some pretty glaring mistakes in both grammar and definition of terms (example: "...*we were abhorred by*"...). Confirming this impression, Gary Edmonds shared the fact with me that Brandon had originally been working for the Moloka'i Advertiser News (George Peabody) before severing that connection and submitting what according to Gary was a "...*poorly phrased and hand-written note asking about employment possibilities with 'The Dispatch'*".

Edmonds was not at all impressed by the amateurish note, despite the fact that there really wasn't a need for any staff journalists at his paper. He also speculated that although MacByte cousin Whittaker told him MacByte had given them a strictly limited amount of money to start the paper, he suspected that additional funds were readily available whenever they were needed to make the paper viable. Gary stated that he and his wife Mary take pains to keep their overhead as low as possible, and he is very much aware of the fact that costs for 'The Moloka'i Island Times' are substantially greater (higher quality paper, more paid staff, etc., etc.) than his for 'The Dispatch'. We also spent a few minutes discussing MacByte's 'former' substance abuse problems and his purported 'Kama Sutra Yoga' activities. Although I could have pumped Gary for many more answers to questions I have about the island, I ended our conversation prematurely, out of consideration for his health, and took my leave promising to send him a few articles to look at for possible publication. It was an interesting and fortunate coincidence to run into him, since I had forgotten to bring over their residence phone number and therefore had no way to get in touch with him other than through email.

Yesterday I mentioned the local wasp that took a dislike to the heel of my hand being placed on him as he perched on the gear-shift knob of my rental car. This morning while showering, I had soap in my eyes when I felt as if some crud from the shower floor had attached itself to my left calf, so I reached down and brushed off whatever it was. Clearing my eyes and feeling a sort of slight sting on my lower leg where it had been, I was amazed to find a *scorpion* lying on the shower floor where I had brushed him off! Looked closely. *Yup.* A real scorpion. No mistaking that charac-teristically arched tail stinger and body configuration. Lucky for me he was only a small one and not some small scorpion's great grand-daddy. The sting soon went away, but it was a healthy re-minder to shake my clothes out before putting them on (especially my short pants with nothing on under them) and ex-amine my sandals for similar visitors before donning them. What next? First a Hornet, then a scorpion, and next up is...a *mon-goose*?

I'm going to skip today's email session at the school, although given that I can't access the internet over the weekend, that's probably not a wise decision. Sitting in there trying to concentrate with all those noisy little kids is just a bit more than I need on a regular basis.

Sitting here examining the sum total of my experience in Mo-loka'i thus far (in the past 5-6 days), I find that I am hungering for some substantial contact with others. More than just the friendly nod and greeting at the grocery store, or the brief chat with Mari-enne at the Moloka'i Visitors' Bureau. Something with a bit more meat to it. Haven't really met anyone to speak of, other than as described here, and it is a bit lonesome not having any friends at all here with which one can relax and feel comfortable with. Mrs.

Baitan is very pleasant and 90 year old Selix is still capable of a friendly nod or two, but even for someone as self-contained as I, the insulated nature of this experience is a bit much to contend with. I find that I am spending much of my time curled up with some of the books I have bought, which while it isn't a bad way to pass time by my standards, still lacks that bit of 'at home' feeling we all crave that contact with others confers.

Once I hear from Suki that the escrow has been officially closed, I'll get together with 'architect' Victor Montero to see about having that water line and meter installed and connected on our new property, since that's an important secondary goal on my list of things to get done before I depart on the 8th of May.

One of the excellent aspects of this 'month away from the mainland' is having so much free time to think and write without the hassle of work to interfere with either available energy levels or the added frustrations of ordinary domestic responsibilities back home. Given the helter-skelter daily work hassles involved with my work for the California State Treasurer's office, I am usually too emotionally exhausted at the end of a work-day to sit and compose my thoughts well enough to write anything. The only real problem I am troubled by right now is the persistent severe stomach and gut upset that has been producing some pretty formidable gas pain. This makes me a little hesitant to eat much of anything, although I do pop cookies and other junk simply because I must eat something. The *simethicone* medication I bought at the drug store does help somewhat, but I suspect my stomach is suffering from the same characteristic chronic irritation that I have had before, after taking a chance on a simple glass of wine (had one about three weeks ago and sure enough, the same delayed reaction I have experienced before is taking place anew—guts upset, severe gas problems, and bouts of diarrhea/loose stools). I love wine, but it doesn't seem to return the affection!

This evening the K'kai community is having an 'Earth Day' celebration downtown (from 5PM through 10PM), so perhaps I'll take a look. Tomorrow is the town's weekly *flea-market-cum-arts-&-crafts* event in the AM hours. Sitting here writing this, find myself noting that the roosters next door have been at it all day long. Apparently the pattern is that one of them a few blocks away will crow a challenge, and that produces a response from the immediate neighbor's flock, which in turn requires another volley of crowing from a block away, etc., etc. Bloody awful racket, without an end, all day and all night. Makes me want to go cut the poor addled beasts' tongues out. I have to also remind myself that astrologically speaking (from the Chinese viewpoint), this is presently the *Year of the Rooster,* so perhaps this is part of the *'trying times and unhelpful circumstances in store for Dog people'* that the Chinese almanac referenced, earlier this year.

Taking a look at the stack of books I have bought while here, I hope their substantial weight won't result in my being penalized when I check in with the airline to return to the mainland! Gulp! We're taking a total of 46 books here, both hardcover and paperback! *Gaak!* All have some bearing on Hawaii and/or Moloka'i, of course. I usually joke with my friends about the fact that I normally seem to go a little crazy in bookstores, but there's doubtless more truth to that than fiction, as if this weren't enough proof of it! Suki would probably think me stark raving mad for buying such a small library on vacation, but the way I see it, you can't find any decent books dealing with the islands back in California (at least not in Sacramento), so this is a unique opportunity to stock up.

Weather has been very windy today, with usual build-up of clouds and scattered rainfall for April (so I am told). The wind was very stiff up in Maunaloa earlier today, which since it is on the windward northwest end of the island...normally quite wind-swept all the time...should not really surprise me. Still, it makes me appreciate the vast differences to be found on Moloka'i, from one end of the island to the other. The southern area is some-what protected and known as the 'dry part' of the island (where our property in *Kamiloloa Heights* is located—2 miles east of Kaunakakai on Highway 450), whereas the western end of the island, at 1050 feet elevation near Maunaloa's summit, is known to be quite windy and exposed. The east end of the island, with its 5000 foot high *Kamakou* volcanic summit, has the most rainfall and is blanketed with lush growth everywhere, from along its coastal shores up to the heights. It is from this part of the island whence most of the island's water comes, carried via a 5 mile long tunnel through the mountain, from the *Halawa* and *Wailu Valley* areas.

Although water can and could be a problem for the island in future, there is presently enough, given the population supported (only 7000). However, I have seen no regard on the part of the residents at all for water conservation awareness. Many have lawns with grass, which has always struck me as really stupid and thoughtless, given their thirst and upkeep requirements. Far better to plant flora that is more well-suited to the semi-arid trop-ical climatic conditions found here and which also requires little or no maintenance. Even back home, where there is no present on-going water problem, I have always held residential lawns and ornamental grass landscaping in very low regard. At such mo-ments of reflection on the uselessness of grass lawns, I am reminded of 70s poet and post-beat generation writer Richard

Brautigan's immortal work entitled *"The Revenge of the Lawn"*. How apropos…

Another argument surfaces for the definite need to remind people of things they would automatically be aware of if they just engaged in a bit of reflective thought, every now and then. One of the books that caught my eye earlier in the week (at the Maunaloa Kite factory) dealt with conservation practices as they apply specifically to the Hawaiian Islands. It was a used book, published a few years ago, but still a very useful and in my opinion important book. However, I added it to the stack and find much in it of relevance.

All of this ruminating over my book habits prompts me to recall that one of my 'other' desires (aside from running a left-of-center coffeehouse) has always been to operate a book store. None of my ideas (coffee, books, bicycles) seem destined to generate any real income (Moloka'i already has bicycle and coffee houses) anyway, but it strikes me that there is a serious need for a general bookstore on Moloka'i. The Kite Factory has books, but they all bear on Hawaiian history and culture (that's a good thing for me, of course). What is needed (in my opinion) is a bookstore in the community of Kaunakakai that deals with all subjects and that offers both new and used books. Since one of the real challenges facing the Moloka'i schools is to get kids to read, and since the influx of new Moloka'i homeowners from the mainland (& tourists) also need things to read, I feel the situation is ripe for a bookstore—small and unpretentious though it may be. I'd spring for it in a heartbeat if I had the available capital to do so, but alas, 'Poor Richard' has no spare bucks to start an almanac! This matter of having to underpin the dreams with financial wherewithal (and being perpetually unable to) has consistently been my chief bane in life, since I have always been and still am quite irresponsible with money. (In that vein, I sincerely hope I haven't dragged

Suki irrevocably down the same path to penury in this latest Moloka'i property deal we have just closed—only time will tell, unfortunately).

It should be mentioned here that Kaunakakai does have a nice little public library, that many use and frequent; it also has a couple of PCs there that visitors may use to access the internet. While it's a nice community asset, I still think an independent book store would be a great addition to the community.

April 16, 2005 (Saturday)

Saturday. Good thing for the roosters or I would have slept-in a bit (irony). Found teeny, tiny ants had discovered my rice bowl after rising, so I washed it out when I took my shower (no scorpions this morning). This AM was the weekly arts & crafts happening on Ala Malama Street in front of the public library, but I also planned to visit the east end today, so I packed up everything and then checked out the vendors (artists & craftsmen). Met Carlo again, the same German national we ran into last time we were here (October of last year) and renewed ties. He has some nice items carved of island deer (Axis Deer) horn again, but I still think the one I bought from him is one of his best. Carlo hasn't changed a bit in appearance—still a scruffy beard and ball cap, with aloha shirt. Couldn't mistake him is a million street bazaars.

Also spotted Richard Eloka, a local Moloka'iian ("100% Hawaiian crafts by a 100% Hawaiian") whose hand-produced crafts I had admired last time. He had two *puniu* on display this time (these are the small hula drums made from coconut shells that strap on to the player's leg with ties made from coconut fibers), as well as two small non-traditional drums that he said he was making for some of the school kids who were learning how to play hula instruments. The *puniu* were $50 each, so I decided to think about it a bit first.

I was half-looking at the adjoining display of aloha shirts, as I chatted with Richard, when I noticed that the shirts were being sold by a very slender, foxy lady of dark complexion (I thought possibly Hawaiian). She started to give me some background on the shirts and since I had my eyes on one very nice, pale blue & white shirt, asked her for the price and got it for $10 (100% cotton and tasteful for an Aloha shirt). It definitely was a color and pattern made for this skinny haole, so I took it.

Turns out she is originally from the Mainland--near Sacramento, no less—so I commiserated with her over that misfortune, but learned she now lives with her husband Bill on the east end of the island (mile19), right next to John MacByte's property. She was annoyed that he had built a large multi-story building overlooking her back yard and it was interesting to get her inputs on the MacByte saga. Name is, curiously, Locinda (never heard of this name for a woman before—must be Filipino), and she is 54, but slender and well put together. Looked very Hawaiian to me. VERY tight jeans, nice butt, slim, trim, and just the way I like 'em. *Yumm!* Very upbeat personality and nice eyes, to boot. In short, I could be interested quite easily. Husband is named Bill Butler and he is 60, a 'resident builder' (not licensed as a contractor, but apparently skilled enough, from what I infer). Can't help but wonder if he keeps this rather *wahine u'i wela* ("beautiful hot woman") satisfied! To say I am feeling rather unsatisfied myself at the moment is understating things. *Susie Palm* and her five sisters are not much comfort at such moments of orgasmic extremis. Whenever I am inclined to feel guilty about thoughts of infidelity, I take some small comfort from pre-missionary Hawaiian custom, which made refusing to have *ai* (coition) with anyone even casually asking for it considered VERY impolite. One doesn't need to speculate what the 'missionary position' on that strongly established cultural attitude was, hee-hee...

Locinda (surely, she must have a shorter nickname than that Filipino mouthful) showed me a few photographs taken by the 60ish artist next to her, a fellow named 'Josh', who was wearing a 'Moloka'i Veterans Club' T-shirt. He apparently served in Korea and has some health problems resulting from his service, but his photographs (all of Moloka'i) were absolutely beautiful. At $20 for each 8 x10 image, I had to think a bit about this also, but there is no denying all of them are spectacular. He has a certain gift...or he's VERY lucky...or it's so beautiful here on the island that it's impossible to take a BAD picture.

At any rate, I enjoyed talking with all of these local residents, but after a bit I got in the car and drove Highway 450 East (this hugs the coast and is more commonly known as King Kamehameha V Highway) towards Moloka'i's East End. The speed limits on Moloka'i vary from 20 mph in Kaunakakai, to 35 and in some stretches to 45 only (no higher). Still, I couldn't help but speculate adversely on the number of people who seem to routinely disregard the limits and drive WAY faster than allowed. Paradoxically, the speeders all seem to be local island residents and not tourists. Additionally, many of the islanders seem to delight in owning and driving those huge jacked-up pick-up trucks with monster doughnut tires that I so dislike. These vehicles are not just large and physically intimidating, the tires also make a huge racket, due to their having all-terrain type treads. One of these guys passed me on a very narrow part of the slim east end roadway like it was race-track. I tried to spot them coming and would usually pull over and let them pass, whenever possible, but it was galling to think of the irony implicit shown in all this erstwhile put-down of the customary *"Slow down; this is Moloka'i"* philosophy.

Most notably today, I had a chance to spend an hour or so on beautiful Waialua Beach, taking in some sun and reading a few of the books I brought with me. One of these is a very interesting and most insightful book titled *'Tales from the Night Rainbow'*, which is a rare recorded oral history of the life and times of an early Moloka'i resident 'Kupuna' (Grandparent or 'ancestor') *Kaili'ohe*, of the Kai-akea family of the Mo'o Clan. This clan traces its ancestry back to at least 800 BC, and Kaili-ohe, born in 1816, was the great granddaughter of Kai-akea. It was through her that the family's oral history was preserved, as she was a person of the learned *'kahuna'* type whose special task it was to learn and know these things.

The picture that emerges of Moloka'i's history is quite different from that most conventionally accepted as part of Hawaiian history. Some of the startling things that one reads are quite revealing, both culturally and historically. As an example, she tells us that what so many regard today as the *'Menehune'*, or semi-mythical 'little people' of the islands, were actually the pre-Ali'i (or original, indigenous) inhabitants who lived on the islands prior to the arrival of the Tahitian newcomers, war-like Polynesians who invaded Hawaii and conquered it. She reveals that the original inhabitants *('Maoli')* were much smaller in stature than the Tahitians and that when the Tahitian Ali'i arrived, the indigenous 'people of light' who could not escape to another island withdrew to the mountain fastness of their islands, where they remained deliberately isolated from the new order of royalty and commoners established by the Tahitian Ali'i. The war-like *Na Ali'i* called the original peaceful inhabitants of the islands the *'Mana hune'* (or 'small power') people, since the indigenous Maoli were peaceful and gentle people, who had not adopted war-like ways. It is not hard to see how this became *'Menehune'*, over a period of time, and the hidden Maoli transformed to semi-mythical 'little people'.

A possible explanation is even offered for the present Hawaiian legend of the ghostly *'Night Marchers'* (as follows). When the Tahitian Ali'i ordered the Maoli commoners of an area to perform a formidable task for them, such as the building of a fishpond along the coast, they would typically set a short deadline for the task to be completed and go away, doubtless cynically amused by the impossibility of meeting such a demand; however, if the task was not completed in a timely manner, the returning Ali'i commonly slaughtered many of the area's ordinary inhabitants. For this reason, if such a demand had been levied, signals were sent out and the Maoli (or pre-Ali'i people) would converge on the scene at night and together complete whatever had been ordered. By the time dawn arrived, the Maoli were all back in the mountains again, thereby giving the Ali'i the impression that the work had been done by the aid of their ancestors. Eventually, these feats were ascribed as work of the 'Menehune', who by then were regarded as mythical little people (not unlike the Irish *Leprechaun*). Since these convergences of the Maoli occurred at night, in the form of many of them descending from the mountains, the supposition is that this was the origin of the legendary 'night marchers', to whom modern literary license have been given dark and ghostly connotations.

Since everyone the world over loves a good ghost story and due to humanity's inherent liking of a good, chilling story of the supernatural, it isn't difficult to understand how actual fact may actually have given rise to what is now an established Hawaiian legend that invariably gives *'chicken flesh'* (goose bumps) to all who hear these tales of ghostly marchers in the night. For someone who is invariably almost painfully skeptical like myself, to hear such an entirely plausible explanation for these stories (Kipling would doubtless call them 'Ripping Tales') amounts to wonderfully logical interpretation of otherwise inexplicable historic circumstances.

Just another example of the value of books. This particular book was pointed especially out to me by Jim Sincher at The Kite factory as being an important and valuably insightful book concerned with little known actual Hawaiian history. And of course, I am well aware that such oral histories not only were the sole means of traditional transmission of Hawaiian history, given the lack of a written Hawaiian language prior to the arrival of the missionaries, but a scarce and endangered source of first-person information about the past.

Today has been fairly warm and humid. It helps me better understand why people living in tropical cultures (and also in the Far East) bathe before bedtime, by preferred custom. In the cooler North American climes, the usual custom is to start the day with a shower (this is certainly my own habit and a day without a shower to start it is somehow uncomfortable for me). In a climate like this, one gets pretty sticky by the end of the day (more so males, I would imagine, with their more powerful stink of testosterone-linked sweat). I well recall days spent in Taiwan, back in the late 80s, in which it would seem impossible to ever get dry after a shower. One would get sweaty, take a shower (when the plumbing was working in our Tien Mou area house, that is), and then never get quite completely dry afterwards. I would imagine the same applies here, but since everyone else in this home takes baths and showers at day's end, I elect to stay with my AM shower schedule. Not nearly enough hot water here, as what little there is runs out in a few minutes; the water heater must hold all

of 5 gallons! Fortunately, the 'cold' tap water is room tempera-
ture, or it would be quite a shock every AM getting under the
water.

Today, in the course of my chat with 54 year old Locinda of
the skin-tight jeans, I learned that her controversial neighbor
John MacByte fancied himself somewhat of a 'guru' and was
practicing 'Tantric Yoga' with his *hareem* of lovely young lady
friends and not what was erroneously referred to as 'Kama Sutra
Yoga' by my real estate broker, Cheryl Apaia. That certainly
would explain the indignant regard which others expressed for
the bloke. Of course, money is a powerful aphrodisiac to start
with, so money + sex = wild & crazy times.

On the drive this afternoon on my leisurely cruise through the
East End area, I was traveling slow enough (most of the time at
only 25 mph or so) to check out the many homes and types of
domiciles erected on the various properties. Aside from continuously drooling over some of the exotic sites clustered along the
stunningly beautiful east end shoreline, there were as many modest homes as fairly pricey ones. Even the ones I would imagine
to be pricey weren't all that big or fancy; most were rectangular
and I am guessing about 2000 feet or less in terms of square
footage. Clearly, most of them were built more than 10 years ago
(and a great number before then), when prices weren't as outrageous as they are currently.

I can't help but draw figurative parallels with the task facing us
on our new postage-stamp sized property, since even a modest
1000 ft sq single story home will cost us about $150,000.00 to
build at current rates. When I told our architect contact Victor
Montero what I was thinking, he pulled out a drawing of a home
that, while it seemed to fit my concepts fairly closely, was still a
fairly simple design, rectangular in shape, and with an interior
footage of about 1000 ft sq. At $150 per square foot, that's not

cheap. I'm starting to think that a prefab home, perhaps in a polygon configuration, would be a good idea (at least financially... aesthetically it would be grotesque in such a traditional island setting, however). There are prefab geodesic dome home designs that come pre-packaged with all materials. Supposedly these homes can be assembled completely by two people without any advanced building skills or specialized construction knowledge (at least according to the promotional materials). If I could have a basic platform constructed on pilings (due to the mild declination of the property at the rear, or seaward end) on the property, then one of the geodesic prefab homes could be built on it by myself, with the help of a local friend perhaps. The next questions presenting themselves would then be: 1) how much to have some bulldozing (or grading) and basic property-preparation done first; 2) how much further cost to put in the concrete pilings and build the elevated platform; and 3) how much to buy the pre-fab geodesic dome kit and have it shipped to the property site from the mainland.

Much depends on what the cheapest but most adequate structure (quality-wise) turns out to be, since we'll be hanging on to the cost factors by the bare skin of our teeth, on this project. One thing I certainly can't be faulted for: when I pick a project, I instinctively know how to spend money like it's going out of style. Few doubtless can excel my inherent abilities in this area of pricey resourcelessness.

Speaking of the anticipated project, I am reminded that Carlo today mentioned in our conversation the fact that existing homes on Oahu can be obtained for a few thousand dollars if one wants to go to the trouble of having them moved to a new location. He stated that the properties they are on are presently being cleared for new development and since the property owner has to assume the cost of having the old structures destroyed and cleared, he apparently hit on an alternative idea of allowing the older homes to be bought very cheaply if the purchaser would assume the cost of moving them to a new location. From what Carlo said, the older homes in reference are still structurally sound and suitable for reuse. Of course, the cost of having a small home on Oahu shipped to Moloka'i would undoubtedly entail a considerable cost (understatement), so that idea—while interesting—appears out of the question.

Dunno...I should probably have my head examined for even getting us involved in this little escapade on Moloka'i, since I'll probably have kicked the bucket well before we have anything erected on our property suitable to move into. Five-to-seven years is starting to seem painfully close, as well, since that's the time deadline we have tentatively set for ourselves before we're likely ready to bail out of California State civil service and retire for good.

People like Carlo are probably the smart ones, who own a live-aboard boat and can tie-up at any wharf anywhere they've set a mind to. That assumes that maintenance costs of taking care of a boat are not enough to sink the prospects, of course. Wooden boats are known money holes, while even fiberglass and ferro-cement have their special cost requirements, as well. Ah well, people like me who have a congenital reverse propensity for attracting money were born to be dreamers, I guess. Folks like MacByte, with gobs of money, can afford not just to dream but to scorn the criticism of others when they pursue their own unique and perhaps exceptionally controversial dreams.

Next door to me, the neighbor's #@$%^$#@^&*$ roosters are already in full cry and it's only 6 PM. I've half a mind to sneak over there this evening and strangle the prime offenders. Funny that I've always regarded chickens as benign creatures, but then, I've never had to live right next to a chicken coop with a couple of raucous and horny little roosters in charge of all the hens before. If there is one productive lesson to be learned from this daily ordeal by cock-a-doodle-do, it must be 'never keep chickens' (let someone else own them—just shut up and enjoy eating them). Sigh.

Heard someone playing the Hawaiian drum (pahu) and chanting this evening. Makes me think about Vince Lorenz' $1250 hula pahu up at the Moloka'i Coffee Plantation. In my chat with Richard Eloka today, he remarked that learning the hula drum technique isn't really very hard—the hard part is learning the many different *hula chants* themselves and being able to recite them (sing, actually) to the accompaniment of the pahu. And so this day comes to a near end. Must make a pot of rice and eat before it gets too dark. With all the windows this room has on ground level, it's like living in a fish bowl after dark, unless one goes to bed when the sun sets (which is what I do). At least I don't have to fret over the quality of today's universally wretched commercial TV broadcasting…with no TV to turn on, that particular peeve is not presently a problem.

To sleep, perchance to dream (probably nightmares about where the rest of the money to fulfill this Moloka'i dream of ours is going to come from).

April 17th, 2005 (Sunday)

The huge Hawaiian bumble-bees that frequent the yard here are delightful. One of those aeronautical improbabilities, with their immense body mass and awkward, bulky conformational appearance, they are nonetheless excellent (if slow) fliers and somehow I seem to greatly enjoy the characteristic drone of their flight as they buzz around the window. These natural entomological counterparts of the Boeing 747 and Antonov An-17 (also impossibly huge and seemingly incapable of flight when viewed as static objects on the ground) are a perfect symbol to me of the local lifestyle...relaxed, in no particular hurry, and yet purposeful in an unhurried, unforced, and largely pragmatic manner.

Speaking of being unhurried and relaxed as an example of the Hawaiian lifestyle, my 50 some-odd books acquired here on all aspects of the Hawaiian culture, history, and what-have-you, effectively constitute what amounts to an immersion course in Hawaiiana. I can see why so many writers appreciate the islands as a location from which to pursue their craft. Clemens, Stevenson, and many others of literary note all found the islands and discovered this fact to their evident delight. In fact, I picked up a book comprised of about 13 chapters of Samuel Clemens' Hawaiian observations (written originally in 1872 as a series of newspaper articles for The Sacramento Union), that were part of a larger series that ended up being used for his book 'Roughing it'.

One of the points that is consistently made about the frustratingly (to market-economy westerners from the mainland, at any rate) slow pace of the Hawaiian lifestyle is that traditional Polynesian culture placed a strong emphasis on communal values. Unlike present-day America, which emphasizes individual rights and suborns collective or communal values, traditional Hawaiian custom emphasized sharing of any surpluses that may have accumulated in terms of material goods, foodstuffs and other items. This custom-generated tendency to spread supportive wealth and material things among others automatically discouraged adoption of the integral western economic principle of accumulation of surplus goods (for use as profit-generating trade), since it was by nature antithetical to the ancient Hawaiian manner of living. Viewed by insensitive outsiders, this would perhaps be pointed to as an indicator of inherent laziness, when in reality it was merely perfectly acceptable behavior congruent with the age-old social norm. Any student of social anthropology would immediately perceive this fact, whereas the average person of limited insight and awareness would probably seize upon the circumstance as evidence of 'flawed' (or culturally 'inferior') economic outlook.

Earlier, I mentioned the fact that oral histories of Hawaiian traditions are one of the most important sources of deeper insight into the traditional Hawaiian culture (this is true for any culture, of course). In particular, *Kapuna Kaili'ohe's* recollected history of her family's history *'Tales From the Night Rainbows'*, as a specially selected and trained *"Kahuna Ho'opio'pio"* (sorceress and genealogy chanter) offers tremendous understanding of the old ways that are now so poorly understood or misinterpreted.

I find myself consistently returning to the chronicle of her collected observations for further gems of awareness, for there are many parallels to be found therein with the present status of cultural transference processes on Moloka'i (and the other islands). In one part, she dealt with the cultural impact of the warlike Tahitian invader kings (the islands' more or less acknowledged *'second wave of settlement'*) on the peaceful original inhabitants of the islands (the Maoli, or "people", also known by the Tahitian Ali'i as "Mana hune" or "Menehune"), and later on the impact of the Calvinist missionaries when they began their own invasion of the islands in 1820 (their arrival occurred conveniently just after 1819, which was the date the reigning Hawaiian monarch finally ended the *'kapu'*—effectively translated, *'forbidden by royal decree'*--system and the old traditional gods were effectively overthrown once and for all).

The resultant status quo in both instances was overwhelmingly one of a uniform rejection of the older ways in favor of the newer ones by the younger generations. In the case of the former, the indigenous people effectively had no choice but to either accept the imposed rule of the new Tahitian kings, to remain on their own islands (but escape to the remote areas of the mountains), or to flee to refuge on *Kaua'i* (which was one of the last islands populated by the Maoli that was subjugated by the Ali'i). In the latter instance, not only had the islanders just overthrown the old religion immediately prior to the arrival of the foreign missionaries (therefore constituting prime candidates for conversion to the new Christian god), but the younger generations were quickly fixated by the 'new' (and 'exotic') western culture of the foreigners. This sequence of events continued to result in a near-terminal process of substantially diminished awareness of (and appreciation for) the old traditional values that, in the absence of a written history and reliance on handed-down oral cultural records, a degenerative process simply continued to the point where today, a preponderant mass of knowledge about the old customs, culture, and civilization has been lost. If it weren't for the diligence of contemporary historians, archeologists, and other researchers of past Hawaiian events and history, we would today know very little at all about Hawaii's earlier centuries.

A modern parallel to this process appears obvious as this last bastion of traditional Hawaii (excluding the *'Forbidden Isle'* of Ni'ihau) that is Moloka'i fights off a similar cultural invasion of the island by the worst aspects of modern Haole mainland culture. Given that (due to the degenerative factors referenced above) most 'native Hawaiians' on Moloka'i have almost completely lost any genuine knowledge of their cultural roots, many of them of necessity reflexively retreat to a feigned (artificial) closeness with their former culture that is probably based upon and vindicated only by the fact that they have a higher percentage of native Hawaiian blood than is found elsewhere in the islands. In all likelihood, they have lost as much awareness of the real cultural traditions as their predecessors, but find some comfort in the fact that their *kama'aina* bloodlines confer MORE legitimacy (albeit superficial and largely insubstantial) in terms of their understanding of traditional culture than those who are distinctly identifiable outsiders (*Haole, Malihini*, etc.).

As I perceive it, the most serious threats that Moloka'i faces stem directly from deleterious aspects of imported pop American sub-culture (including gang affinities, hip-hop and rap music, materialistic techno-artifacts), car culture (over-amplified car 'boombox' stereos, jacked-up monster trucks, etc.) and whatever else has been seized upon by sub-cultural groups as the latest ultra-cool 'extreme' fad (examples would include hip-hop, rap, body-tattooing and piercing, etc.).

All of these unhealthy influences, aided and abetted by the sex and violence that is a common component of today's video and video-gaming, when thrown in the mix with increased parental abnegation of traditional authority and a public school system that brought in culturally disconnected outsiders to teach (*haole* from the mainland, mostly, who were invariably disrespected and even outright ridiculed by the local teenaged students, are bad enough. Toss in the additional (and most serious) concern of rampant substance abuse (crystal methamphetamine is the most serious drug, among several in use) that is now apparently almost epidemic among both high-school aged kids and adults, and you have a set of shear-forces that are quite capable of ripping the island apart.

In this specific, I was discussing local problems with a resident yesterday and was dismayed to hear that the situation is so bad at Moloka'i High School (near Kualapu'u, just east of Ho'olehua) that the students brashly insult teachers and the principal to their faces. As this person told it, there is no restraint at all in use of foul language and very bad 4-letter words are routinely directed towards teachers and the school's staff alike. The predictable result is that many newly arrived teachers are easily intimidated by such shocking treatment and either soon leave, or resign themselves to simply showing up for class, going through the motions without any show of determination to actually teach, picking up their small paycheck to enable themselves to remain in what they had originally and rather naively perceived (like so many visitors to these islands) as an idyllic tropical paradise.

These circumstances reflect many influences, not the least of which are natural adolescent tendencies towards rebelliousness, cross-cultural conflicts and misunderstandings (just mentioned), and the continuous negative background effects of violent, sex-obsessed pop-culture imported from the mainland in video and musical form.

I have noticed myself, as I sit in my rented room and write on a number of occasions, that there are obvious evidences of these things to be found here that I formerly strongly associated exclusively with mainland culture. This includes excessively loud and noisy automobiles, the presence of those maddeningly irritating hyper-bass audio-thumping vibrations that are produced by car stereo systems with several hundred of watts of grossly amplified power, and numerous examples of cars being driven excessively fast and recklessly on these small, curvilinear residential streets after dark.

Only the community's small children ('keiki') appear to still be under substantial parental authority on Moloka'i. It is plain enough that by the time local children have hit puberty (and the mid-levels of the public schools), they have been forever distanced from any and all substantial family ties and lost entirely to the horrid allure of the worst pop-culture outrages the (American) mainland has to offer.

On a note apart (it is now almost noon on Sunday), there is a beautiful wind chime somewhere outside my room (on a nearby house) that responds to the never-ending local currents of the island trade winds with a beautiful scale of harmonic tones. A small positive note among all the depressing observations ruminated upon above, but sometimes it's the small things that are the most valuable and noteworthy...at least in my experience. Perfectly in harmony with my central life philosophy of elegant simplicity (Japanese concept of *'Shibui'*, for example, or the human-scale economic philosophy of *E.F. Schumacher*).

Listening to the wind chime reminds me that there seem to be a lot of dogs in the neighborhood locally. A good number of them sound big, mean, and even vicious in the manner of their barking (if one can fairly base an impression of the dog on the reflexive effect his barking creates). I would guess that many are selected just for those qualities, given the encroaching drug problems here; they all sound like Mastiffs, Pitbulls, Rotweiler, or other physically large and aggressive types (although most are undoubtedly what the locals call *'Poi-dogs'*, or mixed-breed mongrels). Moloka'i seems definitely not the place to bring a dog over to and let him run around free, certainly, although this is the Ranch Camp neighborhood, with its uniquely characteristic flavor and not a conventional Haole haven.

I am guessing that both Ranch Camp and the nearby Manila Camp residential areas of the immediate Kaunakakai vicinity were heavily settled by Filipinos, along with local *kamai'inas*, and a few other ethnic groups (Chinese & Japanese). I seem to recall that the largest single ethnic group on the island, other than people of Hawaiian blood, are the Filipinos. Matter of fact, glancing through another of my recently acquired books (appropriately enough titled *'Hawaii's Pineapple Century—A History of the Crowned Fruit in the Hawaiian Islands'*), I find that Chapter Seven of that book contains a precise ethnic breakdown of a Moloka'i plantation village (presumably at Maunaloa) in the early 1950s. In this data, it is revealed that of the total of 861 'ordinary' pineapple workers from all ethnic groups, over 484 of them were of Filipino descent. This contrasted with 5 who were Chinese, 30 who were Caucasian, 188 who were Japanese, and only 2 who were listed as "Hawaiian". Hmmm. More evidence of the layback island predilection among 'locals', I would venture. Apparently, the Libby Company was the corporate grower responsible for the Moloka'i plantation at Maunaloa, and they ultimately sold out to Dole (the same large commercial pineapple producer that was up to its neck in skullduggery in immediately pre-annexational Hawaiian politics, clear through to the final end of pineapple cultivation in Hawaii in the 1980s).

I've a mind to drop by the town library tomorrow to check on the ethnic make-up of the island during the most recently concluded national census. It probably mirrors the data just cited and will no doubt be quite interesting. Another interesting observation is that one may see many older Filipino men longing around the old storefronts downtown (K'kai). The original old pineapple plantation property at Maunaloa (east end) was bought back by *Moloka'i Ranch* (now owned by a New Zealand firm), a decade ago and has now been developed into a 'theme' residential neighborhood with a central plan governing the construction of buildings and edifices that requires them to bear a passing resemblance to the old Hawaiian plantation style home design. These homes seem to be available for about $350,000 each (including .17 sq acre property they sit on), which while not outrageous for this part of the islands, isn't cheap either. Maunaloa sits at an elevation of about 1500 feet and the wind is always in evidence and usually quite gusty there. One needs to very much enjoy being windswept to want to live at Maunaloa, I

---

think, as it is quite exposed (as is most of the entire western end of the island).

An effort to plan Norfolk Pines there several decades ago, to help reduce the impact of those trade winds on the slopes of Maunaloa, do help somewhat, but it's still pretty gusty most of the time.

The east end of Moloka'i is, in my admittedly not yet fully informed opinion, the REALLY desirable part of the island to live on, since it is a lot more lush and tropical than either the east or southern shore areas. Of course, the prices are proportionately a lot higher on that end, as well.

Traditionally, under the ancient Ali'i customs, the land was divided into long pie-shaped segments that stretched from the uppermost heights on the island down to the shore. These were called "Ahupua'a" and Jon MacByte's recent sale of about 1008 acres on the east end (at mile19) was an Ahupua'a property. It will be recalled that he originally purchased it for about $1.3 million (a few years ago) and realized a $2.5 million dollar profit from its sale at the recently concluded auction.

The east end is chock-a-block full of eclectic characters that include wealthy Haoles escaping from the mainland meat grinder, post-Hippie recidivist new-agers, Yuppie refugees, and just about every possible permutation in between (even including not a few natives—or kama'aina locals, as they prefer to be called). Many of them come up to the K'kai weekly arts & crafts event on Saturdays, so whether you buy anything there or not, it's a good way to strike up a conversation and find out what's shaking on the "happening" end of the island.

I think it's interesting to learn that there apparently aren't many Chinese left on Moloka'i (evidenced by the ethnic detail cited earlier, at least). Cicada's mother (Daphne), who passed away in 2000, was one of a small number who were resident here. Cicada mentioned that there was once a Chinese eatery in town and this corroborates other information I have heard that up until a decade or so ago, a Chinese restaurant had been a long-time fixture of K'kai's restaurant options. Matter of fact, someone else asked if our newly purchased property was anywhere near the relic of an old restaurant that is located between the *Moloka'i Shores* condominiums and the *Moloka'i Hotel*. Checking the area over, I find that there is an apparently abandoned old building there right by the roadside, so this makes me wonder if Cicada's family had anything to do with it (perhaps the Chinese restaurant was owned by her family?) Cicada seemed to think that a Chinese food operation would be popular today and someone else I talked with (in Maunaloa, I think--probably Debbie Sincher at 'The Big Wind Kite factory')--echoed that sentiment when she said '...it would be nice to have a few more eating options on the island to choose from'. When I mentioned this to Suki, she responded (without hesitation) *"too much work"*, which is probably still true even if you are a couple trained and skilled in preparation of Chinese cuisine.

Another muggy afternoon today; highs probably in the mid to high 70s, but it feels hot in the direct sun and the humidity also feels higher than normal. The MS/Word spell and grammar checker sub-program I am writing this on informs me that according to something called the *Flesch-Kinkaid Readability criteria*, I am writing at a 12th grade level (too many fragments and other supposed grammatical errors, it feels). That's probably a comforting thought in some higher esoteric context, I suppose, but I wish I could turn the bloody sub-menu off for the moment. Not everyone deliberately chooses to hew precisely to the King's English (and we're not referring to King Kamehameha, here) when writing, but this fact doesn't seem to have made any impression on the software designers when they came up with this program!

Tomorrow is Monday, and back to regular *"slow-mo, Brah"* business hours. I need to call the escrow company tomorrow and check on whether they received the final closing payment for our property, then I need to get in touch with Cheryl Apaia to determine whether there's anything further I need to do before going ahead with installation of the water line and meter. I should also call Cicada, since Inocencia tells me that Cicada has been by several times (but strangely always after I am in bed, since I typically hit the sack at about 7 PM). Need to ask her a lot of things: curious about her work as a teacher and how it interrelates to the current brouhaha over Moloka'i schools' literacy issues. Also curious about the restaurant tie-in. One other subject I want to run by her is Vince Lorenz, the local pahu craftsman who lives just down the street from her place near our property. Don't want to simply waltz in on him without some sort of tentative introduction, since I'm not sure what the local customs are in this regard.

One final agenda item for Monday is touching base with Victor Montero (architect), if it appears that our escrow is officially closed, and I can go ahead and have the water line & meter installed. I think Victor said he can coordinate that for us, since he has some contacts in the Maui County PU department (as previously mentioned). It's now almost 6PM and I have spent the entire writing, reading, and nursing the mild sunburn I got yesterday on the east end.

Kalikiano Kalei

April 18th, 2005 (Monday)

Read some of Sam Clemens' writing done on his first and only trip to Hawaii in 1866 and any read of his work for me is unfailingly stimulating. Although Clemens was caught up in his vision of the rectitude of America's *civilising* influence on the 'barbarism of the Sandwich Islands', it nevertheless correctly drew continuous humorous parallels between the nature of early (colonial) Hawaiian life and the Christian Yankee hypocrisy that for Clemens was a characterized focus of American culture in his period.

Clemens did not note the indigenously Hawaiian sport of 'wave-riding' in his original series of 26 dispatches to the Sacramento Union Newspaper, but later in *'Roughing It'* he did in fact mention surfing in connection with his first (and only) attempts at the sport. Apparently, he tried to surf twice (presumably two attempts to catch waves on the same day), according to his comments, and failed each time. Clemens went on to say that only native Hawaiians could master the technique of catching a wave and remaining on it as it came to shore with all the *"...blinding speed of a street tram"*. Of course, at that time street trams made a blindly fast speed of about 5 mph.

The typical Hawaiian surfboard was made of very hard, dense island woods (*Koa* comes to mind) and lengths of 20 feet or more were typical; to master such a vehicle required much more than technique only and involved more than a little skillful application of physical strength (it is noteworthy that surfing was equally enjoyed by both men and women both before and after the Ali'i *kapu* originally limiting the sport to royalty had been lifted). One other brief factoid that emerges about Clemens in a foreword to these dispatches from the islands is that Clemens at one point during his stay put a gun to his head that had been loaded with a single bullet, in the manner of Russian Roulette, but survived the event;

74

apparently there were moments of extreme self-doubt and sobering uncertainty in Clemens life that his ebullient writing did not readily reveal, at first peruse.

Clemens seems to use the old Hawaiian word *'Kanaka'* as a vulgar substitute for 'native' (much in the same manner the words *'nigger'* and *'kaffer'* were used in the American South and colonial Africa to describe native blacks) in his writing about the islands. 'Kanaka' translated properly means "person" or "human being". In the definitive Hawaiian-English dictionary authored by Pukui and Elbert, there are a number of interesting definitions of the term, along with a number of specific variants. One that I found particularly of interest, owing to my aviation interests, is *'Kanaka lele'*, which literally means 'flying person', and apparently was formulated to specifically describe the Christian concept of an 'angel'. Another more commonly used derivative is *'Kanaka maoli'*, which means 'a full-blooded Hawaiian person'. Several other related derivatives of interest are: 1) *'Kanakamakua'* = "mature, adult person, or to act like a mature person"; 2) *'Kana Kaloka'* = 'Santa Claus'; 3) *'Kanaka 'e'* = "foreigner, outside, stranger, or heathen"; and 4) *'Kanaka hana'* = 'worker'.

Since I am a great fan of the coffee bean, and owing in no small part to my yet-unrealized life-long dream of operating a coffeehouse (since at least as far back as Berkeley days), I have been keenly interested in what passes for such in Kaunakakai. On my last visit in October of 2004, there were only two such establishments that could be regarded as such, by the conventionally accepted definition. One is *Sturgess' Café and Art Gallery* on K'kai's main street and the other was run by a bible thumper who offered religious tracts in his small, out of the way location near the town's relatively new pizza joint (fortunately, it has since dried up and vanished). As a firm adherent to the concept of the coffeehouse as being a figuratively level field where local intellectualism may flourish (or at least may be sewn with seeds of thought and perhaps germinated), I am a firm believer that an establishment that serves coffee should be more than just a conventional 'café'.

Properly approached, a 'coffeehouse' should be a place where people may gather over good coffee (none of that crappy stuff commonly passed off as coffee by American restaurants) and interact as whim dictates, whether by conversation, or by computer (the modern 'internet coffeehouse' concept). Above all, it should be a place where one feels comfortable, as in a refuge from the artificial outside pressures of daily bourgeois concern. Art and creativity, imagination and broadened awareness all have a strong legitimacy as component aspects of such a watering hole, in my mind.

In a small community like K'kai, I feel a strong need for a place where everyone can gather, but most importantly, where those who are more or less 'Kanaka 'e' (outsiders, such as myself) can find some welcome refuge from the diaspora they have been cast into as island newcomers. The popular Moloka'i tag-line *"The Friendly Isle"* was never a traditional island label, having come instead from the efforts of Haole public relations flacks, who back in the 60s and 70s wanted to create tourist-friendly, characterredolent descriptive terms for each of the main islands. The fact that Moloka'i of today is not (nor has ever been, contrary to widespread belief) excessively friendly to distinctively identifiable outsiders is a concern to more sensitive visitors like myself, who come with eyes wide open and cultural receptive antennae aquiver. It isn't easy to blend in with any group here, if you don't have either dark (or tan) skin, or some demonstrable pre-existing knowledge of island customs and mannerisms. There is a sort of casual acceptance that takes a sort of lessened form of rote, pseudo Japanese modes of excessive politeness—this is typically encountered anywhere one flashes cash and demonstrates a proper tourist-like willingness to help pad out the local economy, but otherwise getting to 'the local source', as it were, is as challenging on Moloka'i for visitors as it would be anywhere else in the world.

Sturgess' Café & Art Gallery is a puzzle in some ways, as it seems to have a sort of superficial Bohemian flavor to it, by virtue of its displayed works of art by the proprietor (Sturgess) and its small upstairs gallery of work by local artists. It also has a computer and allows visitors to connect to the net using the in-house PC. However, beyond this, the *Ti-Leaf Curtain* descends and one is again reminded of the invisible boundary line between locals and visitors. The staff are locals, hired by Sturgess in true 'Great White Father' style, since he is providing some much-needed employment (minimal though it may be) for a few locals on an island which has the poorest local economy of all 5 of the main Hawaiian islands.

Therein lies part of the problem, since the locals are not at all tuned in to the greater picture of world-wide cosmopolitan thought and are about as gregarious in their critical role as baristas as a lump of sullen stone. In almost all coffee houses, the baristas set the style, the tone, and the manner by which the establishment's aesthetic character is measured (and correspondingly enjoyed). Thus, passing any meaningful time of day attempting to cultivate a productive conversation with one of Sturgess' local baristas is a completely null experience. One orders an espresso and pays for it, drinks it feeling slightly empty all the while and then gets up and leaves. There is no desire to linger, to sit for a while and enjoy the ambience, for there really is none to speak of in that greater aesthetic sense I refer to.

Frustrating too is the fact that occasional exotic Haole tourists (or island visitors who may own a condo or have a rental accommodation for a week or so) will drop in and sit there ostensibly immersed in a book and giving off strong mainland vibes that say *'keep your distance—I don't feel at all comfortable here'*. I noted this on my previous visit, when a drop-dead gorgeous young woman and her small sister would drop by for coffee in the early morning. This beautiful dark-haired creature was clearly well-aware of her extreme good looks, and her walk and self-assured LA style mannerisms almost seemed to actively discourage any attempt to strike up a casual conversation with her before she departed, younger sister in tow (and doubtless headed back to the condo). Of course, had the casual converser engaging her been a Brad Pitt clone, I am sure things would have been instantly different!

This past week, I dropped by for a double espresso and somewhat bleakly took a seat, after finding out that the computer was 'down' (I later found out the net had only gone down briefly and was immediately back up again—the barista of the moment was a young high-school age person who seemed to almost rival Calvin Coolidge's legendary penchant for verbal brevity and she hadn't attempted to make this important distinction). At any rate, sure enough, there by the window sat another obligatory, artificially absorbed beautiful young woman, nose deeply buried in a book and giving off all the warm vibes of a block of ice. I drank my coffee and noted this repetition of nuance and left shortly thereafter to take care of some business. Pity, really.

Sturgess doesn't help things by displaying many of his rather excellent artworks on the café walls that he will not sell under any circumstance. Not only is that a bit strange, it can almost be regarded as a form of arrogance. Sturgess advertises in the original local paper *('The Dispatch')* for 'local models' to paint and the subjects displayed on the walls of the coffeehouse are seemingly all of 'Kanaka maoli'. He has one particularly striking painting of a local shorescape and palm trees, depicted under the dark glower of a tropical storm, that much impressed me on my last visit. Of course, it wasn't for sale. Another one that also impressed me was a sympathetic and sensitive rendering of beautiful (hapa-Haole) Royal Heir Apparent Princess *Kaiulani*, as she might have looked, seated in a flowing white dress, just before her untimely death at age 24 on March 6th, 1899. I haven't had a chance to meet Sturgess or talk to him, so I have no idea as to what he is like in person, but his apparent disengagement from casual contact with visiting Haoles suggests much.

If I were able to find capital to support my desire to open a combined coffeehouse and book store (alas, *'neva hoppin'*, as my wife delights in saying), I would certainly try to make it more agreeable and friendly to visitors as well as locals, but the whole idea behind the vitality of any coffeehouse is intelligent interaction between visitors, in support of enlightened thought and the precepts of aware intellect and reflective self-actualisation (however vague and non-specific they may be). Sturgess' is a false start in that direction, and the air of intellectual arrogance (mixed as it appears to be with aesthetic disregard that it gives off) is vaguely unsatisfying and aesthetically sterile from the perceived standpoint of any haole visitor (in my opinion). Sadly, Sturgess' is the only such refuge in the entire town, so well-intended, wannabe island residents like myself still have no safe harbor in which to tie up, for the moment.

One reflection that my reading produced yesterday was the realisation that as bad as the missionaries may have been in their ill-conceived (although well-intended) and ultra-conservative repression of local morals, in their relentless quest to convert the island's 'heathens' to Christianity, they did accomplish a few notable things. Chief among these was the formulation of a standardised Hawaiian alphabet, which enabled the Hawaiian people to finally have a written language (after centuries of having to rely on oral tradition *only* for transmission of their cultural wisdom).This was without question or qualification a formidable undertaking and one that no matter how bad many of their other efforts were (such as attempts to clothe the islanders in totally unsuited western style dress), deserves to be commended unequivocally and completely.

With regard to the latter missionary crusade to cover the 'shame' of the islanders' nakedness with modest garments, Sam Clemens makes some wry observations about the results of their early efforts to get the natives to adopt western dress. Of course, he does so with an ethnocentric bias that viewed nakedness as being inarguably inappropriate, despite the fact that traditional Hawaiian garb (abbreviated as it was) was perfectly suited to the heat and humidity of the climate and heavy, hot western garments were functionally grotesque aberrations in such a non-westernised tropical locale as the islands.

Around noon, I dropped by the Ho'olehua PO and found my camera download cable waiting for me. Suki had sent it out to my new box there (PO Box 536). Interesting lesson in technological advances for me in this, since shortly after arrival and finding that I had neglected to bring this important camera-to-laptop cable with me, I had visited the office of the Moloka'i Island Times to see if they might be able to loan me a cable temporarily. I figured that they must use digital cameras to take images for the paper and in that I was correct. What I hadn't figured on was the fact that they use the latest USB-2 compatible Olympus equipment, gear that uses the newer standard connection (rather than the old USB-1 or serial connector input). Hence, I was unable to use their cable and had to ask Suki to send me the one I have on my desktop PC at home. My digital Olympus camera is only three years old (C-2020 model), but that's enough passage of time for a whole new connection standard to come on line. Technology waits for no man, to paraphrase an old proverbial admonishment. Later in the day I was finally able to get the images of our new property downloaded into my laptop so I can send them to Suki as email attachments.

While out and around in the Hoo'lehua area, I dropped by to see Cheryl Apaia and enjoyed some more exchanges with her. She's a gold mine of information about everything, since she runs a beauty-parlor right next to the Kualapu'u Post Office (out of which she carries on her real estate business as a sideline). As mentioned before, Sheryl is a haole who married a local some years ago (probably a mixed Kanaka/Filipino person, judging from the name 'Apaia')—he passed away 5 years ago—and she dabbles in astrology, among other things. Her hair is permed to death…one of the liabilities of endless hair-styling that requires a 'permanent' hair wave. I keep trying to warm Suki away from this habit (one of her sisters is a 'cosmetologist'), but she persists in it and her hair is starting to get thin in the same manner. What is it with this harsh chemical treatment of women's hair that so destroys it, anyway? *Yuuk!* Give me a woman who lets her hair grow long and straight, and untouched by heat & chemicals, any day! I think it the greatest irony that women such as the Chinese, who are blessed with some of the most luxurious and beautiful hair in the entire world, invariably persist in subjecting it to the wretched and harmful injustices of Western 'perming'.

Among the topics Cheryl and I touched upon were the dire situation at Moloka'i upper level schools (i.e. Moloka'i HS). I have to agree with Cheryl that what that school needs is (in her words) a great big, no-bullshit male principal, preferably one weighing over 275, six feet plus tall, and a former USMC DI, who also happens to have a PhD in education. She opined that it would be great also, if he were black, Hawaiian, or of any ethnicity other than Caucasian. I agree completely, since only someone who is willing make it very clear that he is not going to be intimidated by adolescent 'attitude' is going to be able to successfully overcome the present disrespect and disregard that is so effectively emasculating the school's administrative ability to turn the school around.

The present principal is female, haole (from the mainland), demure, and small-statured. In other words, inconsequential in the eyes of the rebellious post-pubescent HS students whose lack of interest in their studies is responsible for the sad 'bottom-of-the-heap' scholastic ratings the school has garnered in a recent island-wide survey. I really think Cheryl has the right idea here. She earlier told me about a new haole teacher (female) at Moloka'i HS who had passed out a lengthy summer reading assignment to her students. A day or so later, the huge (physically imposing stature) kanaka father of one of the students came to her office and after installing himself scarcely an inch from her face, proceeded to let her know in a loud and angry manner that she should stop interfering with his family's life (*Ka 'ohana*) by giving his kid such 'stupid' things to do in the summer vacation break as a *reading assignment*. The teacher was so shaken by this angry display of violent reactivity that she shortly resigned (as many others have done, upon receiving similar treatment here) and returned to the mainland. Hawaii is no place for meek snowflakes!

After leaving Cheryl's shop, I dropped by the former *Moloka'i Coffee Plantation* shop to take another look at the beautiful 'Hula Pahu' I had seen there, shortly after arrival. I was mildly distressed to find it gone, but found that the drum maker's sister (local Victor Lorenz is a wood craftsman, but his father-in-law Bob Kahiko is the Pahu craftsman) had just taken it back home. At any rate, I bought a nice business card case, a rather simple but elegant brass case with a carved Hawaiian sea turtle etched out of Koa wood on it. I also noted that K'kai local Richard Elokas also had a few of his nice Pu'niau drums (these are the small traditional drum made from a coconut shell and worn strapped to the player's thigh) and hand-carved traditional fish hooks on sale there ($50 for the Pu'niu and $75 for the large old-style fish hooks made from Koa wood and deer antler). These 'Maui's fish hooks' are the essential tourist take-away, by the way, along with those insipid automobile rear-window 'stick family' decals that haoles think are *sooooo* cute!

The woman I was talking to was quite pretty and in her mid-30s (I guessed). Her name was *Kamaile* (which my reference library tells me means *'of the fragrant Maile plant'*, a flowering Hawaiian vine with a luxuriously floral perfume). As we talked, it was quite a pleasant surprise to find her to be a very warm and genuinely friendly person, so we chatted about all sorts of things—mostly related to Hawaii or Moloka'i. She wore, it did not elude me, a beautiful red flower above her right ear—a sign that she was presently unmarried and 'available', in the unspoken gender language of the islands (worn on the left, it means 'taken').

As our chat continued, she told me her son had been immersed in a unique local institution—a school wherein everything is taught in Hawaiian—up through the 6th grade. After that he transferred to the local public school system and as a result now is fluently conversant with both English and traditional Hawaiian languages. The special school referred to above specializes not only in teaching the traditional Hawaiian language, but also in subjects that are unique to the islands (arts, culture, social customs, etc.) themselves.

She was really warming up to our chat, since it was evident that I was not just another insensitive tourist but someone who had a keen and active interest in the old manners and customs of Moloka'i. *Kamaile* also struck me as someone of reasonably acute intelligence, which is always a pleasure to run across. Of course, I couldn't help but be aware of her attractiveness, at the same time I was reminded of ancient Hawaiian attitudes towards mutual attraction. There was no doubt that Kamaile was of substantially pure native extraction—you could see the islands quite clearly etched in her facial physiognomy and figure. I honestly found myself quite attracted to her, despite the relatively brief contact we had (about 30 minutes). She was working in the gift shop that is part of the old Moloka'i Coffee Plantation store, which is how we came into contact, of course. One thing that didn't surprise me was the fact that when I mentioned the fact that I was staying in Ranch Camp with a friend, Kamaile instantly knew who Inocencia was and also that she worked part time at *Moloka'i General Hospital*. This is simply another example of how completely and insularly integrated life is on Moloka'i. Everyone here knows everyone else and there really are ultimately (I would assume) no secrets that could possibly be kept in with total confidence in such a place as this.

Thinking about this encounter later that evening, I reflected that she had made a considerable impression on me. Pretty, intelligent, serious when it was time to be serious, but also able to smile and share an amusing interaction with the most unself-conscious spontaneity when appropriate, I quite found that the spirit of genuine *Aloha* that Kamaile had all about her was genuinely intoxicating. The foregoing is either an indication that there is still a spark of latent romanticism hiding within my crusty, jaded, and bitterly cynical hide (as my Oregon cousin recently described me), or I have an exceptional ability to delude myself. I prefer to think it is the former and not the latter, although the latter is a well-established fact. I have to constantly remind myself that there is no fool like an old fool, and at 58 I guess I am now well-vested in that category.

Although I tend to regard commerce among the sexes far more in sympathy with pagan pre-Christian Hawaiian customs (not being one of those much-despised Christians—like my wife), I probably need to keep a tight grip on my feelings, since old fools can be as easily hurt by romantic miscalculation as young ones. Still, it's lovely to fantasize about luscious Kamaile, even if I can't allow myself any discretionary maneuvering room in her regard. Besides, I never was a very smooth operator when it came to acting *'Mano'* with the fair sex (Hawaiian idiom for 'acting like a shark around the young women')

Moloka'i Coffee Plantation regrettably sold the plantation and closed out its former business on the island about 6 months ago, so the plantation is now owned by *Island Coffees International*. This Maui based business is now importing other island coffee and selling it on the island until they can resurrect the old (Moloka'i) coffee fields (that have now been let go, since Moloka'i Coffees pulled out) and harvest a new crop of Moloka'i-grown coffee from the existing orchards of *Arabica*. This is unhappy news, since I had been mail-ordering Moloka'i Coffee beans by the 5 pound bag up until recently, and now I find that all the existing reserves of indigenous Moloka'i beans were sold on Oahu to the US Navy's commissary (no doubt with a cut-rate price) at Pearl. What's the old French saying? *"Plus la change, ça...etc."* Viewed from the perspective of the *Tao Te Ching*, change is (inalterably) the way…

Kalikiano Kalei

April 19, 2005 (Tuesday)

Had a rough night last night. The roosters were having a convention next door and their screams wailed out into the cool night air like a serious of consecutively set alarm clocks, from dusk to dawn. While commiserating with myself over this, I had some coffee and started reading through Sam Clemens' collected dispatches of 1866. On page 44, I was somewhat mollified to run across the following *tres amusing* excerpt from *'Roughing It in the Hawaiian Islands—Hawaii in the 1860s'*. Although it pertained to the 150 mile sea voyage between islands that Clemens undertook to get from Oahu to the big island of Hawaii, his acerbic commentary certainly has acute parallels to my present landlocked situation, here in Ranch Camp:

"The hold forward of the bulkhead had but little freight in it, and from morning till night a portly old rooster, with a voice like Baalem's ass (and the same disposition to use it), strutted up and down in that part of the vessel and crowed. He usually took dinner at six o'clock and then, after an hour of two dedicated to meditation, he mounted a barrel and crowed a good part of the night. He got hoarser and hoarser all the time, but he scorned to allow any personal consideration to interfere with his duty and kept up his labors in defiance of threatened diphtheria."

Sleeping was out of the question when he was on watch (which was all the time). He was a source of genuine aggravation and annoyance. It was worse than useless to shout at him or apply offensive epithets to him—he only took these things for applause and strained himself to make more noise. Occasionally during the day, I threw potatoes at him through an aperture in the bulkhead, but he only dodged and went on crowing...the above is not an overdrawn sketch!"

Just had a cellular call from Gail Surano at *Title Guaranty Escrow* in Honolulu in response to my request for a call back. I explained the tight time-table we have to get the water line and meter installed on the newly purchased property and asked for some sort of documentation that would probably be needed in order to commence the needed utility work. Gail informed me that they had not yet heard back from the property's seller (Detrick Lee) and that they had sent out papers for him to sign at the same time they had sent ours to us (back in March). This is not cool, of course, since he needs to sign his part of the agreement to effectively close the deal.

We have signed our part of it and also wired the whole purchase amount (since received) to the escrow people. Official closure is not until the 25th (the deadline he needs to respond affirmatively by), so technically we are hamstrung if he chooses to take the full amount of time and technically cannot begin any work (needed or otherwise) without receipt of the officially recorded Maui County deed. I intend to call Cheryl Apaia today to ask her if she can contact the seller to prompt his timely responsiveness, and will also go see Victor to see what our options are, should the closure not come off on schedule before I leave the island. This lies in the realm of regard BEYOND the usual slow-motion island habits and doesn't seem to reflect much concern by the seller to see to it that everything goes smoothly.

Meanwhile, this leaves me fairly high and dry for the moment, since there's nothing else on my list of priorities relating to the property that can be accomplished until the deal is officially closed and the deed recorded successfully. I guess I'll go take a picture of some multi million dollar property east of us and send it back to fool my friend Jack at work into thinking we have latched onto a beautiful bit of the pristine east end coast here for a song (a total lie, since the unimproved property is probably only

TRULY worth about $50,000 max). What the hell. Nothing else pressing to take care of until the deed matter is brought to closure.

Another of the books I picked up at Jim Sacher's 'Big Wind Kite Factory' (which he specifically recommended) is a very unique work by island resident Elsie Adelbert. Titled "Paddling My Own Canoe", her 135 some-odd page paperback book contains a narrative comprised of her series of trips to the isolated (but serenely beautiful) northeastern coast of Moloka'i back in the late 60s and early 70s. Known for its immensely sheer sea cliffs that rise almost 3000 feet from the ocean (these are recorded as being the highest in the world), this stretch of extremely rugged and remote north coast area (located east of the Kalawao leper settlement) is still one of the most inaccessible areas to be found on any of the five main islands that comprise the central Hawaiian region.

Adalbert is one of those rare and insightfully reflective individuals who early on recognized the importance of understanding humanity as necessarily being only a relatively small (if important) element of importance, most properly regarded against the far greater and vastly more important contextual backdrop of the entire natural world (planet, cosmos, universe, et al).

Adalbert made a series of treks back to this extremely difficult to reach part of the island, powered only by per own effort and human-power, that she records for the reader's pleasure. An excellent swimmer, she actually walked and swam much of those trips, although to most people even vaguely familiar with what that rough windward coast is like, such a feat as swimming several miles along it seems almost inconceivable (certainly does to me!). But then, Adalbert was (is) a most unusual woman. Having had 4 children by the time she started these trips (in her 40s), she was not what one would consider 'youthful' anymore, but at

5'6" and 120 pounds, she was possessed of a very functional human machine—her excellent state of fitness.

Adalbert is also a very wise woman—not just conventionally literate, but someone who understands the nature of the individual human being's essential 'aloneness' probably about as well as any person I have ever known or read about. What is most attractive about her, aside from her impressively adventurous spirit and natural competence, is the fact that she is also a very deeply reflective person. I suppose, as a man, another aspect of her that I most appreciate—along with all of these things already mentioned—is the fact that she is not a 'mannish' woman (or lesbian, if you need to pare it down to that essential status); she is a woman who is both adventurously spirited and a very much a 'normal' female. Her descriptions of time spent entirely alone in that vast Hawaiian paradise that comprises the isolated valley areas of *Wailau* and *Pelekuhu* on Moloka'i's north coast are delicious, even if one must share them vicariously by virtue of only reading about them.

Adalbert has many interesting and worthwhile observations to make, not just about the geography and natural history of ancient Moloka'i, but about the spiritual nature of a solitary human being subsisting alone amidst such splendid natural isolation.

On one particular trip in which Adalbert swam just offshore (and pushing a small waterproof float containing her food and spare clothing) most of the route from Pelekunu Bay northwest to Kalaupapa (the famed leper colony), she finally made an exhausted landfall and found a small group of Catholic sisters and visiting picnickers near the shore. Most of the tourists were insufficiently versed in the austere isolation that characterizes this part of the island to realize what an ordeal she had just completed, swimming miles in those unpredictable waters, but one woman from Honolulu did and asked her if she weren't afraid. Thinking the woman meant afraid of sharks, and jagged rocks, and unpredictable surf riptides, Adelbart asked *"Of what?"* The woman continued, *"Oh, of being alone. Uh…some man might have come along and…"*

Adalbert chuckled and answered, *"If you mean wasn't I afraid of being raped, no. If a man hikes 5 miles, swims 10, crash lands on the rocks, and still has enough vitality to be interested in this grubby, salty body, he's welcome indeed!"*

The anecdote above gives a good capsule impression of the sort of spirit that supported Adalbert throughout her solitary adventures, but more importantly, the final paragraphs below convey a higher and far greater insight into what benefits such deeply reflective moments of solitude as she experienced may yield up to the human spirit. I am tempted to cull a few dozen more especially noteworthy excerpts from her book to illustrate this last point, but I'll settle for these summary wisdoms that are found at the end of her book:

"I've learned to live without things and alone. The ability to live in a variety of styles, cities, or countries, with people or without, in different languages and cultures, with enthusiasm for the small luxuries, gives me a power over the future, whatever chaos the world comes to.

There is a sensuous joy in being totally alone—delight in the simple animal pleasure of blowing my nose with one knuckle, peeing in the moonlight, or trying a Tahitian dance step with only myself to snicker. There is a smug ironic satisfaction in finding an ingenious solution to a problem that was caused by my own inadequacy or stupidity.

Men and women are more alike than different. Women, too, need to feel the coyote wilderness, the pleasure of muscles moving in coordination, the sweat and the weariness, and the uncertainty of what the end to all that effort will be.

Always I come back from these trips feeling like a skinned-up kid, feeling like a renewed, re-created adult, feeling like a tiger. All that basic nature, all that use of animal instincts, arouses some very earthly desires. The most delicious comment about these trips was by a sailor-oceanographer who understood the sea both mentally and physically. 'A woman who would do a thing like that', he said, 'is worth going to bed with.' A classic remark— but it said more about him than about me. You don't just make love to a female body. It doesn't matter if she's twenty or eighty; you want the whole person. At least that's the best kind and at least that is what I thought it said about him.

North (shore) Moloka'i is only a 20 mile coast; it is a small fragile area and will not survive an onslaught of people. We have not yet learned that all Hawaii is an equally small and special place that we shall soon destroy with deliberate, carefully orga- nized 'progress'. We do not yet know how to care for it.

And why did I always come alone to Moloka'i? I know why, but the telling (is) hard. Daily we are on trial, to do a job, to make a marriage good, to find depth, serenity, and meaning in a com- plex, deteriorating world of politics, false values, and trivia. But rarely are we deeply challenged or alone. We rely on friends, on family, on a committee, on community agencies outside our- selves. To have actual survival, living or dying, depend upon our own ingenuity, skill, or stamina—this is a core question we sel- dom face (today). We rarely find out if we like having only our own mind as company for days or weeks at a time. How many people have ever been totally isolated, 10 miles from the nearest other human being, for even two days?

Alone you are more aware of your surroundings, wary as an animal to danger, limp and relaxed when the sun, the brown earth, or the deep grass say 'Rest now!' Alone you stand at night, alert, poised, hearing through ears and open mouth and finger-

tips. Alone, you do not worry whether or not someone else is tired or hungry or needing. You push yourself hard or quit for the day, reveling in the luxury of solitude. And being unconcerned with human needs, you become as a fish, a boulder, a tree—a part of the world around you.

The process of daily living is often intense and whimsical. The joy of it, and the compassion, we can share, but in pain we are ultimately alone. The only real antidote is inside. The only real security is not insurance or money or a job, not a house and furniture paid for, or a retirement fund, and never is it another person... It is the skill and humor and courage within, the ability to build your own fires and find your own peace."

Can't thank Jim Sincher (of Maunaloa) enough for pointing out both this book by Adalbert and the oral history I mentioned earlier, titled 'Tales From the Night Rainbow', as important books about Moloka'i that should be on any person's shelf who has an interest in this special island, *Moloka'i nui a Hina ('Moloka'i beloved to Hina').*

Some of the things Adalbert remarks upon in her book remind me of ties to ancient Hawaiian culture. One in particular is the fact that the Kanaka Maoli (original inhabitants of Moloka'i, thought to have been a first wave of Polynesian settlers coming from the *Marquessas* in the south in about 500 AD) were perfectly suited to their environment in terms of their attire and attitudes about their bodies. The later invading Ali'i also maintained similar attitudes, with men commonly wearing only a breech-clout and the women wearing typically only a short wrap of *kappa* (an amazingly durable paper made from tree bark) around their waist and lower body. Most often, whenever bathing or near the water, both sexes went about entirely without clothing. It was a very natural and normal response to as fair a climate as that found in the islands. Of course, the first missionaries were scandalized by this immodesty (viewed by their standards, of course) on the part of the islanders. It wasn't long before the ultra-conservative Christian standards of bodily modesty were imposed on the Hawaiians, a process that resulted in many strange circumstances (as noted by Sam Clemens in his articles about the islands written for the Sacramento Union newspaper) as the new apparel was adopted.

However, it also resulted in such grotesqueries as photographs (starting from about 1860 and onward) that show the typically large-proportioned hula dancers garbed in the voluminous female clothing of that time: to say the sight is simultaneously ludicrous and sad is understating the effect. The 'hula' was originally danced by women in the ancient culture who wore nothing but floral leis and skirts made from *Ti* leaves. After the missionary edicts on appropriate dress came into effect, on those rare occasions when the 'lascivious hula' was even danced, the visual effect must have truly been stunningly awkward at best. Images taken of women posed as hula dancers similarly garbed exist today and one cannot help but despise the Christians in their frantic blue-nosed efforts to impose such things on the 'natives.'

While the Hawaiian 'hula' is far gentler and moderately paced than the sybaritic and rapid, grinding animal sensuality of the Tahitian counterpart, the inherent sensuality of both dances is totally destroyed by the acres of clothing missionary etiquette required. Today's 'tourist hula' spectacular, especially the sort that was until recently put on at Waikiki for boatloads of cruise passengers, finds 'atypical' hula dancers wearing coconut shell bras, grass skirts, and who are probably more of an *ectomorphic* or *mesomorphic* physical type (particular to blended Japanese, Hawaiian, Chinese, and Filipino ancestry) than to traditional (ancient culture) 100% full blooded Hawaiian women of the large framed, big boned *endomorph* type. The reason for some of this effect is the fact that since the old Hawaiian customs are dying off rapidly, only those who willingly wish to come forward to help preserve them study the traditional dance; many of these women likely possess only a small amount of true Hawaiian (Kanaka Maoli) blood and there is a disproportionately great titer of Asian blood in many.

Adalbert's comments on clothing as it applied to her trips is interesting, since if there are no others around, most people would probably not feel compelled to wear clothing at all—except, of course, to protect the body against physical injury or thermal harm. Certainly, way out on an isolated spit of tropical land, cut off from any convenient access by others, clothing would be aesthetically unnecessary for a person of dark-complected skin. For a white-skinned Caucasian, protection from the sun would still require clothing of some sort…as would protection from insectivorous critters, etc.

Makes me think of a few circumstances back in the 70s when I was actively camping in places along the California coast like the *Ventana Wilderness* (Palo Colorado Road access to *Little Sur River*). On a few of these trips, some of us shucked off our clothing to lay in the sun and swim in some parts of the Little Sur River that were dammed up by fallen trees (VERY cold water) and I still have a very funny picture taken of an old friend caught in mid-jump from a log, private parts waving like a semaphore, with his skinny white body standing out against the blue of the sky like some sort of ghost (he is today a successful lawyer, who studies German language *in Germany* in his spare time).

None of my crowd in those days were what I'd call particularly buff physical specimens, of course, and I didn't even discover weight training until I was in the Middle East (mid-80s). It's funny that I was never really what might be termed 'body conscious' until then, but I was always able, nonetheless, to appreciate the sensual aesthetics of a finely tuned human physique or figure. My standard of human beauty prefers the lithe, leanly muscled look of a human figure attractive, no matter whether man or woman, to an overly muscled piece of human beefcake (after Arnold's or other male & female body builders). I have always considered what I call the 'swimmer's build' most appealing, since people with that type of build are usually fit in both a cardiopulmonary and muscle toning context.

I once had a serious attraction to a woman friend in high school who was in fact a skillful swimmer (specialized in the breast stroke, no humorous allusions intended). She was moderately tall and leanly built, but with pleasingly well-toned muscles in arms and legs, and with all the right 'bumps' in the right places, too. The sight of her in a racing tank suit would make me all goosey and the proximity of her at such times probably didn't help me to complete in my own events as part of the men's swim team (I was a breaststroker, too, but alas…not of hers!).

There's nothing, in my opinion, like the sight of a firm, female nipple sheathed in wet clinging nylon (or the same effect of wet nylon stretched tightly against a woman's *mons pubis*, either, for that matter). Hey…can I help it if I am just as shallow and easily aroused by superficial visual sexual stimuli as any other guy? No defense, yer honor! Mea culpa maxima, baby! It's a special talent I have, I think, that I can switch from deeply philosophical concepts to trashy, tawdry trivia in a heartbeat! This same intensely Mercuric polarity was, I am told, cause for being *put off* by at least one lady I was hooked on for many, many years…alas! Ah, the absolute acuity of hindsight notwithstanding, I would still in all likelihood not have changed a whit, sadly. I am, after all, a Gemini born and bred.

This whole day has been spent writing, more or less. Cheryl Apaia called a while ago and said that she would try to reach the seller's mother-in-law in an effort to prompt seller to submit his portion of the closure documents ASAP, so that we can get the water meter and line installed on the property prior to my departure.

Didn't make it to see Victor today, or to the local art gallery (not Sturgess') to see if I can get in touch with Victor Lorenz's pahu-craftsman father-in-law. Since tomorrow is the publishing day for the Moloka'i Island Times, I'll try to get all these things done when I pick up a copy of that issue.

April 20, 2005 (Wednesday)

I am beginning today's entry over again, after having just suffered the incredible frustration of 'losing' more than an hour of writing through an inadvertent failure to 'auto-save' prior to an accidental closure of this document. This is probably one of the most annoying occurrences modern writers using PCs can undergo, since it essentially amounts to sending time and effort into the unrecoverable twilight of creative effort at the push of a wrong key. However, it usually only happens once, before a mandate is entered in the PC's operating guidelines to automatically perform an 'auto-save' every few minutes.

I was just reflecting on how cozy my daily routine is now, after the passage of a week or so on the island. Whereas back home I was used to getting up at 5 AM and being at the office, ready to rock & roll by 6:45 after my daily 5 mile bike ride to work, here I have fallen into a far more unhurried and natural daily rhythm that harmonises perfectly with the ebb and flow of the island routine.

Getting up at sunrise, I immediately put the water on to boil. This is almost reflexive, since I am such an inveterate caffeine addict. Although there is a two-element electric stove in the room, I brought a made-in-Japan plastic water heating pot with me that Suki purchased locally on our last visit to the island in October (2004). That was one of the first things Suki acquired on that trip and I have brought it back with me, ironically. The pot's a plainly redundant object, given that water can be just as easily heated in a sauce-pan, but I also brought a small, folding plastic alarm clock with me—more as a relic of my time spent in the Middle East, when it helped me get up early for the days' scheduled heart cases, than for any acknowledged need. Another truly un-needed object: after all, who really needs to measure the passage of time in paradise, eh? Time here seems to flow as naturally as the strong off-shore currents that perpetually sweep this coast.

That horrible by-product of the highly technologised American socio-economic rat-race—the frantic, inhuman, and unnatural pace of daily affairs necessitated by modern Western standards of efficient productivity—is simply a seemingly far-off and none too certain memory in this relaxed place.

Once the water is boiled, I prepare a large mug of highly con-centrated Arabica bean rocket-fuel (ground from Moloka'i beans in a faithful electric grinder I have had for at least 25 years) and grab whatever book lies uppermost in a carefully arranged stock of works on *Hawaiiana* that I acquired in Maunaloa, last week. A one to two hour reading session follows (until I am reminded that I also need to eat something—usually bananas and oatmeal), that is usually abruptly terminated by the fact that my creative juices have been so thoroughly stirred up by the ingested caf-feine and written input that I have to rise, switch on the laptop, and start spewing forth thoughts and reflections like hot steam from one of *Pele's* local fumaroles.

This morning's read is a collection of stories and accounts of strange experiences recorded in Hawaii from the 1800s through the present ('*The Obákê Files*'). The locals would call these 'chicken-flesh stories', but they include factual first-person accounts of experiences from sober, respectable, impeccably straightforward individuals (Kanaka, Kama'aina, and haole), as well as unverifiable stories and tales from the past. As a life-long skeptic of the supernatural, I have nonetheless maintained a healthy appetite for this type of lore, since one unfulfilled wish of mine has always been to have a single experience or encounter with some irrational, abnormal event that my inherent stores of logic, reasoning, and scientific knowledge simply can't explain.

The locals (kanaka maoli) have traditionally maintained the belief that all objects of nature are imbued with varying degrees of spiritual essence; this is a perfectly proper tenet of ancient Hawaiian cosmology that continues to the present, among a select few who still honor the old ways. Of course, this is not unharmonious or incongruent with other religious schools of thought (*Shrine Shinto* of Japan comes to mind immediately, as an example of ancient precepts of animism). In Hawaii, under the traditional precepts, every rock, tree, plant, body of water, gust of wind, and other element of nature contains this spirit or '*mana*'. It is only in western forms of religious belief (Christianity is perhaps the best example) that man is set distinctly and uniquely apart from this palpable spiritual link with all natural things.

What I find most interesting in such stories as involve local spirits, strange events, and incidents (such as the 'night marching', supposedly ghostly torch-lit perambulations of the departed chiefs and ancient gods that occur on specific days of the lunar month—typically on the 14th and 27th days) is that together with the accounts of locals who have experienced these things, there are an ever-increasing number of non-locals (Caucasian visitors from the mainland and other haoles) who swear they have seen or experienced such things. This suggests to me that either there is something real and undeniably palpable to the cited experiences, *or* our 'sober, reputable and straightforward' honkie chroniclers of such stories are all co-conspirators in a vast, well-coordinated, cooked-up joke of unbelievably huge proportions. Part of me (that part that provoked one of my old nicknames... *'Spockie'*) would like to be able to dismiss all of these stories as perfectly plausible occurrences—the same way I'd like to believe that all UFO encounters are the result of too much drinking and pockets of swamp-gas. However, a more irrepressible part of me earnestly desires to be confronted once and for all with an absolutely inexplicable event that would be, as one of the skeptical writers in *'The Obákê Files'* put it, a figurative *"white crow"* (categorical impossibility or a hitherto unknown thing or circumstance).

My wife Suki appears to carry much of these old customs in her core matrix (perhaps it is even subliminal), despite her apparent expressions of strong faith in a Christian God. As a subscriber in the precepts of traditional *Fung Shui*, she already lives her daily life according to the dictates of one of the close Chinese relatives of basic animistic theosophy. Accordingly, whenever I have expressed my desire to experience the supernatural (hopefully not in any terminal manner, of course), she has been quick to admonish me not to entertain any such wishes, obviously believing in the dire possibilities arising from such forces that might be inexplicably malevolent or 'natural evil' forces (and quite apart from the usual Christian religious 'evils', at that).

At any rate, I plan to visit a few of the older local cemeteries nearby Kaunakakai. Even if the departed spirits have long since found more positive stimulation in working for Walt Disney than in simply scaring the occasional intruder, old cemeteries are still interesting to poke around in for their historic nature. I'd dearly love to be out at night on the east end of the island on the 27th of this lunar month to see if any spirits of long-departed Ali'i are lurking about with their followers, keen for a restless ramble to the sea, but the chances of that happening while I am here are remote (regrettably). Baring that chance to witness any *marchers of the night'*, I'll simply have to maintain my rational equivocations about such things.

One assumption (documented supposition) I've read about the old religion is that since the ancient island customs required fervent belief in the theologies of animism underlying the old religion to enable them, the fact that modern locals have long-since lost any feeling for them at all (in embracing Christianity) has deprived them of their 'mana', relegating them now mostly to just scary stories to give 'chicken-flesh' to listeners of the traditional tales. This of necessity brings up the question of how the still not fully understood power of the human mind interacts with nature to engender cause-effect relationships. We know dimly of the power of 'mind over body' and this fact is almost uniformly accepted by all people. We also know of the supposed power of prayer. It is interesting to note in passing that schools of ancient sorcery kahunas existed on the islands (Moloka'i was perhaps the most powerful and most feared example) that were reputed to be able to 'pray' a person to death. There are also recorded instances, in ancient Hawaiian society, of the average person's ability to select the moment of his or her death through sheer belief in certain things (that remain uncertain or unclear to us rational minded, empirically schooled western observers). As I said before, there are many parallels between these ancient customs and perceptions of reality and modern phenomena (UFO-ology and the occult) that we westerners cannot today fully fathom.

What should be clear enough, even to skeptics, is that simply because we do not understand certain things doesn't categorically rule out their possible existence.

I think back to my first full day here on Moloka'i, when I drove up to *Ka Ule o Nanahoa* (the ancient phallic rock) in the rain and hiked down the hillside to stand near it in the gusts of mist that were pouring through the trees. I put my hands on both rocks (the male rock uphill and the female counterpart that is slightly removed from it, further down the hill), closed my eyes, and stood quietly next to each for about 15 minutes, trying to blank out my conscious thoughts and open myself up to whatever sensations might be forthcoming. There were of course none I could palpate clearly, but while I was so engaged there was a considerable amount of wind evident, blowing the tree tops overhead, and the thick mists of the rain-filled clouds definitely conferred a very mystical impression...*of what?* Mood? Later, in reading over a few of the books I have acquired on these subjects, I was interested to learn that various natural signs such as exceptionally high winds, excessive noise, thunder, pounding of surf (despite the fact that surf might be miles away), etc., were all considered 'voices' of these spirits by the ancients, and usually indicated (to them) the presence of some sort of profoundly supernatural force.

While I cannot vouch for that in my own brief experience up there, the wind was certainly far stronger while I was standing there next to the rocks...substantially stronger and more forceful. It wasn't hard to close the eyes and imagine the surrounding thick cover of forest to contain some sort of strong spiritual substance, although always just beyond real perception by the physical senses. Again, I think the powers of irrational faith and strong positive belief have much to do with these forces and I am not by natural inclination a 'faithful' person (perhaps regrettably, if that's what it takes to experience the unknown). Pity.

The morning is getting older and I still have many things to do and bases to touch. Cheryl Apaia (our real estate agent in Kaluapu'u) called a while ago by cell to inform me that the seller of our property had finally gotten the escrow papers into the mail and basically cleared the way for me to initiate an application through Victor Montero to get the water line and meter installed without further delay. I'll have to get rolling (and here I was, earlier talking about the lack of time constraints and deadlines locally!) and start taking care of the day's agenda…a MOST unlocal thing to do. Then it's off to the market to snag a copy of the Moloka'i Island Times to see if they actually used either of the two possible articles I sent them last week (I'm not holding my breath, having formed a somewhat less than favorable opinion of editor Brandon). Finally, a stopover at the local crafts gallery to check on the pahu makers. I really would like to get in touch with Victor's local father-in-law, who is the acknowledged drum maker of this part of the island. After that? Who knows? Probably time for a few pictures of various places just for the hell of it and finally a trip to the old 'local' cemetery, which is coincidentally located not too far from where our new property is, actually. *Hmm.*

Back at the flat, late afternoon. Managed to find Victor (architect) out, but contacted him by cell-phone (he's on Maui). Victor arranged to meet with me on Friday at 8AM. I told him that we could start the important water hookup and meter installation process, so we will likely get that application filed with Maui County utilities and then it remains to be seen what the actual installation involves.

Ralph, the neighbor dog, is actually a Rottweiler (which figures, given the man-eating bark he has). Last evening the neighbors across the way had a dance (Filipino) and I could hear the *clack-clack-clack* of the *Tiniklin* sticks for quite a while until the party ended. Obviously, everyone enjoyed themselves famously, judging from the sounds of the gala affair, as it carried through the clear night air. Then the shift changed and as the Filipino partyers left, the roosters reconvened their brotherhood and set up a cackle that went on most of the night (again). I may have to gratuitously send a few roosters to rooster heaven when I get back home, to atone for my abiding patience listening to their noise while on Moloka'i.

Moloka'i Island Times did not elect to use either of my offered articles in today's issue of that MacByte backed paper, not that I expected it. Ah well. Did get Victor Lorenz's telephone number from the folks at the *Kamalana Gallery* in town. They told me that Victor's father-in-law is the real master artisan, whereas Victor is just a very skilled amateur who is learning the art. Amateur status or not, that hasn't kept Victor from carving crude (in my considered opinion) porpoises out of Koa wood (about 2 feet long) and asking $3,300 for such a piece! The local artists (painters included) seem to think either that the visiting haole tourists are wealthy and exceptionally stupid, or that they have no sense of artistic discernment at all and think anything hand-made by a kanaka is an antique in the making. Yow!

That pahu I was admiring (made by Victor's father-in-law) is a beauty and a big one, as well (measuring about 18 inches diameter at the drumhead), but the price on it was $1250, and that's probably after a bit of reflection over a previous price that was way beyond $1250! Really a shame that prices aren't a bit more realistic. Right now, they seem to be in the same category as real estate (anything at all in the way of available land is instantly worth big bucks!). Can't say I blame the locals for wanting to gouge the tourists, but they really seem to feel all tourists are short a few brain cells, judging from all the available clues I have uncovered so far. Can't wait to finally retire, move over here, and start cranking out stupid tourist kitsch out of old coconut shells to hawk at the weekly arts & crafts market on *Ala Molana Street*. I was reading recently that tree-trimming is big business in the islands, what with all the coconuts that need to be removed (as safety hazards) annually. Somewhere in the vicinity of several million individual coconuts must be removed manually each year. Even at flat local labor rates, that's a lot of *bazookniks* to pad out a bank account with! Of course, falling coconuts is a major cause of those rare tourists who turn up on Moloka'i (not!).

Managed to visit one of the old local cemeteries this afternoon, but felt no ghostly presences or strange sensations present there. Many people of Filipino, Japanese, and Chinese ancestry planted therein. Nothing too startling to be seen and the graves were not kept in top shape. One had an empty beer can perched on it that I removed, as a small gesture of respect for the departed; I hope it wasn't left intentionally to help keep the departed's spirit nourished (that is the custom more often than not in Asian cemeteries, of course). Like sprinkling Schnapps on a German grave, in Europe.

Nothing too important on tomorrow's agenda (21st). Maybe I'll plan to visit historic and sublimely beautiful *Halawa Valley* at the distal east end—or the *Iliiliopae heiau* (where they reportedly sacrificed a local, every now and then, back in the bad old days).

April 21, 2005 (Thursday)

One of the 'chief' delights (a 'royal' joy?) for me here, is having absolutely no constraints of my available time for reading & writing. Although I have never been an originator of unique ideas and outlooks, even the slightest bit of reading acts as a catalyst to release myriad tangents of thought and speculation; this is regrettably a symptom of a mediocre mind, not a great intellect. With not a small amount of rue, I recall a moment back in 1982 at which time I was going with a Chinese resident at Highland General Hospital named Mei-li, when I grandly stated (in an unguarded moment of exuberant egotism) that I was an excellent writer; Mei-li quickly put my modest literary talents into proper context when she corrected my glaring assumptions by observing that I was an *"OK writer, but not so great..."*.

Since this moment of unexpected candor occurred immediately before she applied some outstanding *omo* on my *pōheo*, I didn't object to the pronouncement, and after relishing the outstanding *omo* she maintained with her *waha* on my *ule lalahū*, I returned the favor with some *ai ikaika loa* in her *okole likiliki nani kōkī*! *Auwi! Auwi!* Mei-li was *he wahine u'i* and also *he kanaka ikaika a pono 'oe*, of course! I still miss her *poho lua likiliki* after nearly 23 years, needless to say. (And if you want to know what all that means, you need to bone up...no pun intended, although it is rather *appropo*...on your Hawaiian language!)

Reading through some of the vast *Hawaiiana* references I acquired on this trip, I have been today grazing in selections from several older histories of the Hawaiian islanders (such as Fornander's classic *History of the Polynesian Peoples* and Hawaiian King Kalakaua's anthology of Hawaiian myths and legends).

Among the earliest recorded myths (most recorded Hawaiian history begins with the second wave of settlement in the islands that occurred in the 11th century) is the story of Ali'i ancestor and high priest *Pa'ao's* departure from *Kahiki* (originally a specific westerly land of origin, generally supposed to be Tahiti, but now a general term that simply means 'foreign place') and his brother *Lonopele*. Due to an altercation with his brother that involved

Pa'ao's son having been accused of stealing fruit from Lonopele's trees, such bad blood developed between the two (Pa'ao had had to 'open' his son's stomach to prove his innocence of the charges, which naturally was fatal to the son; as a consequence, he had Lonopele's son murdered) that Pa'ao was forced to flee in a large canoe to seek a new place to live.

As Pa'ao's outrigger was pulling away from the shore, some priests on the nearby pali (cliff) shouted out to him to return so that they could flee with him. Pa'ao declined, stating that to return would be a very bad omen and if they were really powerful priests and wished to join him, they could leap off the cliffs and "fly" out to his outrigger. Most of the priests were killed when they fell onto the rocks below the cliff, but one was successful in finally reaching Pa'ao.

It occurs to me that regardless of the fact that we do not have any further surviving evidence that the successful priest actually was able to "fly" out to join Pa'ao, this appears to provide sufficient historical substantiation for the establishment of early Hawaiian aviation efforts. According to the language references I have, a flying person would be referred to as a *"Kanaka lele"*. This was also the Hawaiian term used to refer to Christian angels, since *"lele"* translates to 'fly as a bird', and Kanaka is used to refer to 'person'. Shades of Erich von Daniken!

Further stories of human 'flight' survive concerning the volcanic 'stacks' and small rocky island protuberances located just off the northern shores near the *Makanalua Peninsula* (locale of *Father Damien's* leper colony at *Kalaupapa*, that is today erroneously termed *'The Kalaupapa Peninsula'* through common usage), two in particular that are specifically mentioned being *Mōkapu Island* and *Ōkala Islands*. Apparently, several centuries ago, the inhabitants of Moloka'i's northern shore area would either swim or canoe out to these large rock outcroppings and after climbing up them, affix large tree fronds to themselves (their pre-flight procedures are not explained in the surviving accounts) and indulge in a form of early hang-gliding from several hundred feet up and into the sea! It is not known what the success rates were for a survivable final approach and landing, but it's probably not a bad guess that the 'short final' was more the norm than the exception.

Since I have a healthy element of unreconstructed child still latent in my 58 years of (largely) adult life, not to mention equally strong elements of whimsy and imagination, it would seem to me that we have here the basic legitimization for the establishment of a modern day *"Royal Hawaiian Air Force"*. With all of the mid-to-late 1800s obsession by Hawaiian royalty on the superficial trappings of European nobility, what with the elaborate military type uniforms, decorations, orders, and such that were so favored by King Kalakaua and his immediate forebears, the establishment of a Royal Hawaiian Air Force would seem only logical and fitting (from a whacked-out, but constructively whimsical standpoint, of course).

Kalakaua, the last of the Hawaiian kings prior to the reign of Hawaii's final monarch (Kalakaua's sister, Queen Liliuokalani), keenly felt his nation's vulnerability as haole American economic interests strengthened their tenacious grip on his island kingdom. Part of his effort to visibly establish Hawaiian autonomy and to firmly retain the nation's home rule by virtue of formal international recognition—apart from adopting the external visual superficialities of 'royal vestiture' (such as elaborate uniforms, decorations, a 'palace', and other traditional western appurtenances)—was to establish a *Royal Hawaiian Army* (actually more of an honor guard consisting of a platoon-sized regiment of 'household troops', etc.) and a *Royal Hawaiian Navy* (the latter consisted of a few royal rowboats, a handful of royal outrigger canoes, and a schooner, by the way).

However, since aviation had at that time not yet made a broad appearance in the world as a legitimate and widely recognized human undertaking, the possibility of a *Royal Hawaiian Flying Corps* was logically not then extant. I have no doubt that had the powerful American annexationists not succeeded in formally attaching the islands (as they finally did in 1898), Kalakaua would have unquestionably established his own small royal military aviation entity. [Perhaps it is not too late to do so, both out of respect for the King, with his admirable desire to return Hawaii to the Hawaiian people, and my own finely-honed sense of *Dada'esque* whimsy. We shall see about this...]

In passing, one other evidentiary instance of fledgling aeronautical aspirations in early Hawaii is found in the last ruling Queen's (Liliuokalani) book about Hawaii, that was originally published in 1898 as a plea for the dignity of her people and autonomy for the Hawaiian monarchy. She remarks that in November of 1889, she and a party of her retainers and friends were having a picnic in Honolulu to celebrate the birthday of King Kalakaua. Suddenly they noticed that a balloon had arisen from the foot of Punch-Bowl Hill. As it rose higher and higher, it finally came level with the strong upper currents and started to drift rapidly away.

At that point, according to the Queen's narrative, the occupant on the trapeze under the balloon cut himself loose and started to plummet earthward; fortunately, he had equipped himself with a sort of parachute and had deployed it. Unfortunately, the wind carried his inflated canopy out to sea, far beyond the breakers, and not, as he doubtless hoped, to dry land. Several small boats immediately started out after him, but by the time they had reached the point where he had apparently splashed down, he and the chute were nowhere to be seen. The same was said of his balloon, which disappeared windward in short order and was never seen again. Speculation had it, the queen notes, that he provided the many sharks (Hawaiian term: *Mano*) off shore a welcome variation in their normal diet of other fish, although she stated this far more delicately and tastefully than I have. She was amazingly articulate.

The above details, mentioned in passing by the queen, were referent to the attempt made by a pair named the *Brothers van Tassell* (Dutch, apparently) who in November of that year (1898) made two manned balloon ascents. They were preceded, for the honors of making the first attempted manned balloon flight in the islands, by an individual named *Emil L. Melville*, who in 1889 tried to make an unsuccessful hot-air balloon ascent from Honolulu's Kapi'olani Park. Melville (and there's no truth to the report that he was related to the famed author Herman Melville…or that his balloon was named 'Moby Duck' in honor of that relative) regrettably was unsuccessful in getting off the ground at that time.

However, a week later, he tried again and this time was able to rise about 9 meters above the launching site, before being dragged 300 yards sideways through a thicket of *Kiawe* (a thorny shrub) bushes at roof top level and finally being forced to make a spectacular 30 foot dive to the ground (which he survived). Prior to these two manned attempts to fly via balloon, several hot-air balloon launches had been made. The first was recorded as early as 1925, off the *HMS Blonde* (*Hmmm*, an early English 'blonde' joke, perhaps?), but fell on Lord Byron's grass shack setting it afire (doubtless provoking yet another poem by said august personage). Other unmanned hot air balloons were more successful, recorded as having been attempted in 1840 and 1858.

At any rate, and returning to the Brothers van Tassell, on November 2, 1889, when Joseph Lawrence van Tassell took off from the same Kapi'olani site used by Melville's attempt in 'Moby Duck' and reached a height of one mile (no small feat at that time, considering the state of the art), at that point he separated himself from the balloon and came down under a rudimentary, umbrella-like parachute device. Unfortunately for van Tassel, he attempted unsuccessfully to repeat this effort, this time launching from the Punchbowl crater. As already noted by Queen Liliuokalani, who witnessed the disaster, the strong trade winds this time caught him and carried him out towards the sea. Bailing out into Ke'ehi Lagoon, van Tassell (who appears to have badly muffed his basic water survival training course) fell into the sea and drowned.

However, this posthumous hero of early Hawaiian aeronautical history went down in the record books as Hawaii's first aeronaut, first balloonist, first parachutist, and first aviation fatality...not an all-bad three-in-one showing for the intrepid Dutch trail-blazing aeronaut.

This first recorded flight in a balloon and/or use of a primitive parachute in old royal Hawaii adds further stimulus to the likelihood of later development of a Royal Hawaiian Flying Corps, and if the King had lived much longer, he probably would have started such an organization himself (since he had already originated several uniquely Hawaiian societies (examples are "*The Sons of Hawaii*", a secret fraternal order modeled after the Masonic Order, in which he held a 33rd Degree rank). [For the record, the first flight of an airplane in the Hawaiian Islands took place on December 31st, 1910, when J.C. "Bud" Mars made 4 flights from Maunaloa Polo Field (on the 'Big Island' of Hawaii) in a Curtiss P-18 biplane, reaching an altitude of 500 feet on the first flight and hitting 1,500 feet on his 4th and last hop.]

Kalakaua, who was viewed by Dole and the other of his influential American 'Big Four' Hawaiian enterprise cronies as a potentially serious threat to their firmly established economic interests, keenly felt the pressures his Kingdom was being subjected to by the political and economic influence of American business entrepreneurs—all of which pointed directly towards likely outright annexation by the United States. As already mentioned, part of his strategy to counteract and offset these very real threats to his (Hawaiian) autonomy by haoles was to establish Hawaiian home-rule legitimacy as an accepted fact among the other, larger world powers.

In this he was modestly successful. At one point, during a tour of the world to make his point about Hawaii being a viable and autonomous monarchy, Kalakaua even visited the Emperor of Japan, during which visit he offered his islands to that imperial person as a protectorate (and was refused: what a lost opportunity!). This stemmed from his tendency to view the Japanese as being much more harmoniously attuned to the racial, cultural, and ethnic qualities of the Hawaiian people than the Caucasian haoles who threatened to economically overwhelm them at any moment. Since at that time the newly westernised Japanese empire was viewed (even at that early date) as a distinctively emerging threat to future American pan-Pacific economic hegemony (evidence of that was clearly offered in the later Russo-Japanese War of the early 1900s, at which time the Imperial Russian forces were decisively defeated by modernised Japanese *Bushi-Do*), the Meiji emperor, who was keenly aware of the possibly devastating repercussions such an alliance might have, politely declined the offer.

As the next-to-last of the reigning Hawaiian monarchs, David (King) Kalakaua, tried in other ways to put some substance into his aspirations to stave off America's acquisitive intent. This took the form of his active encouragement of customs and practices formerly severely censored by the Christian missionaries and their American economic cohorts. They included a reemergence of the previously forbidden hula and a renewed interest in traditional Hawaiian customs and practices. Although the old pantheon of ancient religious deities had long since been successfully disestablished and rooted out by the Christian missionaries, he encouraged those among his own people and sympathetic westerners (haoles such as Abraham Fornander and his cultural cohorts, who were not just interested in and favorable to the maintenance of the old cultural ways, but in most cases conjugally intermixed with and married to the kanaka maoli Ali'i) who supported and upheld links with pre-missionary Hawaiian society.

At that time (the late 1800s) it was the norm for most westerners to simply cohabit with Hawaiian women, and a formal western sanctification of such a union (Christian marriage) was not viewed as being a necessary requisite for conduct of a normal life in the islands. Of course, this practice often ran afoul of kanaka women who had been successfully brought up by the protestant missionaries to be God-fearing Christians, but on the whole, it was a custom promulgated by common incidence.

Prior to that time (and the coming of the missionaries), the traditional norm was for casual sex among consenting Kanaka couples, wherever and whenever the urge arose (on the beach, in the water, in the hale, etc.). Although it was generally considered rude to reject any interested male's advances, women still had the acknowledged right to refuse to have *ai* (sex) with any man whom the woman was not sufficiently attracted to. Thus, despite the often-castigated limitations of a few of the pre-Christian *kapus* applicable to women (two that are notable were rigidly segregated dining prohibitions—women ate separately from the men—who also did all of the cooking—and the requirement that menstruating women were to live in a segregated hale while they were in *menses*), women were remarkably free and equal to the men. This last point is underscored by the fact that women not infrequently accompanied their men into battle, fought by their side, and undertook similar roles invariably at odds with western (Christian) precepts of proper gender behavior.

Under the ancient customs women did not undertake heavy work—this was always performed by the men—but since the normal island way of subsistence living under balmy island conditions made fairly gentle impositions on both sexes, this is not hard to understand. Men fished, were craftsmen, hunters, and gatherers, and cooked, while women undertook lighter chores such as the making of *kappa* (wearable fabric made from natural vegetable fibers) and preparation of floral leis, etc. Women also did not worship the gods or participate actively in religious activities, but this also conferred the definite benefit of not being subject to selection for the occasional human sacrifice required at the *heiau* (no stereotypical Hollywood 'virgin sacrifices'). Interestingly, this contrasts with the time-honored haole depiction of the busty Caucasian female in pop literature, who has been abducted by the savages for sacrificial offering to the pagan gods. Even the notion of the offering of a virgin by natives to appease Pele, Goddess of the Volcanos, is categorically incorrect. Sorry, Hollywood.

Most frequently, sacrifices consisted of food, flowers, and other non-sentient items. When a more serious sacrifice was required by the Ali'i at a heiau, it would typically be a pig, a dog (of which there were many, having been brought over to the islands by the Polynesians on their voyages of settlement—they were highly regarded as food and were fed vegetables to make their meat more palatable), or some other non-human creature. Only in the most-dire circumstances, such as during a war, a famine, a devastating tsunami, or some other supremely catastrophic event, were human sacrifices required. Those who were selected were usually of a higher rank or greater importance than the ordinary person, since it was felt that use of a common or unimportant person would be construed as an insult by the god the offering was being made to.

Typical also was the habit of using a person recently expired, or, during times of war, the first enemy warriors captured alive. These sacrificial victims were always strangled to death and not dispatched with sharp weapons (contrasting with the usual custom of the Aztecs and Mayas, whom we are told cut out the living hearts of their victims as offerings); another favored manner of dispatching a victim was through use of a heavy wooden club. In the case of death by clubbing, the selected sacrificial victim was restrained in a supine position (spread-eagled) on a rock slab by four priests, one holding each extremity firmly fixed, while a rope around the neck held the head fixed. A priest then smashed the victim in the head (actually in the face from above and behind him) with the club. In the case of strangulation, the victim was frequently pressed back-first against a tree by priests holding his extremities around and behind him, a garrote made of fiber was used by two other priests to throttle him by pulling back on the garrote with their full weight.

In terms of which method is more 'humane' (or less painful), who can venture an opinion? Probably any method of immediate deliberate murder is about equal to any other in terms of the actual physical pain imparted in the process, but most would probably recognise and agree with the fact that the psychological pain of knowing how and when (anticipation) death will occur would be the most stressful aspect of such an act. This is what makes deliberate torture so utterly reprehensible and in my mind far worse than any deliberate homicide resulting from a momentary act of emotional aberrance (although either circumstance is abjectly proscriptive, at any rate).

All of this brings to mind the Iraqi occupation of Kuwait, prior to and during the 1991 Gulf War. Stationed in Riyadh, as I was and associated with the Royal Saudi medical service, I came into contact with a number of people who had been in occupied Kuwait—both as part of the liberating forces and occupants caught there when the Iraqis took that country. Many of the latter had been caught and tortured by members of the Iraqi Republican Guards.

Their methods ranged from merely cruel to the demented and utterly deranged. Most often those who were tortured to death were the Arab civilians who worked the Kuwaiti infrastructure facilities, since their lives were regarded as cheap and expendable. The Caucasian foreign expatriates who worked in Kuwait escaped capture successfully in most cases, but there were a few instances of MIA in which the final disposition of the individuals was never learned; they were, in all likelihood, tortured to death most cruelly and their bodies disposed of by fire.

I have a few volumes at home that describe some of the tortures undertaken by the Iraqis at that time, some with photographs showing the results of these techniques on a few lucky ones who escaped with their lives, and also some with images of those who did not. Most of these cruelties do not bear iteration here, but suffice it to say, they very adequately amplify and underscore that sad fact that no matter how 'civilised' human beings may consider themselves, there are still extremes of human behavior extant that can and will result in such atrocious acts just about anywhere one cares to look (hello, Arthur Schopenhauer!). By comparison to today's modern acts of torture, cruelty, and deliberately calculated inflictions of extreme and insufferable pain on living people as were recently carried out by the Serbs and Bosnians, the occasional Hawaiian human sacrifice that characterised the old 'pagan' religions is almost completely laughable (and at the very most completely disregardable).

It's afternoon and the trade winds have picked up, predictably. The general pattern of south shore Moloka'i weather observed in this brief period I have been here (12 days to date) seems to find nights calm, with cool and gentle breezes (usually a sheet and a thin cotton blanket suffice, I have found, but last night was cooler than most) predominating; in the mid-to-late morning hours the winds pick up, until by noon and extending through to 4PM, they are uniformly quite stiff. As dusk falls, and the air begins to cool off again, the thermal convection effects die down and the evening and night return to the same pattern of gentle breezes mentioned before. The foregoing seems to be pretty much consistent here—at least in mid-April.

I recall October being fairly similar, on our last trip, but the days were warmer and it did not cool off quite as much at night. I recall that a sheet was still a bit too much cover at night, depending on the local hemispherical weather patterns obtaining. I am told that summer can be considerably warmer during the day, but the constant flow of the trade winds helps keep things cooled off beyond a certain level. certainly beats Sacramento, though, with its intensely bone-chilling foggy winters ('tule fog', which is not convection caused, but rather the product of condensation resulting from interactive dew point/temperature factors and thermal inversions in the bowl-like Sacramento Valley that keep the water vapor contained like the lid on a rice pot).

Have to take a healthy dump a few minutes ago and that brought to mind something from John Steinbeck's famous novel of Monterey Bay life in the 30s, *'Cannery Row'*, wherein protagonist marine biologist "Doc" (the real life Ed Ricketts) tells Steinbeck about some of the peculiarities of his aged father, whom Doc has nicknamed *"Old Jingle Bollocks"*. The name obviously referred to the fact that Doc's father's bollocks drooped down substantially (*"bollocks"* = a slang expression in the UK for the American equivalent, "balls") and frequently got in his way, while sitting (surely an observation only a son would be able to make?). Now that I'm 58, aside from the fact that my years of deliberate sun exposure in Saudi Arabia have practically destroyed all the healthy collagen in my skin (stupid of me, really, but fair-haired, Celtic-ancestried old *moi* had to get that dark tan, didn't I?), I find that my own cojones now strike me as being somewhat dangly, also.

Never noticed this prior to this time, so perhaps this is an effect concurrent with advancing age in men, just like flaccid, droopy breasts seem to be characteristic of an elderly woman (not that I have a chance to see many of that type, of course— did see a few, years ago when I was doing cardiac ultrasound exams intercostally, though). This effect would not normally be much of a consideration meriting thought, were it not for the fact that here, as in Saudi Arabia, I do not normally wear briefs under my pants. In the Kingdom, it was accepted as characteristic of good hygiene to let the 'boys' roam freely under one's outer garments, due to the ever-present heat of the desert that worked together with normal *pupal smegma* to produce some pretty stiff bodily fragrances. The heat in Saudi was ultra-dry—usually less than about 4%, which is considered by meteorologists to be 'bone dry'—and for that reason highs of 140 degrees were almost tolerable. Here in the tropics, with much greater levels of humidity (averaging 70-85%), the effects of heat are far more noticeable and at much lower temps.

However, whereas I used to prefer bikini briefs in earlier days, now that I am significantly older, I find that keeping the boys penned up is more objectionable than letting them roam the range unhobbled. The only problem with this is that there are moments when I find that certain postures will result in unanticipated pressure on those sensitive parts of the male anatomy that can be uncomfortable at best and painful at least. Medical researchers will be quick to affirm the fact that sperm production is far more profound when the balls (always hated the term 'testicles', for some inexplicable reason) are allowed to dangle free and away from normal body heat. Tight fitting briefs tend to lessen sperm production due to the same effects of body heat, when the balls are sequestered close in by tight briefs. Bottom line seems to be, the most positive health effects are best realised within the musical context of that old song of the American 'old west', *"Don't pen me in!"*

In the best traditions of psychiatric *'Klang Association'*, these reflections bring to mind a lengthy encounter I formerly had with an exotic expat lady-friend back in Saudi Arabia. She was of Korean-Canadian extraction and as is typical of her ethnicity, was nearly hairless in her private parts and had such a clean *okole* you could probably eat dinner off of it without being offended. Now the accepted protocols for amorous liaisons in the Middle East (as it also is in the tropics) require that one bathe before bed (instead of after rising), since the accumulated effects of heat, moisture, and lack of ventilation in the perineal area of the body can produce some powerfully off-putting odors. [Women of Taiwan whom I met while living in Taipei insisted on wearing western-style nylon panty-hose, despite the fact that these otherwise sexy (in my opinion) garments can block off all ventilation to a woman's *kohe* (or *poho-lua*) in such a typically hot and humid climate; the resulting 'old fish' smell that is the normal product of yeasty human *smegma* can be pretty horrifying, hence (I would presume) the popularity of female hygienic sprays in that Far East land.]

At any rate, this Korean-Canadian fox I knew in Riyadh, a nurse who normally kept herself as clean and sweet-smelling as a hyacinth in full flower, had just returned late in the day from a desert trip in which she had been climbing rock cliffs all day long (it was October, when rock-climbing is possible near Riyadh without dying of heat prostration). Having been in a particularly lusty frame of mind at that moment, I grabbed her as soon as she came through the door and pinned her to the floor (surprise!). She had always seemed to enjoy 'rough sex', and since I was in one of those extremely rapacious moods that only isolation in the desert wastes can catalyse, I literally ripped her clothes off and started to have my way with her. It was pure animal desire that was pulling off her pants, tearing her black nylon bra off, and sliding her matching black thong south off her delectably smooth *Tropic of Cancer*, but she seemed to be a little disconcerted...unusual for her, since she normally met such forcefully physical overtures with a hunger equally animalistic and as impatiently demanding as my own. Not to be dissuaded, I grabbed her butt and turned her over, plunging myself deeply into her moistness without any thought about anything at all but a roisteringly good *FUCK*. PHEW! The gut-wrenching fishy stench that issued forth from her overheated and unventilated *poho-lua* was so profound that to this day I still remember it as vividly as if it had just happened... *Yuk* and double *yuk*! (Always get clean before having sex!)

For this reason, as well as for any other, I quite understand my wife's insistence on bathing before having *ai,* for the stupefyingly strong odor of uncleansed pupal smegma from either a man or a woman can so instantly and overwhelmingly off-putting that

that any further thoughts of romance and/or libidinous activity usually fly out the window so fast you wouldn't believe it.

There were many other occasions when we couldn't really grab each other on momentary impulse, despite the mutually polarized flash of lust that crossed between us—such as in the hospital gym—when instant consensual rape had to yield to barely constrained electric glances and darting looks of pure sexual energy. I well recall the first time I ever met this woman (in the gym, of course, since that was one place where expat men and women in the Kingdom could check each other out without fear of the unwanted scrutiny of the Saudi religious police). Annie, for I shall refer to her as that, had been on contract in the Kingdom several times before (why she kept coming back is way beyond my ability to imagine) and this time she had taken a contract at the King Fahad SANG Hospital (SANG = short for *Saudi Arabian National Guard*). I had been employed for about 6 months and had become used to a daily routine of exercise that included 6 miles of bike riding on the compound, a daily 3 mile run, and two hours of weight training in the gym after work each day. I had also begun destroying my skin by developing a (very unhealthy, but great looking) dark tan. With my sun-bleached hair and tan bod I guess I looked OK, since the weight work was really doing good things for me.

At any rate, I was rather mesmerized into stupefaction by the boring sets of repetitive arm lifts I was doing, when into the chill coolness of the gym pops this slender, absolutely drop-dead gorgeous Asian woman, with beautiful long black hair drawn back and tied with a band at the back of her head. Having always been a push-over for beautiful Asian women, I was immediately aware of her, but found myself hard-put to not make my interest in her obvious, since she had a perfect dancer's body—long, lithe legs with extremely well-toned muscles evident under her tights, two perfectly firm breasts that were tightly sheathed by a black nylon tank-top, and a smooth, flat stomach that you hardly ever see on any woman. To say I practically creamed my shorts is understating it. I may not have a rep as a *mano* with the *wahines* in the normal course of my life, but I still had all the perfectly normal reproductive reflexes of my gender...intact and on tap.

This was my introduction to Annie, the Korean *wunder-fuchs*. At any rate, happy to say, the regard was apparently mutual (she must like tall, skinny, wiry haoles) and when she met my gaze, she back-smiled a very sincere and warm greeting armed with animated dark pools for eyes and those perfectly white and sharply pointed little teeth of hers (*mano wahine*?--a female shark?), much to my wonderment. This in itself was hard to believe, since all of my life I have been one of those painfully shy guys who invariably act too politely, too considerately, and too gently around ladies to ever cause lustful sparks to fly in a woman's eyes.

What I was experiencing was one of those rare occurrences when one meets a beautiful woman, who although she is well aware of her assets, remains an open, friendly, and engaging individual to a strange men she has happened to encounter. There was much *mana lua* behind that gaze, as I was to later find out, for as an ultra-marathoner who was used to running 60 miles at a stretch on occasion, she had far less to fear from me than I from her. Thinking back now about her, those eyes were like deep black holes in cosmic space—a highly trained astronaut could get completely lost in there! Hell, a whole starship like the *USS Enterprise* wouldn't even stand a chance with those sucking black-hole pools of formidable female antimatter.

I shortly came to find out that in addition to running ultra-marathons back home (Canada), she was also a great rock climber, an accomplished gymnast, a classical dancer (western ballet and

Korean traditional forms), and a registered nurse. As she went about performing the most amazing gymnastic exercises I have ever seen a grown woman go through on the gym's wooden bars, I just couldn't quite accept the fact that I had run into someone like this in a gymnasium in Riyadh—about 8000 miles from anywhere worth mentioning.

At any rate, Annie finished up her exercises and in between sets we had a chance to chat, since she was obviously a very open and positive woman. Before she left to return to the flat to take a shower, she turned to say good-bye and in so doing reached over to pull my face close for a kiss, planting a juicy one full on my mouth! To say I was stunned into abject silence is considerably understating things. Something like this had never ever happened to me in the course of my whole 45 years of life to that point (nor will it ever again, I am convinced!). That (and I swear the foregoing is absolutely true on a stack of Holy Korans) was my initial introduction to lovely and very desirable Annie, the white-hot Korean-Canadian nurse I would come to know VERY well in days to come…

But enough about supremely sensuous Annie for the moment (she who must be obeyed! *Woof! Woof!* Move over, H. Rider Haggard!). Obviously, all these reflections on Hawaiian gender behavior I have been making today have made me a lot hornier than I had imagined. With a richly endowed imagination like mine, it doesn't take much of a stimulus to open up locked memory vaults and release powerfully erotic memories and reminiscences of former youth, such as these. One final note here: It still amazes me to think that I had to go all the way to sexually repressed, gender-constrained, and socially constipated Saudi Arabia to connect with someone as naturally erotic and complexly exotic as that absolutely unique and singular woman. It could never in a thousand years happen again; I know that for certain. Clearly, the time, circumstances, and situation must all be in perfect harmony for anything half as amazing as that encounter to have transpired. While I suspect Suki knew about one of my female interests over there, I don't think she ever knew about *Annie* (thank God for that, or we'd have the spirit of famed knife wielder Lorena Bobbitt on the loose again, wreaking major havoc in short order!).

April 22, 2005 (Friday)

Got up earlier than usual, in time to meet with Victor Montero this morning (8AM), who was back from Maui. Victor began the process of having the waterline and water meter installed on our new property. Since Victor (as a resident architect on Moloka'i) has connections, he phoned up his contacts at the local office of the Maui County Utilities Department and found out that the water hook up status at present is thus: There is a 6 inch (very old) water line running parallel to the property front on my side of Kam V Highway (Makai), but is apparently so old that they want to let its functional use expire. Therefore, we shall have to tap into the newer and larger (current standard) 12 inch water supply line that runs along the opposite side of the road (*Mauka,* or 'towards the mountains' side). This involves cutting a trench across the road perpendicularly (through the asphalt road surface) and laying an extension through it that will reach our side of the road (sounds $$$$). At any rate, Victor will have the necessary papers at his office on next Tuesday (26th) so that cheques can be made out to the County of Maui Water Department ($300) and a few smaller ones ($10 & $20, or so) as well. Then, assuming the request for a permit is approved by the county without complications, we can locate a local contractor who will do the excavation work; the Maui County water guys still have to perform the actual hook-up, however. Victor said he is also going to see if he can get the Water Department guys (friends) to do all of the work, thereby obviating the need for a private contractor in the deal, but that's just a 'best case scenario' he hopes to effect (worst case will require a private contractor). The roadway has to be controlled, since access is disrupted during the work, and Kam V highway is a major roadway.

Our seller had indicated that the estimate for the water line installation would be about $3500, so that tells me that he had already looked into this and pretty much knew what the task would require, since he offered to defray the estimated $3500 by $1000. We shall see if it ends up being more expensive than his estimate. The rumor is that the water meter cost will also go up by an additional $3000 at the end of the month (meter installation was estimated at time of sale to be about $6000, in addition to whatever the water line work requires, so if we can't get this done before I leave, that's $9000 for the meter, plus the water line itself). Most interesting, and I certainly wish we had been able to get all of this done earlier. Unfortunately, the escrow wasn't due to close until the 25th, so I have basically only 12 days remaining in my stay to get everything completed before flying back home on the 8th of May. And this is assuming that we don't run into any problems in either the paperwork/permit process or the excavation/installation work, and that there is also no problem in trying to get things done despite possible 'Moloka'i time' constraints (Moloka'i time is reputed to be even more relaxed than 'island time', which is generally on par with timeliness considerations in Mexico, as in "Mañana").

On the way back from Victor's, I stopped by the Kanemitsu Bakery and grabbed some of their famous bread and a couple of cake doughnuts. Found out that Victor was formerly an Italian national who immigrated to the USA back in the mid-90s. His birthday is the 4th of July, so he no sooner became a US citizen than the whole nation celebrated his day of birth! Ironically, shortly after he was naturalized, he received a jury summons from the local court. Talk about cutting edge civil servants! He still chuckles about that 'birthday gift' from Maui County.

Since Kanemitsu's is just a spit from *Moloka'i Fish & Dive* (the island's original outfitter), I dropped by to check out their books. Sure enough, they had a number of interesting ones that Jim Sincher had not had at his Kite factory gallery in Maunaloa, so I started piling up additions to my reference library and talked story with Thom, who with his wife owns the business. They have been Moloka'i residents for about 5 years and it was interesting to learn from him a few of the lessons he had picked up, in terms of getting 'into' the local community circles. His recommendations included becoming involved with some of the local sports activities, going to local school ball games, perhaps attending a church (little old pagan *me*!?) and gradually cultivating contacts and friends through the usual means. There are no strictly 'expat' watering holes, which was one sure-fire method used in the Middle East to establish one's self in a new location. I still think a local book-shop-cum-coffeehouse would be a worthwhile asset to Kaunakakai, for that reason among many. Moloka'i *is* a quick connect to the local deer hunting crowd, since the artificially introduced *Axis Deer* population on Moloka'i has now grown to constitute a serious menace to indigenous flora on the island (along with wild pigs and goats, also not indigenous fauna that pose threats to native species, such as birds and plants *and people*).

Started reading what started out originally as doctoral thesis by a resident of the islands on the ancient and traditional culture of the islands ('*Man, Gods, and Nature*', by Michael Kioni Dudley), in which he examines indigenous (native) Hawaiian cosmology and customs as a necessary cultural context within which to understand the unfulfilled and still on-going quest for Hawaiian sovereignty. As is well known, the last Hawaiian monarch (Liluokilani) was deposed when the USA annexed the islands as a territory in 1898 (passage of the act was finally pushed through to completion, despite a not-insubstantial reluctance on the part of many fair-minded individuals in the US Congress who opposed the move, by the outbreak of the War with Spain in the same year). Today, there is a sustained and determined, although not extremely forceful, residual movement (it has been active for at least the last decade or two) to return Hawaii to the Hawaiians, by granting them sovereignty recognition that they feel should have never willingly dispensed with to begin with. It isn't as looney as it sounds, considering the admittedly underhanded economic wheeling and political dealing engaged in by US haole business interests at the turn of the century to bring Hawaii into the US as a protectorate or territory. Many island people feel it is a long overdue act of contrition for the events of 1898.

The book in reference was written as a broad foundation of knowledge within which to better establish the rationale Hawaiian sovereignty proponents cite as justification for an official return of the islands to the native Hawaiians. But as a discrete reference on ancient customs, beliefs, traditions, and cosmology, it provides a wealth of useful and thoughtful information on the old culture that Christianity so successfully dismembered and nearly destroyed completely.

Among the stimulating awarenesses that one acquires reading through this book, is the singular fact that due to there being no written Hawaiian language prior to the coming of the missionaries in 1820, there was no written history of the ancient Hawaiian culture available to scholars and academic researchers. The Ali'i of the second settlement of the islands (from *Kahiki* in about 1100 AD) relied upon specially trained kahunas who were charged with learning the important historical facts through memorization of chants, which were the only accepted form the oral tradition utilised to transmit knowledge. Since the history of the commoners (the kanaka maoli or Mana-hunes) was not recorded at all, what little existing knowledge we have today of the known history of the islands starts at about the time of the second settlement. Dudley notes that only the most important history of the ruling members of the Ali'i was recorded, usually in a standard, ritualised form of chant that consisted principally of genealogical information on whom the chief or royal person was descended from. Other collateral motifs and leitmotifs may have been combined with the primary genealogical chant to preserve and pass along royal legitimacy of birth, according to Dudley.

Understandably, the demands made upon the chanting kahunas were formidable, since there were no notes available to refer to and everything had to be recorded perfectly by memory. During religious activities at the *heiaus*, word has it that the ritual religious chants were considered so sacred that a simple error in their recitation could be sufficient excuse to have the erring kahuna executed or sacrificed (this would assume that there were other chanting kahunas present who also had the same chant committed perfectly to memory, as there undoubtedly were).

Such feats of memorization are to most westerners almost inconceivable today, given that written (or electronic) knowledge is such a basic foundation of western civilization. The parallel to this of most note exists in ancient China, where similar feats of rote

memorization and recitation were also a common aspect of learning, and even today learning by rote memorization is more the
norm than the exception in Asian parts of the world. Curiously,
many examples are cited in the available contemporary historical
literature of ordinary Hawaiians in the missionary schools of the
early to mid-1800s who would astonish their Christian teachers
by listening to long passages of the bible and then be prepared
to recite them back, word for word and without error. One particularly astounding example of this ability involves a Hawaiian who
listened to his missionary teacher read to him out of the bible for
well over a whole hour, only to have the book put down and then
be able to recite it all back *perfectly*!

Other reading I have been doing recently about the 'kahuna
system' of ancient learning and knowledge makes it clear that the
spoken word, but perhaps also even pure thought, had a very
special significance to the kahunas in association with what western philosopher & guru Dwayne Dyer terms *"The Power of
Intention"*. This presupposes a unifying force, mind-set, and spiritual link (*mana*) between human beings and the entire rest of the
natural world (*'Ghea'*); this offers further supporting evidence of
the ancient belief that all things in life have a certain basic sen-
tience (even rocks) that can be shared. It was this assumption
that was the underpinning behind most kahuna learning and
knowledge.

A modern example demonstrates just how pervasive vestigial
remnants of these attitudes persist today. Owing to the special
power Hawaiians feel words have as a strong form of concentrated spiritual essence, one never asks a local if he is going
fishing. To do so would make the fisherman's intentions impossible, as he will believe the fish have now 'heard' what he is about
to do (thanks to the carelessly expressed verbal utterance of the
questioner) and elude his efforts.

Other curiously associated facts of 'mindfulness' and spoken intent are uncovered. One technique that Dr. Dwayne Dyer makes use of in his previously mentioned book (that clearly must have been borrowed from this set of ancient Hawaiian beliefs) is the practice of writing down a particular word that describes a fondly wished for or hoped-for outcome on a blank card and leaving it in a conspicuous place where it may be viewed regularly throughout the day. Seeing the word each time it is passed by or viewed reinforces mindfulness of what has been wished for, with the result that this becomes a powerful focus of conscious and subconscious awareness. This, in turn, it is suggested, supposedly has the ability to bring the object of the wish into effective fulfilment.

Of course, this one example of ancient Hawaiian outlooks can be quickly submerged in a whole ocean of similar philosophical bits of knowledge scattered throughout the history of humanity, and correlation of such a specific circumstance with even just a few of the billions of similar counterparts in other cultures would be far more of a daunting task than most would care to undertake. Suffice it to say that this is just a single expression of the ancient Hawaiian belief that all things in conscious human awareness (and perhaps even in unconscious or subconscious awareness, also) have strongly linked and interactive *mana* (spiritual force or power), but perhaps one of the most compelling.

I have not yet done much study of the ancient ways of Hawaiian religious theology, belief, practice, and/or learning (as perpetuated through the various specific kahunas who were acknowledged to be adept at each individual task or concern), and I haven't yet even scratched the surface of more arcane areas of Hawaiian traditional knowledge, such as sorcery and spellcasting, but I expect the ensuing reading promises to be extremely stimulating.

It's now high noon and I just had a funny thought (the trade winds are whipping the trees furiously, outside—right on schedule). If a 'platonic' relationship refers to a non-sexual liaison between a man & a woman, would a 'platoonic' relationship imply that a woman was sexually servicing an entire group of military men? OK, sorry ladies. Just a rebellious part of my errant mindfulness following a goofy tangent, stumbled across along the trail to higher, purer thoughts, I assure you...

Returning briefly to that beautiful young local lady I ran across at the former Moloka'i Coffee Plantation a few days ago named "Kamaile" (since I have just figuratively crossed the divide from sober thoughtfulness to near-lustful day dreaming), I did a bit of researching of my references and found that her name means "(of) the sweet smelling Maile". According to Sohmer and Gustafson's *'Plants and Flowers of Hawaii'*, the Maile is a common vine ("Maile" is the Hawaiian name; scientific name 'Alyxia oliviformis', family Apocynaceae) found in most vegetation areas, but most especially in mixed mesic forests. It has a very distinctive and pleasing fragrance and is an important component used in lei making. I will forebear the ill-restrained prompts of my whacked-out sense of humor to make a play of words on the terms "fragrant" and "lei", and will rather instead get back on the straight and 'narrow(tive)', here.

One of the activities I have set out for myself is to go to the east end of the island and search for some of the Maile and take a bit of it back to her when I go up there next time to get some coffee. I think she would find that at least curious, if not purely thoughtful. One can only imagine what that flower lodged gracefully over her right rear ear would likely whisper to her at such a moment (probably telling her to haul in the sheets, weigh anchor, and paddle like a banshee for the lee shore!).

While on the subject of books and more Hawaiiana, I should mention that even though I have no children of my own, I have always been a keen appreciator of children's literature. I suppose this stems from feeling so strongly that children need not just to read books, but to read suitable books to help them learn about and appreciate the world around them. One such book I picked up at Moloka'i Fish & Dive is titled *'The Littlest Paho'eho'e'*. Any worshipper of *Pele*, the ancient Fire Goddess of Volcanism, would tell you that there are many Hawaiian words for lava (probably as many Hawaiian words for lava as the Arabs have for 'sand' and 'wind', or the Eskimos for 'snow' and 'water').

Irregular chunks of flow lava are termed *'a'a'*, while smooth and rounded volcanic ejecti are known as *'paho'eho'e'*. The story is brilliantly illustrated (always fully half of the attraction of worthwhile children's lit, in my opinion) and tells the story of a small round piece of 'paho'eho'e' that finds itself surrounded by antagonistic slabs of 'a'a lava. The story also involves a small boy who has lost his father and mother and is now homeless, without the protection of an *'ohana* (family & relatives) to look after him. Long story short, the local Ali'i (high chief) has just completed a religious heiau (temple) out of local lava rock and has one small niche left in the wall that no rock seems the proper size to fit. He sends his people all out to search high and low for a special rock that will fit perfectly, without success.

Meanwhile, little homeless Kea hears about the search for a special small rock and comes across the littlest 'paho'eho'e', which he brings to the chief. The round, smooth lave rock fits perfectly and as a reward Kea is adopted as a son by the chief and made keeper of the heiau's wall. Thus, both the little boy and the little rock find fulfillment and both live happily ever after (until, that is, little Kea meets and marries a local young wahine, who eventually ends up making his life a living hell, hee-hee).

Intentionally or unintentionally, this book is a fascinating illustration of the ancient outlook on nature that believes all objects, biologically alive or not, share an interconnectedness of spiritual energy. The book was written (obviously) by a local Hawaiian and illustrated, I find to my pleasant amazement, by one of the local artists I ran into at the Kaunakai arts & crafts event last Saturday.

Since there is a very healthy dose of unleavened child in me, I don't need any further inducements to appreciate and enjoy such wonderfully crafted children's books. Although I always smile assent when asked by a bookstore cashier if the book I am buying is for my children, I could verbalise a truthful reply by saying "Yes," since it is in fact for a child...*myself!* One of the greatest sorrows of my life is that I will never have any kids of my own, since I am now too old (58) to realistically entertain having any (that is, unless the current circumstances that obtain in my life were otherwise). When I was young, I rarely questioned the wish I had to eventually become a dad, since having lost my own father at age 4, no one could know more than I (I felt) how important it is for a child to have a father (& mother) as role models when growing up. I wanted that chance to give a child of my own all the quality of interaction that I myself had so sorely missed, growing up.

However, due to the fact that I somehow never connected long enough with the right person, I never married. Although a lovely Chinese-American woman I had a long (& I felt promising) relationship with back in the early 80s did become pregnant, she was still in her medical residency training and the timing just wasn't right for children. Consequently, that little spark of life was prematurely terminated with a D & C and that was as close as I ever came to being a father figure to some lovely little child (I say this trying not to cringe at the thought that, thanks to such criminally aberrant creatures as pop-idol Michael Jackson, one is no longer able to say such things without a slight bit of reticence, no matter how inappropriate—thanks heaps, *Captain Eo!*).

Later, of course, when I finally did get married (in my mid 40s), times had radically changed and I by that time knew that having children in the severely dysfunctional setting of today's typical 'no limits' American culture would be an exercise in mutual futility. Clearly, with all the deleterious influences pre-and-post adolescent children in American are now routinely exposed to (through TV, pop-culture media, extremely graphic sex & violence at an early age, etc.), and also in no small part to the financial demands (associated with schooling) incumbent upon parents today in mainstream America, it simply was no longer wise to have kids.

If I had married a supremely beautiful (spiritually & physically, since the two are inseparable to my way of seeing things) woman whom I had been hopelessly in love with (that sort of wildly romantic outlook was really far more characteristic of my early life than of those I now have are), I would have willingly thrown caution to the wind, but as it was, my marriage (when this finally happened) was built on far more substantial and practical foundations than simple romance. Since there were no allusions to shatter in this regard, no children were forthcoming.

On the other hand, instead of having discovered Hawaii relatively late in life, if I had somehow managed to end up in the islands earlier, there's little question in my wind that I would have eagerly sought out a lovely island wahine with which to let nature take its course in some out-of-the-way rural Hawaiian locale like east Moloka'i. But these are the cards fate deals one and one plays the best hand possible with what one has, at all events. (...pause for big sigh!).

Moving right along, lest the monologue get mired down in self-indulgent melancholy, it is a curious fact that the favorite personal transportation preference on the island seems to be a half-ton pick-up with 6 inch lift, shod with humongous rubber doughnuts that have aggressive all-terrain tread on them. This is probably a good idea during the rainy season, when local flooding can take place in certain parts of the island, but the loud whine of the tread on the roadways is so loud (even at moderate speeds) that they sound just like the DeHavilland Dash-8 twin turboprop STOL aircraft used by Inter-Island Airways out of Ho'olehua Airport. For the past week or so, it seemed that despite the fact that the airport is a good 7 miles away, I could hear these Dash-8s on final every few hours. Came to find out that it's merely the local folks driving their trucks on nearby streets! *Duh!* Another great Moloka'i mystery solved!

Spotted an old beaten-up VW bug on the lot of a service station in town; love to have that puppy for my own wheels. It looks forlorn and abandoned; wonder if it's for sale (he said quietly to himself, knowing damn well that such an acquisition is completely impossible)? I also take pity on stray dogs and cats, in addition to old VW beetles, just in case anyone reads this and wonders.

Speaking of dogs (*ilio*) and cats (*po'poki*), there are a great many cats around here. At first, I wondered about that until I did a bit of background reading and determined that the cats are probably a functional replacement for the imported mongooses that were originally imported to the islands in the med-1800s to help control the rat population. Regrettably, considered with the keen reflective acuity that 100% accurate hindsight affords, the mongoose is a diurnal critter (daytime) and rats are nocturnal (*nuff sed*), so their paths rarely crossed and the rat problem continued unabated. The domestic cat was suddenly a very popular pet in the islands, although they have been allowed to range freely and not responsibly controlled; as a result, the cat population has accordingly shot sky-high (as might be expected). I understand that Oahu alone has some 4,000,000 feral cats! Gaak!

The first dogs (they were apparently relatively small and short-haired) were brought over with the first wave of Polynesian settlements in (the pre-Ali'i Kanaka Maoli) about 400 AD, since they were a favorite food source (poor puppies!). It wasn't until much later (mid-1900s) that community and state agencies establishing rules for humane treatment of animals in the islands finally succeeded in weaning the islanders off that particular staple in their diets. Their teeth were also favored for anklets and bracelets, as well as ceremonial rattles.

Visited the Moloka'i Public Library today for the first time on this particular visit. They have a small library, but a good many excellent reference works on the ancient culture. I took out a 5-year library card, being now officially a property owner on the island, for $25 and found that they have 8 PCs that card-holders are allowed to use on the internet (at no additional cost). If you can manage to elbow your way past the usual gaggle of small (noisy) kids who think cruising the internet is way cool, you can send and receive email on these units, also. Today I found out that the local school is only open for internet access Monday-Thursday, so finding the library computers is great. Only catch is you can't hook up your own laptop and must use their desktops machines (also can't use your CD discs in their mainframe drives, but that's a minor problem).

At least several options are available: 1) Moloka'i Elementary School Computer Community Resource lab (Ethernet broadband connection, with permission to use your own laptop); 2) Moloka'i (Kaunakakai) Public Library (no laptops permitted; must use their machines on their broadband Ethernet tie-in); 3) Sturgess' Cafe and Gallery (on Ala Alama Avenue, must use their two desktop machines—broadband Ethernet). The Moloka'i Elementary

Kalikiano Kalei

School machines and computer resource room was enabled with
John MacByte backing, I think (he donated PCs and peripherals
to the school, shortly after his arrival on the island, if I am not
mistaken).

Walking in to the local library this afternoon made me feel a
stab of both envy and pity, simultaneously. Envy over all those
wonderful reference books on Hawaiiana and pity for the scruffy
reference collection of only 58 books I have barely managed to
acquire by purchase, while here. I think most of my friends know
I have a 'thing' about books. It's been both a blessing and a mon-
key on my back, throughout my entire life. The first 30 years of
my life were spent lugging a personal collection of about 2000
books around with me, as I relocated of necessity from place to
place (as a bachelor). That was never a fun ordeal, but I certainly
loved having all that knowledge arrayed about me, wherever I
was. Having my own home was certainly a major step forward in
that I then at least had a place to keep all of them. One of my few
true obsessions in life, since I can't seem to keep much actual
knowledge *inside* my cranium, I have to rely on having it close at
hand when answers are needed. I've always considered that
there are two basic types of 'intelligent' person found in life: 1)
those who are able to carry most of their knowledge around in
their heads (those blessed with superior memories), and 2) those
who know *where to go* to get the knowledge they need, when
occasioned. Sadly, and lacking the prodigious ability to memo-
rise vast amounts of information like the ancient Hawaiians &
Chinese, I am of the latter, less capable (but no less enthusiastic)
variety.

April 23rd, 2005 (Saturday)

Saturday—arts & crafts on K'kai main street (Ala Alama). Woke with a headache and a huge erection. Rx: Pop an aspirin (or an elixer made from Hawaiian *'Noni'*—*Morinda citrifolia* L., otherwise known as the *Indian Mulberry*) and a lusty whack-off as the sun rises. Result: Headache gone and lustfulness temporarily satiated. An ancient *Kahuna La'au Lapa'au* trick I picked up. A quick check of my palm reveals no hair growing on it; excellent! After a quick traditional Hawaiian breakfast of strong Moloka'i espresso and Quaker's Instant Oatmeal (with artificially sweetened dried cranberries thrown in), the day is ready to start unfolding on the temporal panorama machine.

Funny how the tropical climate here seems to promote or at least enhance these urges. I have never had any need for stupid stuff like *Viagra*, always having been endowed with perfectly satisfactory circulatory function (and normal blood pressure, thank you very much), but there's something about this island place that makes you just get these libidinous urges out of the blue, with no real forethought or vague feelings of horniness required. I can see myself stranded somewhere on a desert island with Miss Hawaii's younger and more beautiful sister (or even her thicker and less lovely elder sister); it wouldn't be long before we'd have our own nation, given the frequency of urges to grab someone's pretty ass that happen of their own lovely volition here, and I'd be the *Ali'i nui* of a new *moi* in short order.

Another absolutely great 'local' book I picked up is a small 150 page paperback with a green cover titled '*Exiles from Time: Stories of Hawaii*', by Ian MacMillin. These are not old stories about the ancient culture, but vignettes about the modern intermixing of races in the islands that goes on right now. MacMillin writes about such things as dealing with the voracious island termites that infest Hawaiian soil on the surface, but subtly explores the preconceived perceptions of one ethnic or communal group towards another on a different level in the same story. There is a strong element of traditional Hawaiian oral history richness in his writing, given the different levels of meaning that he manages to weave into his some of his stories, but on a broader level he is dealing with the same basic perplexities of human interaction that have been part of our experience since the onset of recorded history.

One such story explores the reflections of a man of clearly evident Caucasian Haole extraction, as he copes with his wife (a very literate woman of Swedish ancestry, who edits a small local newspaper), the very 'local' attitudes of his Hawaiian-Portuguese neighbors, and the acculturisation of his children into local island community—all while engaged in a search for termites under his hale. Aside from being skillful and entertaining writing, the issues he weaves into his narrative are stimulating and thoughtful. Truly a writer one could call 'artful' in his craft. MacMillin's book is a very good example of the sort of wonderful and worthwhile writing that one more often than not accidentally stumbles across while searching for other books, that is unique to the archetypal modern Hawaiian experience and valuable learning material not just about the Hawaiian lifestyle, but life in its broader sense.

One of the sub themes in the story just referred to delves into the process of the writer's children picking up island pigeon dialect, despite his wife's imperious insistence that they learn and speak 'correct English'. Aside from being an inherently interesting proposition, it raises larger and parallel issues that today profoundly affect many children in Hawaiian public schools. I already briefly mentioned (earlier in this journal) the recent study

conducted by the state's school system that found Moloka'i public school students (especially at high school level) to be at the
bottom of the barrel academically (in critical math & English skills,
particularly). This problem relates directly to the conflict between
traditional mainland American emphasis on 'pure' language and
learning forms and the radically relaxed (by mainland mainstream standards) island approach to academic study, and
preference among adolescents for the local idiomatic pigeon dialect.

A tougher nut to crack than I admit to having the intellectual
resources to bring to bear against it, the concerns alluded to are
both legitimate and paradoxically conflicting. Most importantly, as
this same set of problems continue to impact the local schools,
MacMillin successfully directs our attention to the fact that these
influences have direct impact on daily life in the islands—that
they are not the exclusive provenance of scholarly intellectuals
and educators alone.

Reflecting on this makes me think a bit about my present situation. I am staying in a spare room in the Ranch Camp home of
a Filipino woman and her 90 year old husband. Having had the
opportunity to listen to extraneous noise and sounds of daily life
coming from neighboring homes, it is evident that a good number
of the surrounding people here in the Ranch Camp residential
area of Kaunakakai are former Filipino plantation workers (and
their descendants) who came here in the 50s to work the pineapple plantations. Several dialects of spoken Filipino are
obvious, even to someone like me, who barely recognises the
main Tagalog dialect. Across the street lives a family that has a
Filipino father and a (mostly) Hawaiian wife, with their multitude
of small children. There are a few (pure) haole families scattered
about in Ranch Camp, but I would be tempted to venture a guess

that most families are of Filipino or mixed Filipino/Hawaiian ethnicity. Then there's recent arrival me, blonde ('dishwater'), green-eyed, and lanky, with the clearly mainland trait of having disgustingly white skin that is untouched by too much sun. Coming from a background replete with very Caucasian pretensions of erudite 'honky' hauteur, I undoubtedly reflect (as much as I conscientiously fight off the influence) some of those racial and ethnic prejudices picked up osmotically from my school-teacher mother (of strict Presbyterian upbringing), whose years of working with Mexican and black minority children instilled in her a palpable condescending regard for these groups. My consequent acute awareness of these cultural shear forces have always made it inordinately difficult for me to interact smoothly with people of distinctly non-Caucasian ethnic groups, since I typically react to them in the same strained and overly constructed manner an ethnologist would to a new and hitherto little-known people (i.e. superciliously polite, acutely—perhaps painfully and uncomfortably--tolerant of cultural differences, practices, habits, language, manners, customs—viz. the "white man's burden syndrome", "Honky liberal response", etc.).

Since I am by nature and by virtue of my 'only-child' upbringing a naturally shy and restrained person (also possessed of a strong sense of politeness and good manners) at first contact with others, this is probably responsible for a strong sense of vague self-consciousness and discomfort I experience at such moments and in such circumstances. All too frequently, extreme politeness and 'good manners' may be misinterpreted or misconstrued by far more relaxed and informally structured people as a manifestation of 'condescending tolerance'. This creates some relatively uncontrollable embarrassment for those like myself in cross-cultural interactions and I am constantly having to remind myself to relax, chill out, and drop the yoke of strictly prescribed (upper class haole) social conventions that I (unconsciously) bear as a result of my childhood upbringing.

Haven't thought about it much, but perhaps that also explains why I have always found the rich differences between the various ethnicities and cultures such an endless source of fulfilling stimulation. What I have to do, of course, is put the magnifying glass and note pad in the drawer more often, and simply experience these things without being so goddamned *quantifying* in my approach to them. A simple set of two words from the post-Beatnik era usually hangs at the edge of my thoughts—just out of reach: *"Mellow out!"*

Of course, I am unable to do this and even find myself (horrors!) thinking about my recently appointed supervisor back at the State Treasurer's Office, a naturalized Filipino named Henrico, who is an infuriatingly and chaotically intermixed confusion of distinctly Philippines-Filipino attitudes and American pop-culture. This chap has been the bane of my existence as a Treasury Program Officer since the department was shaken up once again by our dim-bulb Chicano Division Chief, Rafael Lunes. Henrico has many personal habits that drive me absolutely crazy, such as a tendency to exclaim loudly to himself whenever he is pleased with something (eg. *"Oh...I am liking this now!"*, or *"Ah...I am understanding this now; I am very pleased!"*, etc.). By any normal western standard, such dialogues with one's self would be considered droll at best, schizophrenic at worst. However, with Henrico it is just another aspect of his distinctly 'Filipino' behavior that I have trouble with, since thanks to a life-long touch of ADD (Attention Deficit Disorder) I am unable to block extraneous noise and surrounding noise out of my immediate awareness, and anything spoken within my earshot I am forced to give my full attention to. By my standards, his drivel is pure noise!

Another problem with Henrico is that because he communicates incompletely, through his less-than-perfect knowledge of the English language, he consistently fails to get his thoughts, attitudes, opinions, demands, etc., across clearly in conversation. As the process of unclear intent continues (typically) and it becomes increasingly apparent that he is not being fully understood, the level of his voice will rise as he consequently becomes increasingly agitated by this fact. Of no help at all, and adding considerably to the frustration, is his habit of refusing to let the person he is talking with complete what they are trying to say. Any answer to a question asked by him is met with a staccato barrage of *"No, no, no, no, no, no, no.....what I am trying to say is... what I am trying to say is...",* etc., etc., ad infinitum. For someone like me who has a better-than-average grasp of the English language and who understands all too clearly the importance of being able to communicate or articulate clearly in the communicative process, the resulting frustrations and annoying misunderstandings are horribly irritating.

Unfortunately, Henrico appears likely to remain as our immediate supervisor at work, even though he came to us knowing absolutely nothing about what he is now administrative responsible for; in fact, he has been driving us all progressively crazy with his concerted efforts to learn something about our work from us. We were hoping he'd have the good sense to leave everyone alone and let us continue to carry on our important financial responsibilities unencumbered by having to 'suffer a fool', as the old saying puts it, but worst-case fears came about and now we have him in our faces all day long, having to patiently try to answer his doubtless well-intended questions as we simultaneously try to get our own work demands fulfilled. For some like myself, who only function well in an absolutely quiet and peaceful environment, such unwelcome intrusiveness is absolute anathema to say the least. But enough of Henrico and the presently colossal frustrations of my office back home.

Probably take a shower in a few minutes, wrap up the reading and writing until later today. Maybe I'll even take in a movie at the only theatre on the island, located on the north end of the island in Maunaloa. They are showing the recently released flick 'SA-HARA', which I was given 10 free tickets to see in a special sneak preview, back in Sacramento. I had no time for it then, but I may well pay to see it now. Aside from the subject matter of the vast North African desert locale (a subject made interesting by my work in the Middle East and the fact that I was brought up very near the great Mojave Desert of California), there's a beautiful busty brunette starring in it who has a set of the finest pineapples one could ever hope to lay a tongue on! It might even be a fresh idea to invite lovely Kamaile (with her red flower coyly placed over her right ear) to go with me—strictly *platonic*, of course. I'm sure she doesn't get invited to see a flick with a haole every day (even when he's nearly 59 and old enough to be someone's grandfather by now) and she really is a lovely young (Hawaiian) woman (*Awue!*) who is not (clearly and unmistakably) presently not committed to any *kane* (male) friends. Ah... *dream on*, sweet dreamer.

Speaking of gender attractions, it has always struck me as interesting that smell has so very, very much to do with sexual attraction. I well recall a woman whom I have known for many years, someone I originally met back in the 70s and whom I remain in touch with (remotely) today. This woman was a source of immensely powerful sexual attraction to me in my late 20s, and not just because of her absolutely stunningly lithe, tanned, slender good looks and exceptional personality. I am convinced that a significant part of my attraction to her was, simply put, her natural bodily aroma.

Call it an *eau*, an odor, personal fragrance, natural bodily cachet, aroma or whatever you wish, but there's no denying that her pheronomic chemical essence was fatally attractive to me. I well recall specific moments out in the wilderness when we went on mountain trips. The overall smell of her at such times, which had to be a combination of her skin's odor perfused with sweat, the fragrance of her dark chestnut brown hair, and who knows what else, was simply and indescribably overwhelming to my nose. At those odd times when I deigned to mention this to her, she probably thought I was crazy, since she undoubtedly regarded herself as being terribly smelly after trekking up a mountainside on a hot and sweaty Sierra summer day. I simply couldn't get it across to her that one person's perhaps not necessarily pleasant 'odor' was to someone else the sweetest perfume this side of heaven. Even plunging my face into the damp skin at the nape of her neck, lying covered as it was by waves of her beautiful brown hair, was rewarded with a tingly awareness of some uncommonly irresistible essential chemistry at work, rising through the follicles of her glorious brown mane to transfix me. Lying with her intimately at other times, with both of us sweatily embracing with raw urges of lustful pleasure, was to release a complex aroma of an even more powerful essence from her. But of course, MOST of the time we bathed before hand, LoL.

Few women I have known in my life before or after that time have had the same effect on me. Her smell (and that's as good a term for it as any I can think of) was right: raw, earthy, moist and promising, full of complicated chemical interactions that I can't even begin to guess at. It said: *"Love me, take me, hold me, merge with me, become one living spirit with me, enter my moist recesses, fill me with your hot love, destroy me with your passion...."* and far too much more to go on about coherently here (not that any of the foregoing is actually coherent, of course). Those were moments when I felt as if I could willingly expire from the precarious heights of feeling that arose within me, as I lustfully explored that vast jungle of delicious complexity that was her nature, her physical and spiritual anima.

Sadly, it was the very powerful force of my attraction that she (many years) later explained had put her off, ironically enough. That was not altogether a happy discovery, but as a wild eyed (German-Irish) romantic throughout my life, it is simply my nature to be powerfully aroused by certain complex stimuli. Perhaps it's the blue-painted, savage Celt forebears lurking in my family *in-cestry* (sic); or maybe it's simply poetic licentiousness I routinely take liberties with. Who knows and who cares now? It's all history, past events, and no longer a real concern, but one thing is for certain: I'll never forget the powerful forces her *scent* unleashed in me.

One reads occasionally about the unfathomable power that romantic love can have on human beings. Stories of kingdoms won and lost, lives violent ended or destroyed, are all an important part of our human literary heritage. All I can say, from having had brief moments of contact with these primordially monumental forces of gender attraction is that at that specific instant in time, I could have probably moved heaven and earth with one hand, if need be. Such was the heady (hormonal) stuff that those particular dreams of youth were made of, at the time! Sadly, my wife has no such chemically powerful attractive scent about her and her hair simply smells of too many permanent sets having damaged her long dark hair over the years. And yet we have a reasonably good marriage, a stable partnership, and much to consider as proof that I am finally 'mature enough' as a responsible adult male to not let my wild romantic fantasies and emotions get the upper hand on my conduct of life. Boring perhaps, spiritually stultifying possibly, but stable and conducive to marital perpetuity. (How much rather I would be experiencing extremes of heaven and hell with a dark-haired woman of my dreams, rather than a solidly stable domestic life with a good, reliable, and highly regarded partner, but that simply is not to be. Another of life's many little ironies, I guess.)

It is now somewhat later in the day and I spent the late morning at the arts & crafts street market, held each Saturday on Ala Malama Avenue (main street). Talked a while with Fil, the white-haired (ex-Korean War vet) photographer, and with gorgeous Locinda, from whom I bought a nice Aloha shirt last Saturday ($10). Carlo was also there, selling a few of his always nice items. More tourists this Saturday than last and the usual lovely weather...of course, of course. I am reminded for no particular reason that last night was a wretched one, thanks again to the roosters and also to the neighborhood dogs (of which there are many).

The usual pattern was 1) dogs start barking and howling; then 2) roosters wake up and start crowing; 3) followed by another doggy chorus of howls and growls; 4) in turn followed by yet another round of lengthy crowing, etc., etc. With canines singly rendering melody and roosters complementing with harmony, there was no peace throughout much of the night. I was too lazy to reach out for the ear plugs (or a shotgun) so I just suffered in silence, vowing that whenever the chance presented itself, I'd augment my customary dinner of rice with Turkey SPAM over it with some rooster-stew. You'd think the neighbors would themselves be driven slowly insane by all this cacophony, but they have probably all gotten used to such *grosser nachtmuzik*' by now.

After the arts & crafts mart closed at noon, I got in the car and traveled up to the mail box at Ho'olehua PO, then dropped by the

Moloka'i Coffee Plantation shop to have some espresso. This turned out to be a most interesting stop on my junket, since the chap I sat down next to turned out to be quite an interesting guy. He was a rather large and florid haole, wearing a loud aloha shirt (I liked it anyway), and was having a drink and sandwich as I walked over to the counter.

Waiting for my own espresso included quite a floor show, free of charge, as the same local barista who last time had barely given me the time of day this time was preoccupied trying to train his new female cohort how to draw off coffee drinks from their espresso machine. She ruined several, and after a few more efforts, gave up and let the guy with the 'local adolescent' attitude take over. Meanwhile an obviously touristy haole and his wife were sitting there, waiting for the own coffee drinks and putting on a cheerful façade of *bon hommie*. I thought they might grin themselves to death, having to watch this lamentable amateur show being put on by the barista and his apprentice (No doubt the repeating refrain in their minds was: *"This is the friendly island, so I MUST, MUST, MUST put on the appearance of patient understanding and amicable, good natured tolerance…"*). I too was starting to strain my face from too much good-natured grinning, but fortunately, the doppio was ready shortly after Mr. Cool took over duties and I retreated to the lanai to sit for a spell in the refreshing breeze blowing *makua*.

At any rate, the large aloha-shirted haole tourist turned out to be from Texas (more precisely from Fort Worth, where Lockheed-Martin's General Dynamics' Aerospace Division has their corporate operations), I shortly learned as we started talking story over our coffee. Turns out he is a Lockheed-Martin aeronautical systems engineer, who is currently involved with Mitsubishi Aircraft as part of their aerospace partnership in the Japanese F-2 aircraft program with Lockheed-Martin. He was *en route* to Japan (Nagoya) and had elected to take a one-week stopover at the Moloka'i Ranch Lodge in Maunaloa Town. Richard (since that was his name) had lost his 50 year old wife to coronary disease precipitated by severely advanced diabetes last year and gave me some background on what a complete turn-around his life had taken, when he lost her (she was, ironically, an RN). Sad enough, when it happens, for anyone. It made me realise what a complete redirecting of one's life is in order after one has traded former 'unencumbered single status' for the closely shared partnership that marriage ultimately becomes. He did say that while they had each other, they had a very good life together, since apparently, they were about as perfectly attuned to each other as a couple may be. I envy him that, of course; pity that it all came to such a sad end so prematurely, but again, one plays the poker game of life with the cards the karmic dealer passes out.

Richard was well acquainted with many of the same subject areas in aviation I am, so we really had an interesting half hour chat over the coffee. Earlier, he worked with Lockheed-Martin's shuttle programs and later participated in the development of the Lockheed-Martin F-35A/B/C Joint Services Strike Fighter that is still undergoing pre-production testing. The aircraft is quite an amazing piece of aeronautical technology and I am fortunately possessed of this month's (June 2005 issue) excellent Flight Journal Magazine article on this aircraft, having brought it over with me to read *en route* to Moloka'i.

Richard was entertaining me with a few facts about the archaic computers they had in use for their design development work on the space shuttle. I recall him saying that one of the key microprocessors they used at Lockheed back in the late 70s had a colossal memory of 64 KB of RAM! There were many similar amusing exchanges and we both chuckled over the fact that we had such a strongly shared set of interests, way out here in the middle of nowhere, but stranger things have happened, of course. One of the most-odd was the fact that when I went to Saudi Arabia on my first work contract, back in 1983, they gave me as a flat-mate a fellow I had sat next to in the college band that I played trombone in.

Andre was his name, and I had always regarded him as something of a wimpy 'mama's boy' while tootling away with him on band music. I guess the bad karma of my basic disregard for him as a person was partly at fault for my ending up with him living in the same flat as I did, some 8000 miles from home and almost 20 years later! *Hoo-boy!* Let that be a lesson to me! Never talk stink about anyone! You never know when a few moments of un-called-for arrogance may return to dull your spurs! Hmm...I notice that *Messrs. Fleish and Kincaid* (that automatic writing analysis program on my laptop) now regards my writing ability as being on par with a 7th grader. *Woo-hoo!* Progress!

After a while, Richard returned to the Moloka'i Ranch Lodge (where he said no one else was staying at the moment) and I took the long way home via the *Palau'u Lookout* that provides such a stunning overview of the *Makanalua Peninsula*. Actually, my ulterior motive for coming up there was to do a bit of half-serious searching for the fragrant Maile vine that is used in making floral leis. The wind was brisk, as it invariably is, and the view from the outlook, perched some 2000 feet above the peninsula, towards Father Damien's storied *Kaluapapa Colony* for lepers was spectacular. The sun was out and the clouds, although slowly gathering overhead, had not yet completely socked in this spectacular eagle's eyrie of a vantage point. I spent about 45 minutes looking vainly for some specimens of the Maile vine, but had no luck at all...probably as much due to the fact that I am still not completely sure exactly what it looks like in its natural habitat, despite a few pictures of the vine in a guide book. Well, I really hadn't expected to win the botanical jackpot anyway, considering what a miserably inept arborist I have always been. Perhaps another time.

While driving through K'kai-town, I spotted a very small boy at a crosswalk and stopped for him to pass safely, as is my customary habit here in a place where 35 miles per hour is the usual speed limit on all by the rural stretches of highway. The little boy (he couldn't have been more than 6 or so) finished crossing the street and as he mounted the sidewalk, he waved a very cheery wave and I distinctly heard a childish *"Thank you!"* from him as he went on his way. This just about knocked me over, since he appeared to be a kanaka child, small and very brown, and very 'local'. Serves me right for projecting my biases at him so unfairly, since a polite 'thank you' was the very last thing I'd have expected from a small local island *keiki*. Kid must have had a very, very conscious and concerned mother; I'd still probably make book on the opposite expectation, no matter how surprising this experience was. Too bad there can't be more mothers like his among the locals and also a damn shame that once they hit high school and puberty, any last vestige of innocent altruism likely vanishes like *Maunaloa* in the mists of morning.

Well, I seem to have had one too many chocolate coated toffee Macadamia nuts, I guess, since I've now killed off any vestige of an appetite I may have had for anything substantial for dinner.

Suki just called via cell and asked me to find out exactly why we have been so keenly encouraged (by Cheryl Apaia) to rush ahead with the water line installation. Suki's hypothesis is that perhaps we are being urged to take care of having the new 12-inch water line run across the road (with us bearing this formidable expense ourselves) so that the other adjacent properties will be made thereby more valuable. If this is true and other properties next to us that may be also being brokered by Cheryl Apaia will be potentially more valuable, as a result of our installing critical water utilities that were not formerly accessible, this would suggest that we are being played for haole chumps to some extent in the matter.

I'd hate to think that this is the case (I'm such a trusting person!), but I'll have to question Cheryl about this on Monday. I also need to ask Victor if he has any information on this subject that has any relevant bearing, since if there's no screaming urgency to have this complicated work done ASAP, we can afford to let it go until a more convenient date in the future. Of course, there is the possibility of the water meter going up from $6000 to $9000, as Victor intimated may soon happen, but the matter of whether we first even need to bear this cost entirely by ourselves at this time certainly needs to be broached immediately. This is a perhaps a good example why this journal could alternately be called *"An Accidental Occidental"*, but if I find out there is any conscious attempt in the brokering of our transaction to play upon our gullibility in Hawaiian property sales practices, perhaps a better title would be *"The Innocent Occidental"*... *Auwe!*

April Sumpteenth...uh, 24st, 2005 (Sunday)

It's zero-dark-thirty hours in the early AM (6:30, actually) and barely light enough to see the keyboard. Last night was a lovely variation from the norm, uninterrupted by the usual nightly *a capella* choir of roosters, dogs, supported by the percussive background whine of 4WD all-terrain tyres on the street (as the local guys celebrate the weekend in time honored manner, with cars and babes). I used my earplugs when I went to bed. Although I normally dislike resorting to things like this, I have to admit the absolute peacefulness of zero noise pollution was blissful. Only problem with that, initially, it amplified the sound of my heartbeat and this started me to thinking about that marvelous and absolutely vital muscle. The awareness that it never stops operating, day in and day out, without pause or rest, is both comforting and disturbing, for when it finally does decide to take a break, you in a whole HEAP of trouble, *brah!* Lesson? Love that 'lil lub-dub, whiles ya got it!

Always comforting when you have been away from the normal grind for so long that you've lost track of what day it is. Incidentally, I think I've accidentally invented a sure-fire aid to weight loss. Just buy a pack of chocolate-covered toffee Macadamia nuts and munch about 6 of them first thing on rising; it kills your appetite beautifully!

Given my tendencies to constantly cerebrate about everything in life and unceasingly analyse each small aspect of every personal reflective nuance to an absurd degree, I am reminded of several observations. The first is an old joke in which a Freudian psychiatrist meets a Jungian psychiatrist on the way to their offices in the early morning. The one says *"Good Morning,"* as they pass. The second one responds in kind, but wonders to himself *"Now what did he mean by that...?"*

The other is a quote from Shakespeare's JULIUS CÆSAR (one of several of the immortal bard's plays that we studied intensively in earlier school days—a fact I have since found reason to be grateful for on a number of occasions in my past, despite the fact that our *Anglish* teacher, Miss Whazzername, was a real pain): *"Let me have about me men that are fat and sleek and sleep o'nights. Yon Cassius has a lean and hungry look: such men think too much and are dangerous."*

A third fragment of a quote from some unrecalled source also comes to mind that states that *"The unreflected life is not a life worth living."* Profoundly true enough if one subscribes to traditional western philosophical disciplines without qualification, but anathema to he or she who has come to understand the simple truth that too much analysis and reflection can be decidedly *unhealthy*; and if carried to unhealthy extremes, can actually serve as a barrier to actual immediate experience of the life process itself.

One of my reading books already alluded to (Michael Kioni Dudley's exploration of traditional Hawaiian cosmology and theosophy, *'Man, Gods, and Nature'*) discusses, in the context of his discourse, the controversy over whether or not living creatures other than human kind are capable of rational thought. Dudley cites a number of recent studies that have explored this question to varying degrees and contends that animals do indeed engage in a very low order of thoughtful reflection, albeit a primitively developed process that is often dismissed as or attributed to 'instinct' (itself a poorly understood mechanism by behavioral psychologists).

This contention is part of his interesting argument that western philosophy's departure, since the watershed era of Decartes' (I am reminded here of the Monte Python chorus in their 'Philosopher's Song' that contains the phrase *"Renny Decartes, that smelly old fart..."*) pontifications, from any possible acceptance of nature (in its largest context of being inextricably associated with the entire cosmos, as a mere localized element of the whole cosmological enchilda) as being possessed of a universally sentient logos, has largely acted as a colossal set of perceptional blinders that have kept us from seeing our direct association with nature in terms of the categorical imperative that it actually is. [I'd like to think that the preceding 105 word mouthful is not a run-on sentence, despite what Messrs Fleish and Kincaid seem to think,

153

but what the heck—as Hemingway never said, *'A man's gotta right to write what a man's gotta right to write',* right?].

One of my literary claims to fame is the fact that when I was a child, my mother (a teacher) and I spent our summers with her mother ('Nana' Terhune, a Lake Erie Women's College educated Dunning Method piano teacher) at the old family homestead in Burley, Idaho (near Twin Falls). Since my Uncle, Ma's brother Charles, was the town's senior physician & surgeon (Charles Alfred Terhune, MD…an imposing name if ever I encountered one), he had achieved quite a level of local success in the community of 4000 and after returning from service as an Army medical officer in the North African Campaign, had bought a beautiful tract of land on the Big Wood River that lay at the base of Mount Baldy, on the outskirts of Ketchum, near the famed Sun Valley resort.

During the period when we routinely summered in Idaho (the 50s and early 60s), it was the family custom for everyone in the Terhune clan to gather at Uncle Charlie's spacious two-story log cabin for protracted bouts of R & R. These were fabulous times for a kid of my tender years, as the 'poor cousin' from California, and since the Big Wood River ran right through Charlie's front yard, fly fishing was the big activity of note during these retreats. The Rainbow Trout were always big, beautiful, and abundant when the spring runoff was in full flow and this attracted a good number of interesting people who also had purchased land on the river.

Among these were a few noteworthy celebrities (many of them well known Hollywood movie stars) who had first discovered the charming rustic sophistication of Averell Harriman's Union Pacific Railroad resort, Sun Valley, which Harriman had originally constructed back in the late 30s. One of these was writer Ernest Hemingway, at the time enjoying the apex of his career as a well-known novelist. Hemingway's cabin (near the warm Springs

Ranch section of the river) was not far downstream from my Uncle's place and since both my Uncle and Hemingway were fly fishing enthusiasts, their paths occasionally crossed when the big trout were biting. Although I accompanied my uncle occasionally on these outings as the utility creel custodian I never met Hemingway personally.

However, we were all at the cabin (we referred to it as 'the Sun Valley cabin", even though it was more properly located in nearby Ketchum—I guess the magic of association with such splashy stuff had worked its influence on us commoners) enjoying the fine summer there, when Ernest finally acted out the last chapter in his personal autobiography in July of 1961.

For days afterward it wasn't unusual to see locals sort of unusually hanging out in the vicinity of his cabin, feigning interest in fishing during the worst hours of the day when trout are not inclined to bite, since everyone knew about their famous neighbor and had heard what had happened. As a nearby doctor known to be in residence when the suicide had occurred, my Uncle had been called by the county sheriff to participate in the initial investigation. Although he wouldn't talk a lot about it, I could sense that some sort of melancholy change in Uncle Charlie's accepted outlook on life had taken place; he was clearly reflective, less interested in fishing, and a bit less gruff than was his usual autocratic, imperious manner. I don't want to push the limits of sublimity when I say this, but I think the merest, teeny-tiny bit of Hemingway's creative muse took temporary refuge in our cabin at that time, as a result of Ernest's premature departure that year. Part of my claim to fame, I guess, since for the rest of my life I have been otherwise completely buried in the dross and effluvia that comprises the normal flow of detritus on the river of life.

The Hemingway saga didn't end there, since they planted 'Papa' in the local Ketchum Cemetery. This wouldn't in itself be remarkable, although Ernest was extremely fond of the captivatingly rugged charm possessed by this part of southern Idaho. What raised a few eyebrows shortly after the interment took place was the mysterious fact that the mound of dirt on Hemingway's grave began to sink progressively, no sooner than he had been laid to rest.

What was initially regarded as a natural settlement of the soil over his grave soon had to be entirely reconsidered, for the residual level of the grave's surface kept sinking lower and lower. This somewhat unsettling (no pun intended) matter was soon resolved when an alert person noticed that the many visitors to the Hemingway grave were prone to swiping a sample of dirt from his grave as a souvenir. One out-of-town fellow was even removing shovel-sized scoops of it to fill small vials with the dirt and sell them to Hemingway fans who wanted to buy them.

A fence was consequently erected around the plot, which brought a halt to the strange business, but this seems to highlight a characteristic of human nature. It's a curious fact that people want to be associated with individuals they recognise as being noteworthy, people they admire for one reason or another, or whose feats and accomplishments have inspired them in the depths of their own rather mundane or ordinary lives…even if that association is reduced to a spoonful of the dirt their hero's mortal remains were buried in. I guess this factor of human behavior also helps account for the recent auction of pop-star Madonna's sweat-stained (and I have been reliably informed by the press that Madonna's sweat isn't sweet, like that of the lovely brunette lady friend of my 20s, but *REALLY* stinky) and trademark 'nose-cone' shaped bra for some twenty-five thousand dollars, and a dress formerly worn by Marilyn Monroe for an equally hefty sum. I wonder what a used Jennifer Anniston tampon would bring? Or a condom used by Brad Pitt? Hmm. People are remarkable in the inexplicable depths of their individual eccentricities.

The speculation raised by my wife the previous day concerning the water line attachment to our newly acquired property here in Moloka'i made me pause to reflect on our home in Sacramento (after I had engaged in a bit of protracted worry about the prospect of us possibly being conned a bit regarding the urgency of getting that connection completed).

Our lane in the pleasant South Land Park area of urban Sacramento opens off of a major east-west avenue that joins Interstate Highway 5. Located directly across the street from a nice elementary school, it opens only to the right off this avenue and continues for about two thousand yards until it makes a right turn that continues in a 'U' fashion back to the major cross-street in reference. Before the interstate was built, it was a nice, quiet area of town, which found favor with retired people and a more mature group of residents.

Now, with the interstate access that the major avenue provides, a recent problem has been increasingly heavy traffic—much of it from poorer neighborhoods to the east, mainly black and Chicano—characterised by loud traffic noise, those deep bass infrasonic auto stereo systems that thump out annoyingly intense vibrations, and average speeds that exceed the set speed limits by a considerable margin (limit is 40 MPH, but many routinely disregard the limit and reach 50 to 55). The increased speeds are starting to make it hard to turn onto the major avenue against traffic, since by the time you spot someone coming, they are already right on top of you and it's unsafe to venture out into the lanes. [I am convinced that many of the younger drivers travel at these speeds deliberately, so as to discourage others from turning out in front of them; this seems to be a symptom of today's decorticated obsession with being first, being ahead of everyone else in the mind-numbing rush to go nowhere fast…validation of Schopenhauer's classic assessment of basic human nature…]

The neighbors on our block are as varied as they are anywhere else, of course. On our immediate right reside an elderly couple named Lou and Hilda. Lou is a retired state employee who is in his late 80s; his Norwegian wife Hilda is 85. Both are probably the best people anyone could hope to have as immediate neighbors, since not only are they extremely thoughtful and considerate, they are also quite alert to what's going on in our part of the street and keep an eagle eye out for unusual goings-on. Lou formerly had what is called a 'hobby-farm' on the outskirts of town and grew a great many varieties of fruit and vegetables. Now that he is too old to actively care for such a property, he has limited his botanical interest to things he cultivates in his yard at home. This presently consists of several different types of citrus, Kiwi fruit, and some other things. Every Christmas his wife Hilda makes special traditional Norwegian holiday cookies, a delight always to look forward to, since they bring over a platter of them for us as a seasonal gesture of good will.

Across the street from us are a retired Chinese couple who used to operate a restaurant locally and next to them a husky balding fellow I call *"Outdoor Joe"*, with his wife. Joe is a State Correctional Guard (now; he was doing something else before that) and I gave him his nickname of 'Outdoor Joe' due to the fact that he seems to live out of doors more often than in. Never a moment passes that he is not outside, working on his car, washing it, watering the lawn, blasting leaves (with his 200 HP, souped-up leaf blower), or doing any one of several dozen other 'outside' tasks. I guess it's good having someone like that constantly out there, keeping their eyes open for intruders, strange drive-byers, or whatever, but this quirk of his also irritates me inexplicably. As someone who is far more of a private person who spends most of his time indoors, such a prominent outside 'in your face' posture as Joe personifies is somehow antithetical to my whole nature. Joe's friendly enough, but we have little in common.

I would guess he enjoys beer more than wine. Funny how you tend to casually pigeonhole personalities like that. I may be completely wrong about Joe, but he seems a Neanderthal opposite to my Cro-Magnon nature. Good old 'Outdoor Joe'. His son is a newly vested major league baseball player, which is probably one of the reasons for my disparaging bias (I intensely dislike all major US team sports, due to their highly commercialised status and the ruinous nature of 'big money' corporate sports).

On our other side is Dinick, a slender, late 40ish divorced fellow, who inherited his father's home when his dad passed away a number of years ago. Dinick is a perplexing fellow, who also works for the state civil service. Every morning he can be seen running past the front of our home, late as usual for the local bus to work. With a sort of 'Irvingesque' Ickabod Craine appearance, old style and heavy dark plastic framed 'nerd glasses', and a sort of absent-minded affect, Dennis is easy to dismiss and ridicule as just another unremarkable person—something I tend to do, sad to admit. Dinick is perfectly fine, if a little scattered in his eclectic interactions with life.

My main gripes with Dinick center on three things, 1) his totally out-of-control, post-adolescent daughter (who is a real piece of work); 2) the fact that his backyard is an overgrown jungle that he incessantly over waters, day in and day out (a very wasteful use of water, at the very least, on that thick tangle of overgrown trees and shrubbery that require frequent prunings on our side of the fence); and 3) "Mikey", a mature black Labrador retriever who was originally the dim-bulb daughter's cute little puppy, now long since forgotten and no longer regarded with any special feeling of any kind, who lives in Dinick's back yard completely cut off from any contact with people, affection or other dogs.

In this last instance, and resulting directly from his life of enforced solitude (poor little guy!), Mikey has become a canine paranoid, who barks incessantly at the slightest provocation. Any slight rustle of leaves or other small auditory cue which is lost on human hearing is sufficient to set Mikey off on a barking spree that will last for hours…much to my everlasting annoyance during the night, when I am trying to get some rest (light sleeper that I am). This neglect poor old Mikey has to endure, as a result of being abandoned by Dinick's' now late-teenish daughter, also severely bothers me. Dinick doesn't have much to do with the dog except feed and water him and Mikey never gets to come inside, being a permanent outdoor dog. Although such emotional neglect is better than deliberate cruelty, knowing that the Labrador breed's needs include lots of activity and human interaction just makes it hard for me to accept Dinick's benignly neglectful disregard for the animal he keeps at his home.

At such moments, I reflect affectionately upon my own two beautiful dogs, Laika & Raki, Siberian Huskies and the much-valued companions of my wife and I at home. Since we have no children of our own, our dogs are as much 'kids' as any real kids could possibly be. And with no college fund required for their eventual success in life, all the much better overall! Laika (now 12, raised from a pup) and Raki (we estimate about 9, having obtained him fully grown from a Siberian Husky rescue organization north of Sacramento) are absolutely beautiful animals, who don't just require, but demand constant human interaction.

Of all the working breeds, Siberian Huskies are among the most gregarious, owing to their having been bred for a thousand years or more as the constant companions of the Chukchi natives of Siberia. We previously had a wonderful male named Deejay, who came to us from the breeder as a one-year-old, but who has sadly left us to pass over the rainbow bridge last year. This big guy was a gentle giant of a Siberian, measuring about 25 inches at the shoulder and eventually weighing over 110 pounds (normal measurements are a show standard max of 24 inches and 70 pounds), but one of the most good-natured monsters I've ever known. He had a habit (not too unusual in the breed) of smiling constantly, and was rather unique in a number of fondly remembered ways. Rest peacefully, Deejay, as you will always be lovingly remembered by both of us.

One of the books I have obtained here that I would consider more on the 'quirky' side of the ledger is titled *'Firsts (and Almost Firsts) in Hawaii'*, by Robert C. Schmitt (*no Schmitt!*). While it has little of interest to anyone pursuing the ancient culture of these islands, it certainly can provide some amusing comic relief from all the serious ploughing through seas of facts, figures, and documentation that has occupied most of my reading time here.

Three delightful little tidbits of information that surfaced are the following. The first bicycle ever used on the islands was an old 'familiar' (*Velocipede*) that arrived in Honolulu in 1869. The first 'modern' safety bicycle (a *Columbia*) followed in 1892. The first car theft in the islands took place on the 4th of July 1900, when a drunken local fireman named Pat Corcoran (sure and 'twas a transplanted Celtish lad, such as messef!) jumped onto a local citizen's electric horseless carriage and tried (unsuccessfully) to start it. Failing in this, he tried a push-start, then settled for coasting down the block on it ringing its bells.

Since a member of the constabulary witnessed this first-ever car theft, he chased and apprehended the besotted joy-rider; the judge who tried the fellow found him *"...guilty of trying to elope with the vehicle*" and fined him $25. On another tangent, the first ever bikini worn in Hawaii was modeled by a young lady on Waikiki Beach in front of the Surf Rider Hotel in 1952; the picture taken of her provides ample proof of the fact that this very first bikini was as good as (or even better in terms of how it looked on her at that time) any that has since been produced. Now *that's* a significant compliment, since bikinis can be very ugly, despite showing lots of skin! Finally, although it is unrecorded as to when the first kite was actually flown in the islands, there has been speculation that the ancient Hawaiians attached tapa cloth to sticks well over a century and a half ago, and used twine made from vegetable fiber to fly such a wind-catching device.

A quick read through of this book provides a very interesting and amusing diversion from all the serious stuff available on Hawaiian culture. *Nuff sed bout a'dat, Brah.*

Today being Sunday, the local churches usually see a full house in the K'kai community. One aspect of religion here that intrigues me is that although there are at least one or two parishes for each of the Protestant Christian religions represented and a couple of Roman Catholic churches as well, there is no Buddhist Church at all. I was quite surprised to find this at first, until I checked out the ethnic population mix of the island and found that there are only a small handful of people of Chinese ancestry on Moloka'i. Of the next larger group of Japanese, surprisingly there must not be many Buddhists among them, since Buddhism, along with Shinto, are the only religious faiths indigenous to that group.

The vast bulk of religiously inclined people on this island appear to be members of the parishes started many, many years ago by the original (congregational Protestant) missionaries who came to Moloka'i in 1821, although the Mormons certainly seem to have made up for lost time and opportunity by grabbing a major chunk of the sinners' souls here. As a born-again atheist, the only interest this subject holds for me is the historical backdrop upon which these *brahs* sewed their seeds (*relijus kine, not ai kine*), since it is well known that Satan managed to provoke many of those early God-fearing Christians (obviously against their will) to reach out and grab a piece of the cute local brown ass in their left hands, even as the right ones were holding grimly onto that ever present Bible (witness, oh ye Gods, the many old families of mixed haole/kanaka incestry (sic) that existed prior to the 1920s). James Mitchner's epic novel *'Hawaii'* remains a carefully documented and sizzlingly honest expose of this sort of hypocrisy that was all too often the norm amongst the good Christian fathers here.

One of the things that you will occasionally hear of concerning Moloka'i, back on the mainland, aside from references to the song, *'The Cockeyed Mayor of Kaunakakai'*, is the quality of the bread traditionally made at the *Kanemitsu Bakery* on downtown Ala Malama Avenue (the main drag). For years, even before I came here, I had occasionally heard travelers remark upon how unusually good the fine baked goods (especially breads) were at Kanemitsu's.

"Ono'licious" would be the local way of describing things there, since the word *Ono* means delicious, tasty, or savory in Hawaiian. One is usually admonished to get down there early in the morning to be assured of getting some of the limited amount of fresh bread and other baked goods produced each day at Kanemitsu's.

After several visits and many opportunities to try their fabled bread, encouraged by a strong element of self-fulfilling expectation, I finally have to state (with some reluctance) that the quality of their baked goods is commonly overstated. There's no doubt it's good bread, possibly even *very* good bread, but I have to draw the line at use of the word "great." Unless, of course, you have a loaf fresh out of the oven and still warm. Eaten that way, there's no denying it has lots of gustatory appeal.

I have several loaves here in the fridge, coconut-apple, cinnamon-pineapple to name just two, and half a loaf makes a good, quick, and very tasty breakfast, drunk with a good strong cuppa joe. This beats instant oats every day by a mile. Their doughnuts are unspectacular, but still quite tasty—especially the cake doughnuts, which I have an admitted weakness for. They also sell a rather nifty sleeveless T-shirt with their graphic logo on it, which depicts a surfer shooting a curl with a loaf of Kanhemitsu's *onolicious* bread in his hand. The shirt, which sells for the usual $18 or so, is well worth a visit alone, even if you don't happen to be a bread fiend. Moloka'i does have some excellent surf beaches, by the way (on northwest and southeast ends), although the currents and rips found there can be quite tricky and best not attempted at all in the turbulent winter months, except by locals and really skillful *slydahs* (a *slydah* chick is a surfer girl, in local pigeon).

Kanemitsu's began, by the way, as an adjunctive bakery for the pineapple plantation many decades ago. When the last plantations finally folded up in the late 80s, they remained in business as the K'kai-town's source of baked goods.

At the recent Saturday arts & crafts mart today there were many nice things to admire and possibly buy as quality souvenirs of the island, including great locally grown fruits and vegetables (many people—locals and tourists alike--fill their shopping needs there, instead of at the local stores, in fact). While I am pretty resistant by now to the usual tourist kitsch, I did buy one of 'Fil's' beautiful photographs of the island (already mentioned earlier in this narrative). I also bought a T-shirt, not because I needed a T-short or liked the design, but because of the very funny definition of a 'Moloka'i Perfect Husband' on it (as follows):

Moloka'i Perfect Husband:

1. Favorite saying: *"Honey, you right, as always!"*

2. Nevah touches TV remote control (or get ule *whacked!).

3. Got job (can pay bills).

4. Tell da Brahs his wife one SKINNY wahine (nevah lies 'bout any'ting else....).

5. No got wander-eye (or get black-eye wikiwiki!).

6. No like watch sports on TV ('specially football!).

7. Own his own house (no need pay rent).

8. Do chores witout askin (no need hassle).

9. Got own boat (get plenty fresh fish).

10. Have plenty duct tape (can fix any'ting).

11. Nevah complain (no mattah what).

12. For shoh fall asleep on couch at 8 PM (no bodda wahine wid las minute *ai* wikiwiki ** befoe sleep.

(*"pee-pee" ** "quickie")

Of course, the above is only humor and I have no doubt that it contravenes the real daily basic domestic song, verse, and chorus figuratively sung by most men on Moloka'i. There is also a 'Perfect Moloka'i Wife' variation, but you get the idea.

There's a Gecko in my room here. That's supposed to be good luck, per local customs. For those inexperienced in the ways of these amazing little island critters, they have a characteristic barking sound, sort of somewhere between a small yelp and a bird chirp. I have been hearing this in my room since I arrived, but each time thought it was a bird sitting right outside the window. Nope. A Gecko has taken up residence in the double roof, right above my desk, and every once and a while, he will give out a short string of these little chirping barks. It's kind of cute and in addition to helping control the fly, cockroach, and mosquito pop-ulations, Geckos are beautiful little things to watch as they flit across the ceilings after prey.

One nice thing about keeping a journal is that you don't need to be so obsessive about style and form, since *who gone read dis anyway, Brah? Bumbye, mebbe som frens, but since this one kine story anyway, so who care?*

Tomorrow's list: 1) stop popping so much junk food and eat more seriously; 2) check in with Cheryl Apaia to ask her about the water pipe installation; 3) drop in at Moloka'i Natural Organics to pick up some *Kukui* nut oil, some of Moloka'i's special volcanic red sea salt, and some Noni fruit (all local products. The *Kukui* oil is great for a number of things and along with the *Noni* was spe-cially favored by Kahunas for their amazing healing properties. The sea salt has a special red tint to it caused by volcanic soil elements and comes seasoned and unseasoned); 4) check in at either the library or the school to answer email. Pretty easy list, huh? Still tempted by that beautiful large Hula Pahu made by master local woodcrafts kahuna Bill Pekuni, but at $1250 I would definitely be up for an *'Ule whack'* (Lorena Bobbett's famous trademark) on return to mainland, so I *bettah be one da kine careful haole hubby*, eh?

Over 12 days here and still relatively pasty white, since I've been writing so much of the time. I really need to take a day and go out there with some SPF 2000 and take a stab at getting some patina. Won't do at all to return from a month in the islands with the same shade of haole-white skin I came here with. *Foh shame, brah! Shoulda brought sum dat instant tan stuff, so I could blend in better wid'out all the painful* (and definitely un-healthy) *skin abuse. Um. Thassa bout it, foh Sunday.*

One las'ting befoe endin dis: I spotted a copy of a new book recently released, titled *'Da Jesus Book'*. It is, believe it or not, an entire copy of the Christian New Testament translated into Hawaiian Island *pidjin English*. Aside from all the trouble the preparation of this took, it is just an amazing feat in and of itself. A serious book, it supposedly was undertaken so as to provide a copy of this part of the Christian Bible for those whose standard English skills are not that good. For those unfamiliar with 'Hawaiian Pidjin', this is the 'lazy' short cut local dialect that is the lingua franca among hard-core islanders. It compares superficially to what is regarded as 'Black American English', but is far more complete in terms of being a whole dialect and not just a collection of if loosely connected idiomatic terms. I had to have a copy, if for no other reason than to revel in the sheer novelty of this book. *Wot you tink, Brah? Ass sompin,or wot? Auwe!* [PS: I just checked and the end of this sentence makes the total in this journal about 50,257 words to date, and in exactly 14 days. Not bad for a third-class word hack, I think. *'Auwe'*, indeed!].

'Pidjin' originally began, by the way, as a common, simplified means for all the many different plantation workers from China, Japan, Portugal, the Philippines to communicate with each other, with native Hawaiians and with their haole bosses. Many decades later it was co-opted as the 'cool local' language and locals resent mainland haoles who come over here try to use it.

April 25nd, 2005 (Monday)

Monday morning. Rooster fillets, rooster cutlets, fried rooster, rooster steaks, rooster a la flambé, scrambled rooster, rooster fricassee, rooster barbeque...the endless possibilities for payback drift through my pre-caffeinated mind as I roust myself out of the sack, silently cursing the one earplug that slipped out during the night and got lost in the bed covers. I briefly think about the teeny little brown mouse that was hiding on the other side of the curtain as I brushed my teeth before turn-in last night. Would have missed him entirely, had it not been for a subtle little motion of the fabric hanging over the window's inner surface. Thinking it was a gecko, I gently pulled back the edge of the cover and was surprised to find the little brown mouse there. It was so small and fuzzy that I gazed as bemusedly at it as it doubtless did at me, for a few moments, then it quite casually slipped off and down behind the washing machine. The field rats hereabouts are MUCH larger.

Ian MacMillan's stories (*'Exiles from Time'*) of modern Hawaiian life are as valuable to think about as they are inherently interesting and readable, for they deal with the same basic proposition man has been faced with since the dawn of recorded history: the dynamics of ethnic intermixing and cross-cultural relationships. As someone who has always found other cultures and social customs particularly intriguing, reading through some of MacMillan's stories serve as strong catalysts that make me mindful of a number of personal experiences of my own.

In one of MacMillan's stories, a young haole boy starts to interact with the local kids in a natural, unforced manner at the beach, a process that is enabled by mutual interests or participatory activities (in the narrative, fishing is the unifying dynamic that helps the haole boy and the locals draw together as peers, helping to put their obvious ethnic and cultural identities apart and approach each other harmoniously); this in turn forces the boy's straight-laced, rather inhibited, and culturally constrained parents to face the same issues—whether they like it or not. This is a central theme MacMillan employs successfully in many of his stories about locals and mainlanders co-existing together on the islands and it is a theme that remains rich in further possibilities for cultural exploration.

Curiously, as I sat here drinking my concentrated rocket fuel and staring at the laptop's liquid crystal luminousity, I started dredging up some long-suppressed episodes of my own that mirror these themes. A number of them took place when I was a child, being raised by my school teacher mother in small California valley towns (I am whimsically reminded here of various 1970s 'Firesign Theatre' parodies on small town names, like 'Smegma', 'Whoops', etc., and also a number of actual California Gold Rush town names, like 'Weedpatch', 'Last Chance', 'Bumpass Hell', and oh so many more...).

Since Ma was an elementary school teacher, this made the process of blending in with the local kids a bit harder than usual, as they all knew I was marked from the git-go by the stigma of being 'the-school-teacher's-kid'. The fact that we relocated twice didn't help much, since small towns of the size in reference (usually about 3000 or so) were very tightly knit communities where everyone knew everyone else and you were dauntingly challenged by the need to fit into the existing adolescent social hierarchy as smoothly and non-traumatically as possible.

The small San Joaquin towns where Ma taught were typical of the communities of that region of the lower 'great valley' of California in that they had large populations of farm laborer families, as well as significant sub-populations of blacks. My basic nature of being a somewhat 'protected' single child, who was considerably well advanced in terms of learning and awareness over the locals, made it harder than normal for me to fit comfortably in, at least in school. In the neighborhoods we lived in there were the usual neighbor kids with whom you palled around with and got to know a bit more intimately, but in school there were definite social hierarchies and cliques that posed stiffer perplexities.

Kalikiano Kalei

I seemed to have a particularly difficult time relating to the black kids, principally due to that fact that we were so radically polarized in terms of social backgrounds. I am guessing that this natural polarity was not in the least aided by my mother's Presbyterian austerity and a perhaps unconscious cultural bias towards ethnic subgroups that led to her regarding and treating the little black kids in her classes with somewhat less than obvious equanimity, since by the time I got to high school, I seemed to be on the list of preferred targets for a number of these little delinquents.

Sadly enough (talk about emotional scars) I can still remember the names of some of my chief tormentors of that period: *Ulysses S. Demery, Alton Brown, Alonzo Jeffers, LeRoy White*, etc.). They were all at the bottom of the social food chain, of course, but that didn't keep them from taking cheap shots at me whenever the opportunity to bully presented itself. Being somewhat socially naïve and trusting myself, I was easy pickings. Since they were clearly kept at the extreme periphery of the community's social hierarchy, they typically seized upon the only leveling mechanism they had available to them to somewhat offset that disadvantage: sports. All of those little black kids, who were absolutely illiterate in terms of their academic and social abilities, blazed fiercely on the track and in the gym. Most of them were excellent runners and all of them could shoot hoops like pros. None of them played tennis (white kids' game), only a small handful were on the football team, and none swam (the swim team, which I was on, was another *honky* franchised sport).

Since I had been brought up to be ultra-mindful of manners and 'proper' behavior from my earliest years (thanks to Uncle Charlie's austerely autocratic reign, as head of the family in my father's absence), I was an unusually gentle and well-behaved kid. While the other kids were used to having the tar whaled out of them for endless daily infractions of behavior (getting into fights, raising hell, pulling dumb pranks, and in general simply behaving as any 'normal' kid would), I was the atypical paragon of propriety. A verifiable child saint, I guess, and far too smart for my own good, since intelligence, preciousness, and creativity were always looked down upon by the other kids (I see the same trend today in our public schools, where a great number of 'below-average' kids are so disenfranchised by the prevailing white 'system' that they withdraw furiously to the opposite end of the behavioral spectrum and take pride in being ignorant, rude, and social outcasts; they take their bottom-feeder status out on the 'nerds' & geeks, unfortunately).

At any rate, I was pretty helpless to withstand the concentrated social and emotional bullying that I was exposed to, as a particularly sensitive and bright kid who suffered from a mild case of *Attention Deficit Disorder* (ADD, which wasn't even a recognized syndrome when I was growing up; I was just labeled another one of those perplexing 'underachievers', which was how the school dealt with bright kids like me who ironically never seemed to excel, grade-wise). The effects of this are still with me, as I expect the scars ran pretty deep. Occasionally, throughout my life, I seem to have been sensed to be an easy target by blacks who for no apparent reason I can understand 'pick up' on these vulnerabilities and seize on my image of being a reserved and erudite appearing honky (doubtless a *fucking liberal*, too!) with a vengeance. And this occurs in the absence of any overt or deliberately condescending mannerisms on my part...I just get sized up as an easy target and personally attacked, much the same as (I would guess) a shark would instinctively go after a wounded seal, without politely asking *"May I?"*, first. It's probably a far more refined & highly tuned sense for 'body image' than most honkies like me have, on further thought. They can 'read' you better than 'we' can.

This is, I suppose, the reason for my having been cursed by a perpetually conflicting sense of who I am as an always underlying check on my actions and behavior...the same split identity I referred to earlier that is such a notable characteristic of the Arabs—partly superior and party inferior--with no clue from minute to minute as to which half is ascendant. The emotional wounds that constant conflict between surges of supreme self-confidence and troughs of severe self-doubt can inflict are enough of a handicap to be a major behavioral inhibiting factor in one's ability to simply be one's self, naturally and without any apparent effort. A simple enough wished-for goal in anyone's life, of course, but forever just out of reach in mine, I think. This explains the sometimes near-morbid self-reflection and preoccupation that is a characteristic of my life. If that's interpreted as simple vanity, more's the pity, but it is really a deep, very deep, and perpetual (perhaps emotionally unhealthy) analysis of the *uncertain self*, viewed against a backdrop of life that is a constant challenge to successfully understand and interpret.

At the end of it, I suppose you could view the above as just another very good fucking reason why even everyday ordinary life can be so very challenging to simply get through intact...especially in the cross-hairs of a specific multi-cultural context, fraught as that usually is, with conflicting assumptions, projections, aspersions, and pre-conceived notions.

OK, got that out. Does it feel better? Not necessarily. So much for the benefits of post-Jungian self-analysis, but huzzah for Schopenhauer's & Nietzsche's conclusions about life being an essentially unhappy experience.

Next door among the families that live near Inocencia's house is a family with three small children, probably aged between 4 and 6. They are a real handful, with their constant, furious play and shrill little voices. The din is substantial, even 100 feet away, and I can imagine the daily toll in terms of energy depletion that their mother feels by the end of the day. Anyone in the present world who still thinks that raising children is a trivial undertaking, not worthy of simultaneous consideration with 'a real job' as constituting genuinely hard work, is hopelessly out of touch with reality. Such parental duties are probably not *just as challenging* as those responsibilities incumbent in a professional occupation, but perhaps even more taxing, since you are not even dealing with a human mind that functions (at least partly, it would be hoped) on a basis of logical awareness and lucid reasoning. While it drains me to some mild extent to simply sit here and invisibly witness this process of parenting that is going on next door, it helps me keenly understand the often glossed-over or completely unconsidered requirements of proper parenting.

For this reason, among many others, I cannot for the life of me understand the reasoning of today's professional 'mommy', who takes an 8 month break from her law career to have her child, then returns to work, leaving the real work to a mother surrogate or daycare stand-in. To my mind, the only really workable lifestyle that takes these things into consideration adequately is the traditional model wherein one parent works while the other takes care of the family (i.e. children's) needs. That should be further qualified by a presumption that it takes place within a simpler, traditional economy, and not within the confines of today's highly stressed, highly structured, and highly technologised western (American style capitalism) model.

Such a lifestyle was once enjoyed by the ancient Hawaiians, of course, before the white man descended upon the islands and forever polluted whatever natural harmony or equilibrium had previously existed. Knowing what I do of the course of this incursion by 'western' man into the lives of the native Hawaiians, and seen against the backdrop of history's millions of examples of similar socioeconomic patterns of exploitation throughout history, I would probably favor the existence of some sort of unifying world-wide system of governance that put strict limits on such things as procreative rights, economic activities etc., etc. It goes without saying that under this strictly controlled and administered system, not everyone would be allowed to mate and produce children. Genetic selection would be actively practiced to determine intellectual, emotional, and physical hierarchies and only those in the highest levels would be allowed to breed. Social Darwinism? Yes. Artur Schopenhauer considered it the highest priority of the individual to deliberately *not* create children as a means of 'disarming' the endless predations of the *Will*.

This would take care of a lot of problems we face today, such as ugliness (everyone would be genetically created to be beautiful), ignorance (everyone would be genetically endowed with brilliance), and emotional illness (everyone would be made serenely self-actualized and emotionally stable). If course all this would preclude such eternally troublesome elements in human life as religion, superstition, and faith in the intangible, and therefore could not and will never obtain on this very human planet of ours. In fact, as long as there is a single religious sentiment still in circulation, the entire prospect is completely and absolutely impossible. Hope and/or desire are the culprits: both chiefly perpetuated by religions such as Christianity.

The highest hoped-for possible good (according to pessimistic dogma) that would result would be that the whole human race would come to the only logical, final conclusion: *that the planet would be best served by the absence of humanity altogether.*

Thus, everyone would voluntarily turn themselves in to euthanasia centers set up to bring this about and much in the manner of the famed story *'Soylent Green'*, take their painless generic Hemlock to start their voyage to infinity and thereby rid the world of all its pesky little human parasites once and for all. Earth would, suddenly relieved of its damnably irritating highest sentient parasitic life form, happily lapse back into a comfortable and natural harmony consistent with the forces of nature and their effortlessly natural rhythms of action and counteraction.

If it seems that I am being critical of our vaunted singular human gift ('reason'), as the chief self-justification for our supremely egotistic regard for ourselves as the ascendant & highest life form on Earth, I am. Our death-grip embrace of the precepts stemming from the classical *Age of Reason*, as a primary product of our pure Western school of philosophical empiricism, appears to run counter to any possible understanding of the planet as a vast, living, and cosmologically sentient part of a greater (sentient) cosmos (despite the best efforts of Christian right-wing conservatives, Islamic radical terrorists, and who knows what other partisan religiously affiliated groups, to preclude the spread of any such awareness). Of course, thoughts like this would probably make my long-gone relatives positively writhe in their graves, but since I've always been a black sheep in my family any way, why break ranks now, and not shrink from the depressing, daunting task of considering the ultimate questions in such an unenviable state.

It's about 10:30 AM now and another of the huge local 4WD pick-up trucks, with their infrasonic stereo systems and huge vibrating treads, has just passed nearby. My initial impression is still one of a dual turboprop Dash-8 warming upon the Ho'olehua flightline; the similarity is uncanny. It's enough to make one unconsciously head for the 88mm FLAK battery with a mean glint in one's eyes

Since I am staying with a Filipino family here, I am reminded of many things associated with this. One was an incident in Saudi Arabia, involving the Filipino wife of a haole friend. There were millions of Filipinos working as expats in the Kingdom, due to the extremely poor employment prospects back home, and we were all accustomed to working closely with them in the medical field. Ray's wife was a slender Filipina whom he had met at the hospital we both worked at, at the time (Al Hada Hospital in 'At Taif', the Saudi summer capital perched on the edge of the Hijaz). Florence was an EKG tech from the Philippines and Ray was a non-invasive cardiovascular tech (echocardigrams).

Since I had purchased a Russian Lada Niva 4WD vehicle and found it to be an excellent little vehicle for getting around in, Ray decided to buy one also (mine was desert tan, his was a queasy shade of gastric bile green). One weekend we had decided to take the 'Christian Bypass' road (past Mecca, which is off limits to infidels), over and down the 6,000 foot rocky edge of the Hijaz and across the barren desert wastes of the coastal Tihama desert (that sandy waste populated only by camels and scattered Bedu encampments that lies between the Red Sea and the sheer face of the Hijazi escarpment) to go reef diving off the Jeddah coast. Despite the fact that Ray lost his muffler halfway there (in 140 degree F. heat)—something he strangely held against me thereafter, perhaps as subconsciously projected anger at himself for having bought a Russian car instead of the customary Toyota 4WD expat vehicle, Isuzu Trooper, or Mitsubishi Pajero—we all arrived safely and set up a camp on the Red Sea shore, just south of Jeddah.

Later that day, Florence, who had been drinking lots of diet Pepsi throughout the day, was standing out on the reef, about a hundred yards from shore. Suddenly she started screaming something, but the on-shore winds were too strong to make it out exactly what her words were. Meanwhile, she was pointing down at the reef and gesturing somewhat wildly. *Hmmmm*. Cause for concern? Finally, after some intent and anxious listening, Ray made out her words. She was yelling *"Popper piss! Popper piss! Popper piss!"*

The only understanding we could come up with was that all that the Pepsi (Coke was still forbidden in the Kingdom, due to the fact that the Israelis had made a deal with Coke to grant a franchise distribution in Israel) Flo had been drinking was now causing her so much pressure in her bladder that she felt the need to take the mother of all whizzes ("popper piss"= *"whiz or burst"*, maybe?). Of course, there was no place out on that reefy promontory where she could take a lady-like whiz, of course, since to do so would involve a very visible strip-tease within eye-shot of a bunch of nearby '*siddiyks*' (Arabic for 'friends', usually used sarcastically by expats as a term for the locals), who were always overjoyed to see an exposed and nicely-shaped western female bottom (or the Flip equivalent).

Mildly perplexed, but too comfortably ensconced at our camp on shore with chilled glasses of home-brew, we decided to let Flo take care of this problem the best way she could think of, unat-tended, gallant (and mildly inebriated) paragons of knightly virtue that we were.

After a while Flo finally calmed down and no impromptu floor-show was forthcoming, neither did she make any effort to relieve herself; so when she finally waded back to shore an hour later, we strove to define exactly what had transpired out there that had caused all the ruckus.

Flo very carefully explained, clearly thinking us all at least VERY stupid, or at best VERY much under the cumulative influence of the home brew: *"I was out there on the reep, looking at all the pisses and thinking how good they would be in a prying pan, when I suddenly saw this little bitty piss suddenly grow very, very big!"* This little bitty inflatable piss was, of course...what else?...a *"Popper Piss"* (i.e. 'Puffer-fish').

The other incident that comes back to me occurred in 1988, when I had returned from my first Saudi contract and was working at the Santa Cruz Heart Institute (then part of the Santa Cruz Community Hospital on Frederick Street). Before I was able to find the beautiful little 4-room beach cottage that I ended up living in at Sunset Beach State park, I had moved into a sort of slightly seedy old quadruplex complex right on the coast near *Steamboat Lane*. The old place had several small suites or studios in it and I had one of the studios next to a slightly larger flat that consisted of two rooms, plus kitchen and bath.

In the adjacent flat lived a couple whom I never met, throughout the term of my 3 month stay there (most likely because of our work schedules), but they left their windows open to catch the sea breezes and as a result of that, every single sound from their flat carried into my small adjoining room (as did all the cooking smells, since I also had to use nature's air-conditioning in the hot summer months to stay cool). Still not knowing what either of them looked like, I began to overhear a predictable series of conversations and sound effects that seemingly repeated themselves each day like a tape recording.

She got home first in the afternoon around 5 and he arrived slightly later. His arrival would invariably provoke a series of loud complaints and bitchy comments from her, none of them constrained or cloaked in restraint, and all accusatively directed at him for various reasons. After suffering through this predictable fusillade of invective that greeted him, he would (I am guessing) start drinking beer and shortly after the effects took hold, would start returning her sniper-cracks in equal measure. These loud, sustained, and unholy exchanges would typically go on for an hour or more, at which time the smell of fried fish would start flooding through my window with enough power to simultaneously gag and entice even the most undemanding and undiscerning cockroach. Finally, the level of the remarks would subside as they sat down to dinner. After dinner, a more or less continuing series of exchanges would continue, although these were more subdued by the background noise filter of the TV. Finally, after 9:30 the lights would go out after a final bang and rattle of dishes, pans and pots announced the end of the evening. It was clear enough, from my close-hand box-seat observation point that the fellow was a white male and his partner was a young Filipino woman.

At that point, the stars were quite bright and before long all the vast forces of heaven and earth would seemingly start to shake the flimsy walls of the old place. I gathered that their bedroom was directly adjacent to my one room and also that the walls were insulated by air and nothing more. Amazingly, I think I must have learned at least three dozen new and interesting variations on how to reach orgasm during my short stay at that place. No groan, gag, gasp, shriek, thrust, wiggle, squeeze, bite, lick, nibble, suck, grasp, stroke, pinch, giggle, howl, choke, or audibly juicy lunge was filtered by that damnably thin wall, and this astounding auditory and tactile display of yeomanlike coital fireworks continued—as regularly as the hourly venting of Yellowstone's Old Faithful geyser (an appropriate simile, to be sure) for at least a solid hour every night after lights out. So masterful was this feature act that I at one point briefly considered selling tickets to the daily performance and actually did on one occasion even take a few notes for my own edification.

To say the lady was what we gentlemen refer to as a 'screamer' is severely understating things, and there were times when one could isolate and single out the exact level of coital excitement being experienced, purely by the timbre and decibel level of this *backdoor Nightingale's* husky song. I had to restrain the urge to clap spontaneously on several occasions of particularly astounding cocksmanship by her *squeezeee*, due to his seemingly endless and demonstrably admirable restraint in not prematurely blowing his wad until long after she had started hitting notes several octaves above high-G.

Angry sex. All in all, it was better entertainment than a TV, and although I had a small one at the time, I by far preferred to keep it off and would tune into this live nightly event that was being conducted just inches from me through the thin wall of the flat. Of course, there were moments when the massive and wave-like thudding vibrations of King Kong (having his evil way with this *a Capella* Faye Wray surrogate) got to be a trifle annoying, but they were rare enough. On the whole, if there had been a local amateur hour in Santa Cruz, I would have enthusiastically nominated both of them for winning contention.

It wasn't until shortly before I moved out of that flat that I actually saw both of them for the first time. He was a very large, red-haired Caucasian male, who I think was retired US Navy, and his lady friend was probably one of the most breathtakingly beautiful young Filipino women I have ever seen (obviously not from a 'better' family, but with assets like that, who really could care?). She was slender and moderately tall for a Filipina, but had a gorgeous posterior (usually sheathed, from what I was able to see, in tight jeans), a lovely full mouth set in a pretty face, and a natural set of firm and protuberant *chi-chis* that would make any man's mouth water from the mere thought of getting his 30 mm of negative pressure on those babies. I must confess, after having heard all the sound-effects, but never having seen her before in the flesh (perhaps a poor term to use here), I instantly succumbed to a terminal case of lust. *Oooogh*! Even today, I still recall those hot summer nights of hurtling Tagalog invective, suffocating vapors of frying pan *piss*, and hours upon unending hours of coital explosiveness that would probably make the writers of the *Kama Sutra* feel like blushing Tantric neophytes in the comparison.

Ah, memories. I may no longer be much of an excuse to catch a woman's eyes at age 58, but at least I have my share of memories to think back on at such moments when the sap rises precipitously in the branch (and it still does!). Most amusingly, several days ago I dropped in at the local Kamakana Gallery (not Sturgess' but another in which local crafts and artwork are displayed & offered...unlike Sturgess' personal work). Met the two women (haole) who work there and had a nice long chat with them, and a local named Glen who is on the Moloka'i Community Water Conservation Committee. I mentioned in passing that I had talked to a young local lady there on my previous visit back in October and at first they couldn't identify her. When I further described her as an extremely good looking young local woman, they both instantly remembered her and one remarked *"Ah, she was trouble!"*, with a wink in her eye. Apparently, this beauty had prompted all the wrong customers to drop by the gallery regularly—those men who were equally young and without jobs or money (hence the allusion to trouble).

Then one of the two women (she is middle aged and plump) remarked amicably *"Good thing you don't work here or you'd be trouble too."* The full impact of this didn't completely register until a few minutes later, but I perceive it as being a sideways compliment. After I had a chance to reflect on this, I simultaneously felt both mildly elated and mildly depressed, since it meant someone was still interested in the goods; but if she is representative of the type who are now interested, my strong and well-developed sense of gender aesthetics probably would be best served if I kept my mouth shut and my powder dry. [This reminds me of another encounter I had with a Canadian lady doctor while staying in Zermatt, back in the mid-80s, but I'll save that for some other time.]

Speaking of recollections and memories, I am just reminded that I haven't had breakfast yet and it's now noon. Funny that I don't feel hungry, though. The trades are blowing pretty stiff outside and it will soon be time to finally switch this off, take a shower, eat something, and fulfill a few of my few appointed tasks for today.

It's now late in the day, time for a good old-fashioned Moloka'i traditional dinner of rice & frankfurters, topped off by chocolate covered toffee macadamia nuts, a banana, and a diet Coke. Local custom has it that an islander that strictly adheres to the above diet for a month will not have any health worries (or any other da kine worry, since *bumbye he be one maka brah, brah*!).

Actually, the ancient Hawaiian's had certain taboos (*Kapu*) against bananas—especially for fisherman and women. Fisherman were not supposed to let any bananas come on board their canoes, since the banana was one form of appearance assumed by the Hawaiian god *Kane*. Also, women were not ever allowed to eat bananas, and not because of any phallic proscriptions, either. In fact, the banana *kapus* had nothing at all to do with the fact that a banana bears a certain linear resemblance to an erect male *Ule* (another fascinating tidbit to file away in the completely useless file). Since the banana is also yellow, one can't help but wonder as to the possibility of anything being 'Royal Yellow' being off-limits to certain classes.

Bought a few groceries just before 6 PM this afternoon. This is the time of the day when otherwise sleepy little old Kaunakakai comes about as close to rush hour traffic as a peaceful little island ville of 3,000 people can. The Friendly Market is pretty much crowded *wid wahine an luawahine an uddah shoppahs, buying stuffs foh make dinnah*. The malihini (like myself) stand out, no matter how hard we try to blend in—has something to do with skin color, I think. Also, very amusing pastime watching the locals shuffle around the store, in no apparent hurry, as the visibly disconcerted & up-tight tourists glower, wishing things were more efficient like they are back in Manhattan. Some of the tourists are pretty interesting studies in advanced hurry-sickness, but a few actually manage to chill like they have been told to.

This evening, I was standing just ahead of a tourist couple— probably staying in a time-share condo up the road—and watched them casually out of the corner of my eye. The guy was typical mainlander, overweight with a big gut, white hair, and hairy legs—maybe corporate lawyer or *sumtin* back home—while the wifie showed signs that her hubby's big bucks were behind her superfox, shark-like affect, equipped as it was with a set of huge of *papayas* that seemed to beg someone to bite into them. She was checking me out behind her shades, since although her corporate lawyer *kane* was her life-support system in terms of bucks, he clearly was interested in younger game (of which there were a few in evidence, in line). Ah, the human mating game! *Ya brings dah stuffs to mahket* and enjoys da window-shopping.

Tomorrow is Tuesday and no particular agenda, other than meet with Victor at 8AM. Try to get to the bottom of the water line & meter installation. Should be interesting. Cheryl today told me that she knows of no especially pressing reason for hurrying up this process, other than the fact that the county may up the price shortly. I still wonder about that, however. Anyway, this has gone on way too long and it's time to eat.

Stardate: April 26, 2005 (Tuesday)

The story so far: It is another sunny (ho-hum), beautiful (what's new?) day and the trade winds blow gently across the deserted sands of *La'kano'oki Beach*. Our protagonist idly scratches his *huahua*, as he leans back against a *kukui* Tree, and wonders what marvelous adventures in Maui County public utilities planning wait in the offing for him today. But first, a quick sacrificial offering of some chocolate covered toffee macadamia nuts at the nearby *heiau*, as some sharp remembrances of Betty-Jo Bioloski's (or was it Mildred Weenfinkle's?...or perhaps Audrey Farber's?...) exceptional *chi-chis* cause the sap to momentarily surge in his *ka'peha ule nui*.

Speaking of *Ule* and *Kohe*, it is amusing to recall that the early Christian missionaries were often sorely perplexed in their efforts to collect and preserve some of the old Hawaiian (pre-contact) legends and folk lore, since many of the tales dealt inextricably with sex and sexual acts. Instances abound in which those prim old worthies had to do some quick and highly creative repair work in the course of preserving many of those tales, due to frequent allusions to *Ule, Kohe, ai,* and many other natural acts and interactions engaged in by the pre-Christian *kanakas*. More frequently than not, stories contain segments in which a goddess in reference might physically remove her *Kohe* (ordinarily, this would be quite a feat for any mere mortal *wahine*, given the intimate permanence of such a private bodily part) and fling it at an antagonist, thereby protecting some follower from harm. Good thing mainland feminists have not learned mastered this trick!

Other activities, such as *ai* with the nearest handy *kane* at any given moment, were quite common. Since lustful *ai* (or even in fact procreative *ai*, distastefully engaged in by missionaries simply because God ordained it as a necessary prerequisite to 'being bountiful and multiplying') was not a polite topic of conversation in any missionary household, one can only imagine the mental feats of figurative gymnastics required by these chroniclers of ancient legend, in the advancement of their literary recording efforts.

It has always seemed ironic to me that Christians and in fact most religiously obsessed individuals are deeply perplexed and sorely troubled by the fact that sex is simultaneously a basic and natural act and a subject of strong *kapu* (taboo). The ancient Hawaiians (or for that matter any of the Polynesian peoples) had no trouble at all dealing with the subject of sexual interactions. Perhaps it has something to do with the almost womb-like climatic environment found in the tropics--a balmy, benign environment that is conducive to love-making—that seems to naturally encourage intrinsically pleasing and satisfyingly hedonistic activities.

Unconstrained and completely uninhibited sex on a tropical beach, whether under the soft and subtle shone of a full moon or the full and furious illumination of a blazing sun, has to be one of the most sensually stimulating and erotically fulfilling actions anyone could possibly engage in, in my humble opinion. I recall one such event in my own life with such sharp and distinct recollection, that despite the fact that that moment now lies buried among many other memories of past years, it could have happened yesterday. While it wasn't actually in the tropics, the climate was very close in approximating the sexually invigorating aspects of balmy tropical weather, and the experience was simply overwhelming.

The woman I enjoyed this rare experience with was of all remotely possible things) a French helicopter mechanic in the employ of France's Aerospatiale (one of that nation's principal aerospace companies) and the venue was a remote stretch of beach on the Red Sea, at one of the expat dive areas just south of Jeddah.

Danielle Celine was a most unusual woman, even for a French woman. Originally from the Brittany sea coast, along the channel, she had a slightly darker tone to her skin that most women of her nationality, but it had of course been further deepened by a year spent living under the hot Arabian sun in Riyadh. Working as a helicopter mechanic would seem somewhat of an odd occupation for a woman (no matter what her nationality), but Danielle was not a usual individual. She once told me that her grandfather had been one of the early French aviators, many years ago, when planes with wood braces and doped fabric skin were the norm; a love of flying therefore ran in her family, so she reasoned. A very tomboyish girl in her youth, she had always enjoyed unusual challenges and unconventional experiences. Unfortunately, her vision was not good enough to allow her to train to be a pilot, so instead she had settled for the opportunity to be around airplanes that certification as an A&P mechanic would provide. This ultimately led to a contract in Saudi Arabia with Aerospatiale, in support of their *Allouette II* and *Llama* helicopters based at Riyadh.

Danielle was moderately tall for a woman, with long, beautiful arms that ended in small, but perfectly formed hands, and had long pianist's fingers (she told me that they enabled her to reach into tight places and perform delicate work on complex engines that was denied to some of her more strongly built male colleagues). What had captured my attention at first glance, the very first time I had seen her (which was at an embassy dance), was her gorgeous mane of dark chestnut brown hair that she normally wore long, but tied up to allow her to work around machinery safely. That first evening at the embassy, however, her hair had been unbound and I recall that it cascaded from her shoulders like so many waves of restless midnight surf, as she danced with someone else. Of course, I couldn't help but also notice the languid motion of her well-shaped thighs and the natural undulations of her beautifully firm butt, hardly hidden at all by the soft silk fabric of her side-slit little black dress. One of the amazing things about her was that although she looked drab and ordinary during the day, when garbed in a baggy tan Aerospatiale work coverall and smeared in grease, at night she came absolutely alive, metamorphosed from her dull cocoon into a scintillating, dark-hued butterfly of exceptional beauty and sparkling vivacity.

The fellow she had been dancing with when I first spotted her was a muscle-bound US Marine I had seen before at the embassy parties, but I soon came to find out later that she had no particular attraction to him or his muscles; he was merely a conveniently handy person with whom to dance and enjoy the relaxing effects of the embassy's rather good imported wines (Danielle was very egalitarian and discriminated not at all in choosing others to enjoy weekly social occasions, I also came to note). How very 'left-bank', I thought!

At any rate, I saw her from across the pool several times after that, each time at an embassy party here and there in the diplomatic quarter, but never had had a chance to dance with her or even meet her, since I am such a terribly awkward dancer and social disaster. One weekend, however, I went along on a Red Sea dive trip with a number of others from the Lockheed compound. To my great surprise, Danielle was one of the people who had also signed up, although someone told me she had never dived before (and she later admitted to me she was somewhat afraid of the ocean). I suppose it was a social opportunity for her to escape Riyadh above all else, since in Saudi Arabia no one turned down such occasions for obvious reasons.

I have done some modest free-diving in the past and had been active in water-sports in school and throughout my adolescence, so I myself enjoyed the fantastically beautiful and rich variety of sea life found on the Red Sea reefs. During the day, on this trip, several dives had been organized, one of which I went on. But for the rest of the day, I remained on the beach, where Danielle had also elected to stay. Since I am not among the most bold and self-assured of men, I anticipated that passing the time there in the intimidating presence of beautiful Danielle would be a bit awkward, as I am all too accustomed to the typical 'guy-gal' scenario in the States, in which muscle-bound guys attract beautiful women and ordinary guys are invariably ignored completely.

I was quite surprised to find that in this aspect, as in so many others, Danielle was quite atypical. We talked at great length about many things, sitting there in the shade of the sun-awning with the warm humid breezes blowing in from the sea. I was amazed to find that here was a very different woman indeed, not just a woman who engaged in a considerably iconoclastic occupational endeavor. This absolutely breathtakingly beautiful French woman with whom I momentarily shared the beach and some warm Pepsi, was not just a knock-out to look at, she was also a very intelligent and deeply reflective person in her own right, revealing very strong bohemian tendencies underneath her poise and gracefulness. As the afternoon wore on and the others continued to dive, we lingered behind to continue getting to know each other, for she apparently found my way of looking at life to be equally fascinating (this has never EVER happened subsequently, or even before that time). I was almost shocked speechless by this discovery, but I managed to contain my surprise. This was, after all, the Middle East, where everything and anything off the norm *was* the norm.

We got along famously that afternoon, the tall and skinny American pseudo-intellectual and the stupefyingly attractive, dark-haired gazelle who was Danielle. So well did we mesh, that by the end of the day our degree of achieved interpersonal harmony and empathy was quite beyond rational expectation; to say I was completely intoxicated with her unique spirit and lush sensuality is understating things.

Later that night, under a full and beautifully pale moon, Danielle and I went for a walk on the beach, away from the dive camp and in the opposite direction of a group of local Jeddah *Sidiyks* who had set up camp close-by, hoping to catch some glimpses of exposed expat female bodies. She was softly singing the words of an old Brittany song from her childhood, as we walked along the water's edge, drinking in the shimmering reflections of the moon's luminescence. The tide was in and few of the little crab-like sea creatures were in evidence on the soft sand as continued walking. We were heading unintentionally towards some out-of-the-way dunes that lay back away from the beach, not talking to each other, but merely flowing along with the moment and enjoying the soft and languid mood of the Arabian desert coast.

Upon reaching the dunes, I turned to say something to her and was startled to find that she had already pulled the halter free from around her firm, ripe breasts and was unfastening the Polynesian style *lavalava* that she had tied around her hips. The folds of the lavalava fell away just as I glanced down at it, to reveal the lush and undulant curves of her soft brown body in the soft sheen of the full moon. Her physical beauty was breathtaking, as I gazed with no little stupefaction at the unveiled spectacle of this moon-maiden from far-off France. The awkwardness of the moment did NOT pass gently, as I continued to stare at her, uncertain as to what this all meant; for once in my life I was absolutely speechless…no words could possibly come to my mouth, given the unexpected nature of what seemed to be unfolding between us.

I remember very well how the moonlight shone on her from slightly behind her left side, illuminating the hollows and valleys of her unbearably sensual form, the soft brown wisp of hair just below her belly standing out between her legs in shadowed relief. Then she spoke.

"Come. I want you and I know you want me. Make hard, passionate love to me. Here. Now. Take me, now! I want to feel your heat inside me, I want to take you into me and hold you prisoner within me; I want to squeeze your maleness between my thighs and feel your stored-up force explode inside me. Show me that you are the person I think and intuitively feel you are. Take me under this full, pagan moon, and caress the empty spaces of my waiting body with your hot tongue. Do not let this moment pass a moment longer! I can feel you in me now, even though you are still dressed. Do not delay. Let us make wild and pagan love under this forbidden moon before this passion I so acutely feel fades, as it naturally must and will!" Or highly accented words to that effect, as she was quite gifted with natural eloquence herself.

What followed was one of the most wildly unrestrained experiences of my life. As I tugged my shirt and shorts off, now thoroughly engorged with the prospect of what she was offering and fully beyond any further need of such oddly poetic words of encouragement, she lay back against the sand on her cast off *pareo*. Offering up her moistness invitingly to me, she arched her back and held her lithe brown arms out to embrace me as I eagerly fell upon her. Her full breasts were unusually firm—perhaps silicone?—but the swelling curves of her hips were what captured my full attention, as I drew myself to her and grasped my erect penis, ready to plunge into her. Gone was all worry about hygiene, health, or STDs. I was about as close to being a rude, wildly powerful, rutting animal as I have ever been in my life then, as I entered her...

She gasped and arched her back even more as I thrust into her surprisingly tight receptiveness. Even before I was fully aroused myself, she was seemingly off on another plane of awareness, as each thrust provoked further gasps of greedy delight from her. There was no one else around for at least a quarter mile and even the thought of the very real and possible dangers presented by the poisonous Arabian sand spider was completely forgotten in the urgency of those wild moments. Neither of us worried about making sounds expressive of unconstrained love.

Not long after I had entered her, I grasped her slim waist and, turning her over, took her full from behind, withdrawing quickly and then lunging back into her in a posture that allowed the full length of my hugely engorged erectness to cleave her narrow recess like a sword. As my initial thrust passed fiercely into her innermost depths with a sucking sound, she shuddered and her full breasts fell free, swaying from side to side. She instinctively reared back into my spear with a matching and deftly erotic rhythm of her own that made each thrust that much deeper and harder. Her slender arms were now outstretched before her, her swollen nipples gently brushing the top of the sand with each lunge, such was the force of my lovemaking. I felt some sort of a strange blood-lust raging throughout my entire body, then, as I clutched those magnificent breasts with my hands and gripped them firmly; a wildly intoxicated feeling of absolute power over her femaleness that must have verged on true madness filled me completely, dimming my vision.

More minutes passed as we both shuddered and bucked with the powerfully paroxysmal hammer blows of my groin smacking loudly against her lush and beautiful bottom. The small spurts of juice from her female core were now regular as we both rode this wild stallion of primal pagan force together. And then...we both came more or less together, she holding back to meet me on that same plane of intimate physical intoxication at almost the same instant. I felt her shudder deeply, a spasm of her vaginal muscles unconsciously squeezing me in a vise-grip of desperate passion, as she arched her back to reach up then, to enter my mouth with her probing tongue, despite the acute demands such gymnastics required. We both collapsed soon after that, lying spent and wasted on the dune, each of us smeared with the moist fluids of our love-making, also now unavoidably congealed with the gritty grains of desert sand. Listening to her gasp (she smoked *Galloise*, unfortunately) breathlessly on her back as I lay near her, I gazed up into that part of the star-filled blackness of the night sky that lay opposite the moon and wondered about all this. *Oh man, did I _wonder_!*

At that moment, I felt as a god must feel, having his godlike way with his goddess' most intimate favors. I can say, without a moment's hesitation, that it was the wildest, most passionate, and most instinctively natural sex I have ever had the good fortune to have ever experienced on this earth. Fortunately, I had enough good sense and style NOT to sully the experience with needless words, questions, or expressions of more mundane moment. I merely accepted this gift from whatever powers there are in the Universe quietly, gratefully and soundlessly, as the breeze cooled us both off.

We walked back to the camp in the same sense of individual, yet intensely shared reflective quietude. The next day we all returned to Riyadh and although I saw her a few more times thereafter at parties, we never again shared such unimaginably primal intimacy. After a few months, contract ended, I heard she had rotated back to France. Someone told me later that she was sharing a yacht with some fellow, anchored in the green depths of the *Cote de Azure*. I can only imagine what has happened to her after that, and of course we never attempted to remain in touch. She had perhaps sucked me absolutely dry of every ounce of that highly personal power that lays within each of us, in that one, wild act of animistic joining.

Perhaps she was a modern-day witch? One can only speculate, but her powers of physical and spiritual love, overwhelming in the scope of their natural force and unleashed like a white tidal wave of lust by that full moon, gave me an everlasting respect for the awesome potential female *mana* (or spirit) that whatever forces of nature exist have conferred upon woman kind... I instinctively know it can never be the same with anyone else, ever again. Regrettably, I also understand all too well how our uncontrollable sexual urges work against any full realization of Schopenhauer's admonitions that procreation is a denial of preferred pessimistic theory. Sex, viewed in this light, is death, since only without sex and the creation of new life can the meaninglessness of life end its cyclic pattern.

Among the things you don't do in Moloka'i: 1) Never give a fisherman some bananas to take with him in his boat and NEVER give him those bananas in a red plastic (or any other material) bag. 2) Never ask a fisherman if he is going out to fish, either (correct question would be: going out, eh?). Reasons for the foregoing are that certain trees and fish are forms often assumed by the ancient Hawaiian god Kane and bananas are sacred to him (same reason why bananas were forbidden to women—kapu!). Red is also a color sacred to Kane.

Things one *never* sees here that you see all the time back home; 1) People spare changing you on the street (to do so is *'foh shame!'*); 2) frowns or *'stink eye'* (bad looks flashed at someone else); 3) people cutting you off at turns or trying to get ahead of you in a line; 4) people ignoring you or trying to appear as if you are not standing right next to them; 5) stoplights (there are stop signs, however); 5) book stores (reading does not seem to be a favored pastime here); 6) fast food; 7) car alarms; 8) locked front doors; 9) slender, weight-optimised locals; 8) people in a hurry to go somewhere for no apparent reason; 9) wrist watches; 9) small and modest proportions served for meals; 10) snakes of any kind (except one benign type that is blind and only an inch long); 11) gang violence, homicides, car theft, graffiti 'art', and gratuitously malicious vandalism; 12) Black racists (and mother-stabbers, father-rapers, et al); 12) Howard Stern type trash-talkers on the local media.

Things you *wish* you didn't see here, but occasionally do: 1) pushy tourists from the mainland or other Hawaiian islands; 2) 'Infrasonic' (heavy amplified bass) car stereo systems (the kind that you can feel vibrating while still blocks away); 3) kids in cars driving fast after dark; 4) kids and adults wearing 'reversed ball caps'; 5) young and good looking girls who think they are too sexy for their clothes; 6) people on the main road (speed limit 45 mph) who tend to push you when you are at the speed limit (sadly and ironically, these are usually locals, rather than tourists, the latter of which groups seems to respect the local speed laws); 7) public drinking (after dark, it has been suggested to me that it is not really safe driving on local roads, due to common DUI); 8) articles in the local community newspapers (*Militia of Moloka'i Advertiser, Moloka'i Island Times, The Dispatch*) warning against the seriously threat of methamphetamine (*Ice*) spreading in local schools; 9) increasing displays of disrespect for parents, grand-parents, and elders of the community by adolescents; 10) increasing real estate speculation by outsiders (from the other islands or the mainland); 11) increasing lack of knowledge of or interest in traditional Hawaiian culture, customs, and heritage, by young locals; 12) monster pickup trucks with high lifts and huge off-road tires (although they admittedly may come in handy once or twice a year when heavy rains cause some local flooding); 13) a profusion of Evangelical Pentecostal or congregational protestant churches; 14) scorpions and centipedes; 15 large, un-friendly (or noisy) dogs; 15) ROOSTERS; 16) ROOSTERS; 17) AND MORE ROOSTERS; 18) cell phones (although they are nei-ther flaunted as status symbols here or used to excess and may in fact be quite handy to have when way out of reach on the is-land, somewhere); 19) teenagers with excessive *attitude* 20) high food costs; 21) right-wing conservatives; 22) NRA gun nuts (there are a few, but no many).

Things you see or experience here that you are damn glad you do: 1) many beautiful flowers; 2) lots of interesting birds; 3) foxy women (although only occasionally, and usually not 'local', sad to say); 4) cool trade winds; 5) continually comfortable tem-peratures, year-round; 5) occasional evidence of the indigenous, very ancient and naturally harmonised older civilization; 6) the most amazing sunsets and sunrises; 7) deeply instilled aware-ness of the importance of slowing down to relax and smell the flowers; 8) people smiling and waving at total strangers for no good reason other than that they choose to; 9) happy little kids at play;10) excellent locally grown *Arabica* coffee; 11) bicycles (although DUI motorists make riding bicycles after dark some-what hazardous on the island); 12) an abundance of healthy, locally grown tropical fruits (papayas, breadfruit, bananas, guava, pineapples, etc.) and vegetables.

These lists are far from complete and really just constitute an innocent bit of time-passing on a slow afternoon, but all things continue to change and evolve and I have no doubt that Moloka'i shall as well, although to date it has not seen much, continue to change in ways less positive and less aesthetically pleasing than one would wish for.

The latest poop on the continuing saga of the water line and meter installation: Met with Victor this AM, my naturalized Italian 'not-quite-a licensed-architect-but-close-enough' friend in down-town K'kai. He tells me that his friends in the Maui County water & utilities department have informed him that the main water line does not lie across the road, as had been originally thought, but on our side of Kam V Highway. Further, he says that the new property owner on our right side (*mauka*) has already filed for a permit to install a water line and meter on his adjacent parcel. Since the main water line is on our side of the highway, this means most importantly that no excavation of Kam V Highway is required (hence less expense), but he suggested that in view of these findings we wait for the water line and meter installation. The reasoning is that if the other parcel owner (lot #23 on our right) puts in a line and meter, Victor can ask to have them install a 'split' or dual off-take that our line could be hooked to. In es-sence, this is exactly the reasoning Suki had suggested might be a concern, if the water line was indeed located on the *mauka* (seaward) side of the street. The fact that the water line doesn't lie on the mauka side somewhat obviates that particular point, but there might still be a further benefit to wait until after the Par-cel #23 owner has installed his line & meter. At any rate, Victor suggested we sit tight and wait, since we will not be building on the property for another three years, anyway. I need to call and relate this latest twist to Suki, who will undoubtedly be happy to hear this (thereby saving an expected additional $9,000 or so in expenses).

Meanwhile, that changes the prospects somewhat for my getting that beautiful sharkskin-head pahu made by Bill Pekuni that I was earlier admiring, and it also alleviates some of the pending financial pressure posed by Fulk Nerra's Lockheed F-104 C-2 upward firing ejection seat that he wants to send me from Germany for a total of $1750 delivered (to Sacramento International Airport). One never knows from minute to minute, seemingly, what to expect.

Overcast deck of clouds outside and no wind to speak of, which is unusual for this time of year here; humidity is up a tad, too, although still not unreasonably so. Roosters in full cry all afternoon long; GOD, I would so like to go settle their hash. It's highly ironic to think that the Tahitian settlers of 1100-1200 AD brought chickens (and roosters) over with them from their homeland, so this animated form of concentrated local noise pollution has been native here for at least 8 centuries! *Gaak.* They also brought pigs, rats (rat stowaways or perhaps a pregnant female on one of their sea-going canoes, probably), many types of fruit and vegetables (most important among them *Kalo,* aka *Taro,* and several kinds of yam), along with certain types of tree and other botanical specimens not found indigenously on the Hawaiian Islands.

Tried some of the local supermarket hotdogs last evening! What a mistake. Even worse tasting (bland) than mainland varieties. Oscar Meyer *Smokies* are the only decent frankfurters to eat without a hot-dog bun and I should know that. Ah well, I suppose it will be nice to return to some sort of normal (healthy) eating fare at home. My diet here has so far been admittedly terrible, despite all my good intentions to stick to the straight and narrow, cuisine-wise. I did, however, buy some concentrated essence of the *Noni* plant yesterday at the local organic food store (yes, K'kai has one). The Noni is a uniquely Hawaiian plant, with fruit that has a lengthy history of use by the healing kahunas of the ancient local culture. Too many positive health effects to go into here, but suffice it to say the list of its positive systemic health effects is substantial. Only drawback is that it has the smell of over-ripe cheese, hence its other nickname, *the Limburger Tree.* There are a great number of fascinating plants and natural herbs that were used by the ancient practitioners of healing back in traditional pre-contact Hawaii. I have bought several good references on the subject of the Hawaiian herbal pharmacopeias with me, which I intend to give to Suki, since she uses traditional herbal medicines and has an interest in such things. So do I, but the subject is a lot lower on my list of interests, given that I have so many of them as it is.

April 27, 2005 (Wednesday)

Traditional Hawaiian recipe for *"Mea 'ai no ke kakahiaka (oka)":*

1) Grasp bag firmly (beginners may wish to use both hands); 2) tear open with slow, ripping motion; 3) pour contents into wooden bowl (made of Koa wood); 4) add boiling water (tastes best when used with rain-water brought by bamboo pipeline from highest *pali* on island); 5) stir thoroughly; 6) eat bowl of Instant Quaker Oats with soy milk. [May also be eaten with fresh, firm local *Mai'a* (men only, however: *kapu* for women).

According to Frank Midkiff, President of the Kamehameha Schools, in 1933, the ancient Hawaiians, although literally a 'stone age' civilization in that they had no iron or pottery tools and utensils, had a generously endowed sense of humor. This is not generally characteristic of other 'stone age' civilizations. For example, the Hawaiians had no less than 7 words or phrases relating to the breaking of wind (Benjamin Franklin would have beamed warmly, were he to have known this fact). The word 'fart' is generally understood to be (in its several dialectical variations) *"Hi'u", "ho'ani", "makani", or "palale"*. "Silent but deadly" was *"Hio", "Ohio"*, or *"Puhihio"*. "Sputteringly" was *"pi"*. "Foully" was *"'enakoi"*. And "Slyly" was *"uene"*. [Note: it is likely that the term "One-cheek sneak" did not have a common Hawaiian term of reference, since the Hawaiians did not usually sit on hard, flat surfaces, but rather squatted or assumed a hunched down posture.]

The actual sound of a fart was described as *"palali"* and the act of breaking wind was described as *"pu'u puhi'u"* (which bears an amazing similarity to the richly onomatopoeic English slang term *"Poo-poo"*—by the way, the Fleish-Kincaid literacy index which MS/Word automatically applies to all MS/Word documents now suggests my writing level is at 'Grade 6.5', amusingly enough). Ben F. (if he were still alive) would probably be the first to suggest that the ancient Hawaiians were indeed an advanced civilization (despite their lack of iron tools and pottery pots) in light of the above revelations.

What the old culture of Hawaii cannot claim credit for is a determination of the effects the physical dynamics of the passage of hydrogen-methane gas through a human anal sphincter had, when subject to the varying constraints of the fleshy folds of human skin on the human buttocks and affected by the compressibility variables of positional orientation. Without invoking the more complex physical laws of *Venturi's Theory of Compressed Gas Frequency Modulation*, suffice it to say that a landmark study conducted by the noted Polish anatomist Yarislaw Brezshinski in 1939 found that the extreme variation in fart tone, pitch, timbre, and harmonics observed among human beings relates directly to the compressibility threshold farts are subjected to by the folds of the human gluteals lying closest to the anal sphincter itself, when they are passed.

Further (Brezshinski noted), the presence of human hair follicles around the anal sphincter act in a manner that either amplifies or mutes the audio dynamics of a fart, depending upon abundance there-at: hence the broad range of fart-like sounds, noted by the Hawaiians (eg. Sputtering, hissing, snorting, abrupt, prolonged, rising tone, et al). It may be reasonably hyposthesised, thanks to the break-through analytical studies of Doctor Brezshinski in the 30s, that the discernible variance in audibility between categorically compensated male and female farts may be attributed to the fact that females generally lack hairy assholes, whereas males generally have a profusion of hair in the gluteal fold (this fact relates directly to hormonal differences between the genders, of course). [The fact that, after enjoying an immoderate amount of wine at the local university pub with some of his less-advanced students one evening, Dr. Brezshinsky offered up the opinion that the presence of hair around male assholes is *"...circumstantial evidence that God has a serenely sublime sense of cosmological humor"*, is perhaps apocryphal.]

But returning to a more serious note, in actual truth, the lack of iron and clay deposits on the islands of the Hawaiian chain of volcano tops is a notable determinant in the fact that ancient Hawaiians had to use what we would consider primitive implements, by comparison with artifacts in evidence among other civilizations. Since they lacked iron ore to make knives and clay from which to make pottery, they were compelled to rely exclusively on other readily available local materials (namely wood and stone). Hawaiian weapons were made from dense varieties of wood, but often incorporated naturally sharp components of animal anatomy (e.g. shark teeth) in their wood instruments (whether for domestic or warlike applications) and stone. Containers to hold food and water were of necessity constructed from calabash gourds.

Cooking was considerably affected by this lack of iron age resources, the typical Hawaiian method of cooking food necessarily being use of the *Imu*, or heated-stone cooking pit. Without pans to cook in, almost all Hawaiian food preparation requiring cooking was performed by the men using these pits. Since men were exclusively the cooks, and since they had to prepare meals for men and women separately (using separate Imus) due to the *Ali'i kapus* placed on this aspect of daily life, cooking with the Imu method characteristically involved several hours of work each day and seems to have been a moderately time-intensive responsibility.

Fire seems to have been relatively easy for the ancient Hawaiians to produce, although I am amazed to find that in all of the 53 books I now have on Hawaiiana immediately available to hand, not a single one directly references fire as a distinctively important subject, worthy of note in their indices. Not even in Fornander's formidable compilation of ancient facts and knowledge is there a reference to one of what I would image to be the most ascendantly central concerns of any ancient society.

A separate but related subject in this line of thought is the nature of how the genders were regarded by the ancients. On the whole and in the most general sense, women were considered quite equal to men in many ways throughout ancient Hawaiian history. The fact that women were constrained from doing or participating in certain things in ancient Hawaii was likely not a reflection of discrete or inherent gender inequities, but a specific manifestation of the animistic religion that regarded the basic 'mana' of men and women to be different. This resulted in certain *kapus* against the equal participation by women in certain activities. Women were not allowed to eat with the men, nor were they allowed to work with them. Women were also forbidden to associate with their families when in menses and lived temporarily apart from the rest of the group in a separate hale of their own for this brief period each month. These distinctions have often been pointed to as evidence that women were unfairly discriminated against by men in the old culture, but in fact another interpretation has been offered to explain this that makes much sense. It is the view both of highly credentialed individuals like Dr. Michael Kioni Dudley ('*Man, Gods, and Nature*') and less conventional individuals such as supernaturalist and 'Wicca' practitioner Scott Cunningham ('*Hawaiian Magic & Spirituality*') that this segregation of genders was perhaps due not to a basic male bias that women were inherently inferior or intrinsically less worthy, but a *fear* of the excessive natural *mana* (or spiritual power) possessed by women.

If one considers the fact that women are both the figurative and actual repository of the procreative life support process that engenders, fosters, and nurtures all human life, a better understanding of the awed regard this realisation might have provoked may be attained. The segregation and isolation of women during their menstrual period was therefore more likely the result of a fear of the special mana such a physical event evidenced and a fear of what (harm) that powerful mana might do to male mana, rather than the result of fear of contamination by something deemed unclean. Misogyny? Of course!

Other recent evidence supports this surmise. It is a known fact that Hawaiian women not infrequently accompanied their men into battle, fighting side-by-side with their mates (a custom also practiced by the ancient Germanic tribes of the Roman period) in ferocious hand-to-hand combat. Unfortunately, the figurative 'ethnic cleansing' that resulted from the post-kapu Christian missionary period was so effective that much of the old cultural knowledge has fallen away completely; were it not for individuals such as the early Hawaiian historian *David Malo* and others who recognised the importance of preserving ancient Hawaiian knowledge and history, very little would still be known about these core attitudes and central awarenesses of the ancient Hawaiians.

Mental note: I do not like the smell of dried rice & turkey SPAM that lingers in a dirty (uncleansed) bowl, the morning after. Further mental note: Must make an effort to clean dishes right after eating, rather than the next day. Turkey SPAM is bad enough as a 'drop-in' component of rice when it's warm, but the residual odoriferous essence doesn't suppress a gag reflex the following morning.

OK. Time for a break from the laptop. There are many heiaus (ancient Hawaiian religious temples) on the various islands. One of the most famous, reported to be a place of human sacrifice later in its history (*Luakini Heiau*), lies not far from K'kai at about half-way between Mile Marker 15 and Mile Marker 16 on the mauka side of Kamehameha V Highway (east end). I am overdue to visit this site and experience first-hand the supposedly palpable mana that many claim may still be felt here.

The *Ili'ilio Pae Heiau*, located at *Mapulehu* just off the Kam V Highway, is the site of reputed human sacrifices, which were normally only made under the most severe of circumstances (such as in times of war or famine), but this is contested by some sources. If there were such sacrifices made at all here, these rites were probably undertaken much later in its history, after the Tahitian Ali'i came and took over the island. The Ili'ilio Pae Heiau was originally built by the early inhabitants of the island (the ka-naka maoli or Mana Hune), long before the 12th Century invasion of the Hawaiian Islands by the Tahitian Ali'i. It is a colossal, ele-vated, and flat-topped structure, with terraces made of carefully fitted volcanic blocks brought over the mountain from the Wailau Valley coast; measuring originally almost a thousand feet in length and several hundred feet in width, it was used exclusively as a school for training the earlier 'ohana type kahuna (sorcer-ers), until taken over by the Pa'ao kahuna 'ana'ana of the Ali'i.

I have been dying (poor choice of words, perhaps?) to view this site for some time; problem is it lies on private property, alt-hough it is possible to hike about 15 minutes up the access road to reach it on foot. We shall see. The thought of being inter-cepted, en-route, by a local who resents uninvited malihini intrusions into a sacred area is always an unhappy one, but I owe it to myself to see this site first-hand.

Just returned from my trip to see Ili'ilio Pae Heiau. As a fighter pilot returning from a mission without success would put it, no joy (roughly, "enemy not sighted"). There are no clear markers on the road, for obvious reasons (no one wants a bunch of lookie-looies poking around such sacred sites without an escort). Hence, the usual way to see this site is through a local company that offers wagon-rides to it. The site is located about a quarter mile west of the road. I drove east along Kam V Highway and passed by the site (it's impossible to know which small jeep road to take off the main highway unless you have been there before, due to there being no obvious markers), then back tracked to what I thought was the logical spot, parked the car, and took off on foot. I followed a jeep trail that led basically straight upwards to an elevation of well beyond 1400, feet with no luck spotting the heiau at all, and since I had neglected to bring any water with me,

I started getting pretty dry toiling away in the noontime sun. Finally, after checking my wrist altimeter (1450 feet) and decided that I had climbed WAY above the site, I headed back down. The views of the reef, fishponds, and Pailolo Channel (between Moloka'i and Maui), however, were spectacular, heiau or no heiau. Fruitless or not, it was a beautiful and scenic hour of good exercise.

Returning to Ranch Camp, I note that in Meg & Todd Cranston-Cruebas' book *'Moloka'i Notes'*, they give directions to find the Ili'ilio Pae Heiau trail as follows: *"About 5/10ths of a mile past Mile Marker 15, you will cross a small bridge. Look for a fire hydrant on your left and the dirt road about 15 feet before the hydrant. Park off the highway and walk down this dirt road towards the mountain (you'll know you are on the right dirt road when you come to an old abandoned shack to your left). Continue walking for another 10minues until you come to a salmon colored house on your right with two coconut trees in front (this is Tutu or 'Auntie' Pearl's place—her phone is 808-558-8113 to call beforehand for permission to cross her land to get to the heiau). Directly to your left you'll see a sign indicating the start of the difficult Waiau Trail, which heads over the mountain and through to Wailau Valley on the north coast of the island. Don't be put off. The walk from here is short and flat, although you may get muddy crossing a small creek bed. After crossing the creek bed, you'll see what appears to be a terraced wall of large volcanic rocks. Since the heiau is overgrown with vegetation at this end, walk around to the right side and up a slight incline to get the most impressive view from the top."*

According to Meg & Todd, the sacrifices (non-living and living) were made on the eastern end of the main heiau platform and then burned on an alter (or *lele*) nearby, but again, this information is contentious and more than likely there were no human sacrifices carried out there until the island was conquered by the Ali'i in the 16th century (it remained free of the rule of Kamehameha I until that time, when he finally succeeded in subjugating all the islands under his monarchy). Perhaps I'll go back tomorrow to try again. At least I now know more precisely where the start of the heiau access road is. I had the same problem with the Matterhorn (a peak in the Sierra Nevadas) in the 70s; took me three trips to the Sawtooth Ridge area on the eastern border of Yosemite before I was able to orient properly, locate the peak and climb it. Good thing I was never called upon to do duty as a navigator. If it had been me on that 11th Century second wave of Polynesian voyage of colonization from the Marquesas, they never would have made it!

One last data point for today: It's reasonably certain that the likely first 'western' discovery of the Hawaiian Islands was made in about the year 1555, when the Spanish apparently stumbled across them. However, proof of their discovery appears to have been lost in their navigational logs and records, since they never made public notice of this fact. Thus, it falls to James Cook's voyages of discovery to claim the most generally recognised credit for finding the Hawaiian Islands in 1779. There are also intriguing Hawaiian tales about a legendary 'long iron knife' (one of these tales is recorded in King David Kalakua's book on ancient Hawaiian legends), stemming from what may have been a Japanese samurai who was shipwrecked on the islands, a few hundred years before the undocumented Spaniard encounter. There are several equally intriguing clues to suggest that although the ancient Hawaiians did not have iron ore, they at least knew what it was and were apparently aware of the superiority of iron weapons. This collaterally supports the theory that Japanese and Chinese sea voyagers who were blown off course may have made brief or accidental contact with the Hawaiians in the distant, pre-Cook past. Of course, there are also those who maintain that not only were Chinese seafarers the first to discover the California coast in the 1100s or so, they also left the remains of one of their ships there (recently discovered artifacts support this theory).

April 28, 2005 (Thursday)

I awoke to rain this morning. It had been a terrible night from start to finish, for no clearly apparent reason. I hadn't been able to sleep most of the night, owing to a number of things: roosters, dogs howling, the neighbors partying, a slight sunburn I had received in my fruitless search for the old heiau, thin pillows that I just couldn't get properly adjusted, earplugs that kept popping out, and also a hasty dinner of strawberry yogurt (just couldn't face another night of SPAM over rice).

One of the neighborhood dogs has a ghastly eerie howl. It starts as a slight and soft warbling sound, then gradually builds into a rising and falling modulation of such strangeness that an Irish banshee would probably be proud to claim it. It is a howl quite unlike any howl I've ever heard any *canus familiaris* give out, and I've heard enough dog howls in my life to be as expert on the subject as the next guy.

The beautiful stillness of the late evening continued (if you factor out the sounds of the neighbors a few houses off having a party) till about 9:30 last night and although I wasn't at all tired (I'd made the mistake of having some coffee late in the day), I relished the cool breeze from the window as I integrated myself gratefully into the tranquil mood of the lush silence. The earplugs were slipping out, but I thought "…perhaps I won't need them tonight". It was that perfect Moloka'i moment that is today on the endangered list (at least in Ranch Camp and the other small and closely clustered residential enclaves like this one in Kaunaka-kai). This natural, gentle moment was what I hoped to find on the Island of Moloka'i and here it was…all 30 minutes of it, until the dog I mentioned above sent off his supernatural appeal to the moon to keep all the visiting haoles awake to hear his concert.

So strange is this particular dog's howl that it always takes me a few minutes to recognise it as a dog howling (and not the protest of some poor ancient spirit, doomed to forever haunt the island)--the same condition that obtains for the jet-turbine like roar of the locals' all-terrain tyres as they drive by in their jacked-up pickups. No sooner had that recognition clicked, however, then the roosters next door answered his call to harass the haoles with a vengeance, and within a minute every rooster on the island was in full cry. This pattern continued throughout the night and the roosters are still at it as I write this, strong coffee clutched grimly in hand at 6:30 AM with the sort of crushing death grip I'd use on a rooster's neck (if one were conveniently at hand).

I recall a couple of dreams (unusually). One had to do with my bank account being overdrawn, but the older clerk with the spin-ster-like edge to her voice that I talked to at the bank had surprisingly taken care of things for me without complication. When I had asked her if there was anything I could do to keep several cheques from bouncing, I remember her replying (strangely): *"Well, I can take a quarter from the jar!"* She had the voice of that well-known actress (*Margaret Somethingorother* is all that comes to mind), who played the part of the '*Wicked Witch of the West*' in the 1939 screenplay of Baum's *"Wizard of Oz"*.

There was another dream, fairly complicated and unusual as they tend to be, in which all I recall was a short sequence in which a human figure in white hovered just outside the window; it wasn't clear enough in the dream (nighttime) to see more than that and I couldn't tell if it were a woman or a man even, but it had the bulk of a large man's outline. I have no recollection of what it represented or what my response to it was, other than uncertainty.

And this morning, rain; strange thing, really. Yesterday, up there high on the southeast side of Kamakou (the east end's lushly overgrown volcano that reaches nearly 5000 feet into the sky) and 1450 feet above the water, I made one final attempt to spot the old heiau; both my arms were dripping with blood, due to the numerous sharp thorns that the undergrowth have (and the fact that I use about 650 mgs of ASA daily, which thins the blood and reduces clotting time) and would have looked pretty strange to any passer-by, I guess (the sight of an older haole toiling up the mountain, steaming small rivulets of blood mixed with sweat would appear unusual, but no one else on the island is likely crazy enough to be up there in the middle of the noontime heat).

Before turning back, I assumed what I thought to be a proper attitude of reflective supplication and addressed the old gods, the forces of nature, and whatever existed so long ago that has today been forgotten or replaced by the spiritual idiocies of modern Christian religion. *"Give me sign, a glimpse of the heiau, anything at all to help me believe that there are larger, wiser powers at work in nature than the human mind can conveniently conceive of...!"*

I waited patiently and receptively, little paragon of a pagan neophyte supplicant in training that I saw myself as, in my mind's eye at that moment. The wind was rising and the spectacular view of the fishponds and reefs just offshore was achingly beautiful, despite the sun's aesthetically unfavorable angle directly overhead. I could imagine only the barest tiny little glimpse of what might have gone through the minds of those ancients on the heiau, as they surveyed the vast and harmonious handiwork of their natural deities. There was no discernible answer, of course.

Finally, with no apparent indication that the old gods were listening tome (or even present, after so many years of disregard), I asked a local vine if I could take a cutting of it (for that is the suggested custom) and restrained my urge to take a whiz on the old trail (this is deemed as being ill-advised, since one never knows what ancient and holy ground one may be desecrating in the doing.

There is a well-documented instance of a Honolulu television crew that once visited an ancient heiau and deliberately desecrated it—one of the crew *defecated* on it to 'prove' that all the superstitious beliefs of the locals were nonsense! A month later, all 5 of the people on the crew who had participated in the documentary were dead. Coincidence? Well, I'll let you draw your own conclusions.... Moloka'i was not formerly known as *Molola'i o o'pue'le* ("Moloka'i of the powerful prayers") for no reason, long before the Hawaiian State PR folks interested in boosting tourism to the islands came up the smarmy "*The Friendly Isle*" tag it now (unfortunately) is stuck with.

Later that evening, just after I went to bed, I suddenly and for no good reason had what would appear to be a nonsensical flash of a thought: give the vine cutting I had removed from the mountainside some water. Since it would ultimately wither away and die, I reflected for a moment on the inevitability of this fact, but then I got up and placed the cut stem in a small cap full of water and propped it up next to the bed. Just exactly why I did this, I don't know, but the likely (western empirical, rationalist) explanation is that I couldn't sleep, so why not indulge in this irrational whim?

Then this morning the rain. Dark, brooding, boiling stacks of clouds directly centered over the island and no wind at all (unusual!), just hushed silence as the rain fell steadily for an hour or so. Although it's still overcast, the rain has ceased and the breeze has begun to pick up again, slightly. Curious thing and probably has absolutely nothing to do with my watering the small vine from the mountain side, after asking for some sort of sign from the ancients. But still...one can't help but wonder....and wish it were a tangible expression of some hidden reality, instead of a mere coincidence. That's the damnable thing about human reasoning and intellect. Nothing in all of our experience is ever capable of being absolutely and unquestionably *quantified* beyond all possible doubt.

I am reminded, in the telling of this, of Somerset Maughm's famous short story, set in the tropics, titled *'Rain'*. It was one of the stories we all had to read in high school English lit and I well recall at the time that I found it hard to 'get into'. The inherent dreariness and depressive flavor of the story certainly was palpable enough, but I didn't enjoy that aspect of it and found it somehow unsettling (perhaps that was the author's intent, even though his presumed target audience was not comprised of 18 year olds). The prostitute's spiritually natural triumph over the straight-laced missionary did come across palpably, however; perhaps I should go dig it out and re-read it now, some 40 years after my first (and only) peruse of it.

Just before bed also last evening, I revisited that unique oral history from Moloka'i, *'Tales from the Night Rainbow'*. The Kaula kupuna whose recounting of family history forms the essence of the work has a great number of immensely relative observations to make. It should be noted that the original inhabitants of the islands (Moloka'i is only the example in focus, since these reflections relate to this family's specific and unique historical genealogy), presumably settled the islands as far back as 2000 BC (according to one source) and belonged to a very different group of people than the Tahitian Ali'i who came to conquer the islands in the 11th to 12th Century.

These original inhabitants (I have referred to them previously as the kanaka maoli or Mana Hune) were very different from the war-like Ali'i and were a peaceful, gentle, family-based people, harmoniously adjusted to and with the world they lived in. Their religious heiaus were regarded more as centers (schools) at which the ancient knowledge and understandings of traditional ways could be transmitted to offspring, in order to perpetuate the old ways. It was only after the arrival of the farmer-priest Pa'ao from *Kahiki* ('Tahiti') that the absolute rule of the Ali'i was established, and only after that time (11th/12th Century) that the pre-existing heiaus were adopted by the Ali'i to reflect their more aggressive, warlike religious outlooks.

Whereas prior to the arrival of the Ali'i the ancient heiaus had no carved wooden *Ki'i* (Tahitian word would be "Tiki"), this practice was adopted by the post-Ali'i priests, as was the ritual of human sacrifice in extremis. Since Moloka'i was among the last of the islands to be influenced by the latter Ali'i group (and somewhat feared for its strong, inherent spiritual mana—e.g. *"Moloka'i o' opu'ele"*, or "Moloka'i of the powerful prayers"), its inhabitants strongly reflected the original, ancient, pre-Ali'i culture. These original, pseudo-indigenous peoples regarded themselves as 'light carriers', stemming from their belief that each soul was born with a spiritual 'bowl of light' that equated to their innate nature or essence. These prefaced understandings having been stated, the context for the following should be clearer.

Among these many, many expressions of natural animistic wisdom found in '*Tales of the Night Rainbow*' emerge a number of concepts such as the following, which relates to the changes suffered by Moloka'iians after the 'invasion' of the Christian missionaries.

"(by 1900)...the children wanted to do things the ha'ole way. Many parents felt shamed by their children, so they discontinued *(the teaching of) the old ways. It was not so much the missionaries that changed things, as the younger generations."*

And…. *"(the children)…listened to my lessons (of the old wisdom), as their eyes followed the ruffled dresses, the finery and the petticoats everyone else wore. My words were often unheard. I kept explaining that 'things' detract from soul growth and seeing with the 'inner eye'. Everyone seemed to be living by different value systems. It was safer to keep what I felt and believed to myself. Grandchildren were coming along and we welcomed them. I wanted to teach them (the harmony of the old ways), however I found that my grandchildren would not listen. They wanted to learn all the wrong things. They wanted to 'be clean', to listen to their ha'ole teachers (and to disregard their elders and parents at home), they dressed and acted like the foreigners. They fought with each other and sassed (talked back to) the elders in the family."*

The epilogue of this 112 page compilation of one traditional Moloka'i family's ('ohana) history reflects much of my own intuitive belief in finally stating: *"Ku (the primary ancient Hawaiian deity), God, Jehovah, Allah, Inner Light, love—one eternal truth. What does so great a power care what we call Him/It? Little minds put tags on things and people; Love accepts and encompasses all matter and all beings. Humans have been given the right to make choices—to be good or evil—to be gods or stones. We are all born with that perfect power to do and be all things. We have the right to with it whatever we wish.*

If we keep our bowl free of rocks (note: the ancient pre-Ali'i inhabitants of Moloka'i regarded their spirit as a 'bowl of light' and called themselves 'light carriers'—a 'rock' in this particular context was a detracting belief or outlook), we can go forward or backward in time, walk with the angels, climb the heights and live in paradise. It is everyone's decision whereas what he is. We are all one, each a part of the eternal whole. There is no line that divides one from the other, or those in body from those in spirit. When men say they believe only in this or that they put blinders on their (awareness). Blinders hide the beauty and majesty of what we all apart of—Children of the Most High! Inheritors of the Universe!"

Even if we can somehow successfully separate the spiritual sentiments from the physical facts of the influence of western culture on ancient Hawaii (which I don't think is really achievable), there is much about the harshly invasive impact western culture on the old Hawaiians that is today reflected by present trends...and not just on the islands but on the mainland. One of the major differences between the immediate post-contact Hawaiian period and today is the fact that the worst aspects of our western-based culture are driven by powerful technologically driven forces. The advanced science underlying and enabling modern technology has facilitated its accelerated dissemination throughout the world and exponentially amplified its effects, among its most directly attributable consequences.

This unhappy effect, sinisterly co-opted and exploited by modern secular corporate powers, has had the most deleterious effects on our whole civilization, since much of its purely profit-driven activity is targeted squarely at those who are least able to understand the severely disadvantageous cultural consequences of it: children and adolescents. Since children at and immediately after puberty are instinctively rebellious, this inherent vulnerability has been mercilessly seized upon my market-driven economic forces to create profits...completely and utterly without the merest regard for the considerable cultural or social aesthetic consequences.

Although the impact of the missionaries on post-contact Hawaiian society was bad enough, a distinctly similar set of forces (albeit of several orders of magnitude above that of immediate post-industrial European society) are arrayed with perilously accurate precision at today's youthful susceptibilities. The results are worthy of serious concern, although it is a one-sided battle that is immensely difficult to fight. Such modern economic 'warfare' waged by private enterprise against that moral and ethical cornerstone of society, the family, is reprehensible to the extreme. And the ancient kaula of Moloka'i thought *they* had it bad...!

It is a quiet Thursday. I had thought perhaps of going down to search again for the *Ili'ilopae Heiau*, but thought twice about the need to call first to obtain permission from 'Tutu' Pearl, the proprietress of the land it sits upon. There has been considerable sentiment voiced recently about the issue of respect for the old artifactual sites and ancient family 'property rights' (even though such actual legal rights may be contentious or questionable, by modern definition). The issue stems down to a basic question of 'modern legal property owning rights' versus ancient and traditional interpretations of the rights of the people to their own land.

One of the most serious issues faced by native Hawaiians back at the time of the *Great Mahele* in 1843 (the kingly rescinding of traditional Ali'i kapus against private ownership, and the resulting division of all Hawaiian lands into three parts by Kamehameha II) was the fact that even though this finally enabled individual Hawaiians to physically own their own property, legal documents were required (with the owners' names on them) to effect this entitlement. Since Many Hawaiians didn't have what we would consider *regular* (read: Western) names at that time, and in many cases had only casually adopted 'Christian' names that they later disregarded or didn't bother to maintain, the actual legal ownership of land fell into a state of uncertain chaos. Hawaiians were also completely unused to the newly introduced western system of 'private ownership', since all Hawaiian land had traditionally been the exclusive property of the King. These factors, plus the widespread practice of native-owned land leasing to haoles (foreigners), resulted in many native Hawaiians losing their land when legal documents could not be provided years later as proof of their original ownership. It goes without saying that the *Great Mahele* was the result of tremendous pressure brought to bear on the Hawaiian monarch by haole businessmen (sugar cane plantation operators, etc.) in the first place, and these same sharp western operators clearly and maliciously took advantage of the natives to skillfully exploit the legal issues in such a manner as to retain permanent custody of the land they may have originally only been leasing from Hawaiian natives.

Although these nuances of Hawaiian history are now long passed, their eventual consequences and the modern effects of this are still being acutely felt today. There is no question that the Hawaiian people themselves were deftly cheated out of land that would otherwise today be theirs. Instead, much of Hawaii not owned by the state is in the hands of private mainlanders and other powerful private (haole) individuals on the islands. Today on Moloka'i the most recent spark has been created by multi-millionaire and anti-virus software guru John MacByte, when he last month auctioned off one of his large property tracts (1008 acres of *apuhua'ha* land, that constituted a traditional pie-shaped slice of property extending from the highest point on the island all the way to the shore) for 3.2 million dollars through an advertisement in the Wall Street Journal.

MacByte, whose interests and activities are alleged to include Tantric Yoga (*Kunalindi* sexual yoga) and other exotic disciplines, bought the property three years ago for 1.2 million dollars. From what I gather, listening to various expressed opinions here on the island, MacByte (who donated computers to local schools and also supported the community in other ways with his wealth when he originally came to the island), erred most by using an Alabama auction house through which to sell his property that advertised it as being *'excellent investment property, with great potential for residential subdividing'*. Whether true or not (most of the property is located at some elevation and cannot be easily or inexpensively built upon), this was seized upon as constituting a gross and insulting disregard for the indigenous island inhabitants, who are increasingly concerned (legitimately) about outside real estate speculators swooping down to convert Moloka'i into another Maui or Oahu. One person I talked with stated that if MacByte had not been associated with the advertising firm's extremely poor decision to use that term to describe the property, it might not have been viewed as the highly inflammatory and contentious matter that it ended up being regarded as.

Whatever the facts, MacByte finally succeeded in selling the property to unidentified persons and made over two million on the deal, despite a large if rag-tag coalition of islanders (led by island activist and part-Hawaiian Winston Rider) who showed up to strongly protest the event. An interesting sidelight is the fact that a new island newspaper began operations concurrent with the start of the whole affair, named *'The Moloka'i Island Times'*. The publisher of the paper is listed as the "Moloka'i Island Times Publishing Company", but in fact it is John MacByte's money funding the new publication, since MacByte gave his British cousin Daniel Whittaker an undisclosed subsidy to start it up and operate it. Whittaker is listed as the paper's 'Advertising Manager', and he ostensibly is 'co-owner' with Brandon Putzer, a former southern Californian who apparently has a journalism degree from Chico State University in California (formerly working with the island's third paper, 'The Militia of Moloka'i Advertiser' and George Peabody, owner/publisher).

The editor/publisher of the island's original newspaper, Gerry Anderson, in a recent conversation we had, shared his observations with me that Whittaker had a history of being in trouble with the law (*"...in and out of prison"* was how he phrased it). While this may in fact relate to some personal problems with illicit drug use or similar statutory law violations, Anderson's opinion of Whittaker was distinctly uncomplimentary. I met briefly with Whittaker, who seems to be in his late 40s), just after getting here and he seemed genial enough; you'd never suspect anything out of the ordinary about him from casual contact, although he clearly had a distinct British accent.

Brandon Putzer on the other hand (when I met him a day or so later to give him two submissions to consider for publication), struck me as being about as open and genial as a Saharan Hooded Cobra. He is young (in his late 20s or early 30s), and has a curiously distinctive appearance with his dark curly hair. I immediately decided that Putzer and I would never develop any mutually amicable understandings and certainly Chico State (with its rep as a party college, along with UC Santa Cruz), is not highly regarded as being among the best of places to obtain a serious foundation in the journalistic arts.

I suppose I should call up Winston Rider and get his opinions on all this, since he seems to be the local activist who is most out-spoken about the MacByte affair (and any other related matter appearing to have serious impact on the island's community). I think it is amusing to note in passing that the island, whose overall population doesn't exceed 7,500 souls (not including several thousand roosters and hundreds upon hundreds of dogs & feral cats....*grrrr*), now has three more or less serious newspapers— each contending for the right to 'speak' for the island.

Of the three, *'The Dispatch'* was first on the island, the *'Militia of Moloka'i Advertiser'* was second, and the *'Moloka'i Island Times'* has now been active since about February of this year. Anderson's paper, 'The Dispatch', is a fairly good community paper, seemingly well suited to the island. The 'Militia of Moloka'i Advertiser' strikes me as being more of a personal venue for the extreme viewpoints of its editor, George Peabody (who lives on the east end at around Mile Marker 16 with his Asian-Hawaiian wife Susan), than a balanced community paper, and so far the 'Moloka'i Island Times' has shown itself to be a fairly nice, fairly balanced, and politically neutral community organ.

Peabody is a definite anomaly who is a bit harder to understand, since he is clearly a person with extremist views, with his unequivocal sympathies for the gun lobbies; judging from his rambling editorializing, he is a pro-gun, strongly pro-2nd Amendment supporter who feels the present Federal Government is the most serious threat to our individual American freedoms. I guess that would make him extreme or ultra-rightwing in his views and I've no doubt the FBI and other Federal agencies have him under reasonably close scrutiny.

Ah, the small-scale passions and highly contentious issues a small little and relatively remote island community such as Moloka'i is capable of producing! *Whoda thunkit*?!

April 29th, 2005 (Friday):

"Friendly Isle" or not, after last night's repeat performances by the local neighborhood rooster & dog musical ensemble, I am definitely not feeling friendly at all towards those two gross violators of the domestic nocturnal quietude. The roosters keep at it all day and all night, brainless little horny critters that they are, although the dogs have enough good sense (& intelligence) to lie in the shade all day and chill. For roosters, with their teeny, tiny intellect, the pattern is simple and repetitive: strut, crow, fuck, eat, etc. My earplugs are clearly technological failures, since they do not remain firmly planted throughout the night and regularly require reinsertion. Since I am, by Chinese astrological determination, a 'Dog' and Suki is born under the sign of the Rooster, I cannot help but think that the symbolism implicit is ironically interesting in the context of the above circumstances.

As I continue to read through my Hawaiiana resources, I continue to stumble upon useful, often delightful and often illuminating little tidbits of information. Among today's are the Hawaiian name for small bits of property (such as the 50' x160' postage stamp sized parcel we have just purchased, in the Kamiloloa Heights area just east of Kaunakakai): *"Kuleana"*. That would appear to make me *"Ka Kuleana Ali'i"*, or figuratively interpreted, *"Reigning absolute monarch of a very, very small kingdom"*. This is fine, since I had always been intending to succeed from the State of Hawaii and start my own autonomous fief, anyway, in the very finest traditions of the ancient Hawaiian tribal custom.

Among the books on Hawaii I considered less substantial is one titled *'Little Known Tales in Hawaiian History'*, by a fellow named Alton Pryor. His link with the islands is less than slightly tenuous, since he spent 4 years here while in the US Navy and thereafter remained on the Mainland. His book is full of well-known aspects of Hawaiiana, as one might predict, but at the end of it, he does go into a subject that is surprisingly not as fully covered by many popular chroniclers of Hawaiian history (e.g. the sort of book about Hawaii that one would pull off a shelf in book store hereabouts). I refer to the matter of James Cook's claim to fame as the official 'discoverer' of the islands.

While Cook's distinction as the individual who made the first major and important western contact with the Sandwich Islanders remains intact, it is increasingly clear that the Hawaiian Islands were discovered by others long before Cook's impromptu impression of the ancient god *Lono* was pulled off in January of 1778. While I had been led to believe by my various readings that this surmise was not supported by factual documentation and evidential data, I now find that there is actually quite a lot of circumstantial evidence arguing in favor of this theory.

What is apparently missing is a declaration by the Spanish (or Dutch) voyagers of the 14th & 15th century period recording that fact. There does appear to be something of that sort among the old Spanish navigational charts of the 15th century, in that these do indicate a small group of islands in mid-Pacific named (by the Spanish *"Las Mesa"*, *"Les Monges"*, and *"La Desgraciada"*. One source states that Cook's navigational chart, used at the time of his contact with the Hawaiians showed these islands. Further, we are told that there was actual discussion among the officers of the Resolution over whether Cook's islands were these same islands. Cook's decision, given his lack of time in which to look into this unexpected problem, was to have both sets of islands drawn up on his map of the Pacific and left to others to investigate further.

Since the Spanish had a colony in the Philippines from the 14th through 18th centuries, which their galleons traveled to and from via the South Pacific from the American continent, it is likely that they were the *actual* initial discoverers. In the records, it is recorded that at least 7 of their ships were lost *en route*, so the logic would dictate that at least one of them occurred at or on the Hawaiian Island chain. So far, no such Spanish shipwreck has been found, but it is an immense area to search and resources would be sorely stretched in any effort to locate such a hypothetical wreck (if it even occurred).

Other circumstantial evidence is even more intriguing. A French explorer, landing on the island of Maui in the late 1700s found evidence that some of the natives showed signs of *syphilis*. Upon examination by the ship's surgeon, it was determined that several in the group showed signs of having quite *advanced* forms of the disease. In Europe, given what is known about the course of the disease, it would have taken 12 to 15 years for the disease to have advanced that far. The fact is that Cook's visit had occurred only 8 years earlier, which tends to preclude his sailors as the *original* source of contact with the disease. In another instance, the skeletal remains of a young woman (recently) found on Oahu and known to have died before 1664 (determined by various scientific assessments, such as carbon dating, etc.) was shown to have a form of congenital Syphilis.

There are also a number of references to pre-Cook contact with white foreigners appearing to be the source of some oral histories of Hawaii that have been collected and preserved. Even as early as 1823, a missionary by the name of William Ellis was able to determine that there were at least three accounts of foreigners arriving at Hawaii before Cook among local natives. Since that time much more evidence substantiating these facts has been recovered and there are even accounts of shipwrecked survivors who appear to have been Japanese, blown off course and perhaps adrift at sea before landing purely by accident on the islands. Further of interest is the fact that several of these accidental 'visits' by foreigners resulted in the foreigners having remained with the islanders and intermarried with native women; in some cases, the foreigners were remembered as having become part of the ruling classes as chiefs.

Finally, there is actual physical evidence of pre-Cook contact. Among these is the fact that although the Hawaiians did not have iron, they were apparently well aware of it before Cook landed. After he landed they referred to it by the word *'Hamaite'*, which it was noted by a few of Cook's officers, bore similarity to a Spanish word for iron, *'Hematitas'*. The Hawaiians even offered Cook a few iron artifacts that they had as gifts (considering their rarity on the islands, quite valuable!), one or two appearing to be much worn and used bits of steel blade from a cutlass or sword that had wood attached as a handle. A few other clearly iron-fabricated artifacts were noted by Cook's crew and recorded as having been possessed by the Hawaiians when they arrived.

Other recorded evidence is equally intriguing, such as that noted by one of Cook's officers: a pantomimed representation by one of the Hawaiian Ali'i of the Spanish having set up a cross on the shore, after a previous visit. Further, in 1599, the two Dutch ships that provided the actual historical basis for James Clavell's novel *'Shogun'*, crossed from the coast of Chile to Japan. *En route*, the log records that they came across *"...certain islands at about 16 degrees North Latitude...whereupon 8 of our party left the ship...and remained with the islanders"*. It is curious to note that when Cook's vessels neared their anchorage of the Hawaiian coast, several canoes full of natives paddled out to them. One of Cook's officers commented that *"...a few of them seemed to vary from the standard islander's native look, with skin colors and visages being not unlike that of Europeans."*

Considering the frequency of Spanish and Dutch sea voyages throughout the world in the 14th & 15th centuries, and factoring in such likely contributing factors as accidents (storms & other natural hazards), navigational errors, and such, it would have to be likely that a number of earlier western (and eastern) contacts were made before Cook's voyages of the late 1700s. It is further very likely in the minds of many that the blood of these accidental or inadvertent foreigners was already mixed with that of the ancient Hawaiians through these encounters (via sexual interactions, since marriage as a formal or ritualised institution in ancient Hawaii was almost non-existent: a man simply 'took' a willing, available woman and lived with her, having sex with her that resulted in her bearing children, etc.), well before Cook arrived.

Thus, by the time Cook and his men had arrived, it isn't unreasonable to suspect that there was already a small, but appreciable admixture of Japanese, Caucasian, and perhaps even Arab blood flowing among the ancient Hawaiians. Interesting stuff, to be sure. The fact that there was no formal written history kept by the Hawaiians, there being no printed language (a situation further complicated by the fact that only the personal history of the Chiefs was recorded verbally and passed down from generation to generation), makes the process of determining any specific sequence of actual facts and events a very, very daunting if not impossibly sketchy task.

It is important to note that the motivations of the various western explorers were quite different, one from the other. The Spanish and Portuguese were principally concerned with the discovery of fabled ancient treasures and the spread of the Christian (e.g. Roman Catholic) faith among so-called 'primitives'. The Dutch were more secularly prosaic and concerned themselves exclusively with developing trade, while the English were interested principally in scientific discovery. [Note: The Americans came about later still and seem to have been mostly obsessed with Christian bible-thunping, cellular phones, pop music, real estate deals, and automobile sales....].

Only 9 more rooster-plagued days to go before I return to the mainland, with its incessant and unavoidable hard-sell media advertising, political correctness, car-culture and overall pall of technology-enhanced Yankee economic exploitation. *I can hardly wait* (roosters notwithstanding, this is intended principally as irony). Haven't watched a TV since I arrived and what a blessed break from the mainland's usual artificial reality that is! Also, have not really listened to any radio stations, other than the local island PBS affiliated station briefly (Honolulu) and an island station located on Maui (*Waiaka*), broadcasting at 940 AM that plays only Hawaiian music. Having brought an old Sony shortwave receiver of mine with me (last used in Saudi Arabia), I enjoyed the relatively primitive process of idly dialing through the various short-wave bands and picking up foreign signals. I was sad to find the same smooth media advertising techniques being used on several of the island stations to sell the usual 'stupid stuff' in the same crass manner used on the mainland; only difference being that the adverts were dripping with honey-coated local allusions to the allure of the Pacific. Last evening. I managed to tune in to a marvelous long distance radiocast of the New York Symphony playing Franz Liszt's *'Faust'*. It was a serene treat, perched out here 2400 miles from the mainland on the top of a submarine volcano, to have this available to put me to sleep—even if the sound was a bit tinny and monophonic.

On my trip out to the east end of the island a few days ago I forgot to mention the profusion of Mongooses (not 'Mongeese') evident everywhere. These slinky little ferret-like mammals dart across the road everywhere, suggesting that there are a great many of them about. I've already mentioned the fact that they were artificially introduced as a method to help control the rat population by the sugar cane producers. That 'great idea' fell flat when it was found (to everyone's embarrassment) that the Mongoose is diurnal, while the rat is nocturnal. Today you can see them everywhere. They are well adjusted to the presence of humans and are not aggressive, unless cornered and threatened. The Mongoose can inflict a fairly painful bite, so I am informed, and if they were famed in India for their abilities to hunt and kill the deadly hooded cobra, I guess I have no argument with that bit of fact. Today they are found on every island except Kauai, since when a few mated pair were brought over to that island, the local authorities refused to allow them and they were thrown overboard to down.

Failed to get in touch with the local pahu maker (Bill Pekuni) this morning, although I did get a strange cell-phone call last evening before bed that may have been him. The caller hung up after saying something about a miss-dial or something. The thought has occurred to me that since the local papers don't appear to find any of my submissions of interest, perhaps I'll write up an article about Moloka'i for the *Sacramento Bee*. Which also reminds me that I bought a case of beer (*Bud-Lite*, the island's apparent favorite, so I am told) for Victor Montero last evening and really should get that over to him (as thanks for his recent help with the water line issue). It's out in the car, where it will undoubtedly be VERY warm by now, however, he can always chill it at home and use it later (Suki's idea, bless her…since Victor didn't charge us anything for his time).

Still stiff from my climb up the volcano a few days ago. Not a very welcome effect, and a definite sign that although I try to stay in shape with my daily bicycle ride back home, as one ages one has to try twice as hard to remain in good shape, given the general physical deterioration that is part of the aging process. Speaking of that, there is a beautiful young island girl who monitors the local school's computer resource lab each day. She must be all of about 14 or 15, and is a lithe, lovely, and well developed young thing. I get the feeling that she doesn't quite know how to act around me, since while I am obviously a 'gray-beard', I still must not seem to fit the standard youthful impression that an 'older guy' has to be grossly overweight and physically repugnant. She obviously feels a little awkward around me (although courteous enough) and my vanity is trying to reassure me that this is not because I am an (irredeemable) 'old haole guy', but because there's still enough about me that is young and reasonably well-preserved to constitute some sort of attraction for her. I'll never know, of course, since she's young enough to be my daughter, but if this were ancient Hawaii, where age made less difference in mating potential than the ability to get up a thick, stiff *Ule*...I'd be after her like a shark after an Ahu. Talk about one lovely lissome island wahine! Regrettably, she's not the norm around here, as the local culture seems to favor VERY heavy-set, VERY large mamas (and papas). Too much rice with dinner!

At the local Maui County Library (actually part of the State of Hawaii Public Library System) I was curious as to what I'd find there, in terms of what the librarians were like. My ideal concept of a formidable (female) librarian has always been someone on the order of the mind of *Sylvia Plaith* (or Emily Dickenson) merged with the body of TV program 'Friends' co-star *Courtney Cox*. In other words, a bright AND sexy woman, despite the fact that acute intelligence has always been regarded by both men and women alike as a distinct disadvantage within the context of female sexual appeal. At any rate, I hadn't gotten my hopes up and sure enough, no aspersions were dashed to the harsh rocks of reality. The main librarian had that characteristically stereotyped thin, maiden aunt look written all over her, with her white hair all done up in a bun, replete with the expected severely dessicated, spare manner of talking. Poor thing probably just needs a good stiff, regular, and rigorous *rogering*, but that's not my concern. Isn't there some sort of a mythical Librarian's *God of Books*, who appears out of a dusty mist occasionally to take an elderly single librarian and ravish her in the stacks? Must be! With the unabridged Oxford Dictionary of the English language propped up on top of Gray's Anatomy, under the small of her back, so as to give her pelvis the proper angle of lordotic receptivity? Gotta be! That would have to make this fantastical Patron Saint of Female Librarians *'Saint Peter of the Oaklike Whanger'* (or maybe just *'Saint Pud of the Prodigious Peter'*), I reckon, vaguely recalling my ancient post-Roman (e.g. Dark Ages) mythology. Wonder if Somerset Maugham had equally trivial moments like these when he was facing blank sheets of paper with volumes of weighty and thoughtful prose to produce, idly wondering how he could *possibly* meet his publisher's deadline?

Places to go on Moloka'i to meet attractive young women: *nowhere*. Things to do in order to be introduced to lovely young local beauties: *nothing*. Not that this is a major item on my agenda, but it would certainly be nice to have someone interesting and attractive and female to talk with occasionally during this creative hiatus I am presently on. One gets the impression that interesting single people (i.e. women) do not come to Moloka'i as a rule. Typically, families or couples may vacation briefly here in time-share condos, an'da local wahines hang wid da local Brah. Moloka'i is not, of course, known as a fun hangout for wild and crazy singles, so that is all as it seems to be. Still, can't help but wish there were at least a few brainy Courtney Cox or Elizabeth Montgomery surrogates around with which to strike up a stimulating conversation. The few half-way attractive ladies I have seen have usually been at the Saturday arts & craft event held on mainstreet and they are invariably very much 'with' someone. The island code of the local women wearing a flower in their hair to indicate availability (left side = taken; right side = available) is a lovely and definite plus, of course.

It occurs to me that I have been so preoccupied with writing that I haven't gotten much of a tan over here, despite my three+ weeks of residence. Part of this stems from an awareness that the effects of too much sun on the skin are, far from being healthy, very bad. I ruined my skin getting a humongous suntan in Saudi Arabia, deliberately flaunting that knowledge and now I must ruefully and not unbegrudgingly accept the fact that a 'sexy tan' just ain't high on my priority agenda any more. It has always been a source of ironic contemplation that while haole people such as myself consider being racially 'white' a genetically superior status to that of the other, naturally darker races, we all still can't wait to acquire a patina of dark shading (called a sun tan). *Go figga, brah!*

Meanwhile, snippet of background conversation floating through the window on the soft trade breezes as follows: *"...bark-bark-bark-bark-bark-bark-rowf-rowf-rowf-rowf-rowf-cockadoodledoo-bark-bark-bark-bark-bark-bark-rowf-rowf-rowf-rowf..."* and that reminds me it's almost time for lunch (sharp Cheddar cheese sandwiched between Ritz Whole Wheat Crackers...yum!). Dinner last night was remarkably improved over the previous efforts, since I finally found those Oscar Meyer smoked wiener links I had been searching for. The ones I found were short, stubby links about an inch long...perfect to dump on top of the rice while it's still simmering in the rice cooker. The result was more than just filling; it was actually almost tasty, although I managed to burn the rice. 'Afters' was about 5 big tablespoons full of Strawberry *Yoplait* yogurt. Yum! Gourmet dining at its finest! Suki would probably get physically nauseous just thinking about such stuff.

Let's see...what to do? Had coffee, whacked off, visited ancient temples, ate chocolate covered toffee macadamia nuts for breakfast, climbed volcanoes, read a lot, wrote much trashy and utterly inconsequential stuff, listened to the birds & bees, savored the sea breezes, conspired openly to annihilate all species of roosters, wished vibration-thumping car stereos were strictly *kapu*. Not much left except take another slug of Diet Coke with Lime and wistfully wish I were actually marooned somewhere on a desert island with a beautiful, wanton young island wahine, instead of figuratively cast adrift on one without same. Idle thought: Wonder if R.L. Stevenson had such insecure and uncertain moments as these, between his paroxysms of tubercular coughing while he over here cerebrally masterbating his creative neurons (probably...*cough-cough, hack-hack*...not, on second thought).

Probably the one person in the whole (very small) world of my acquaintances who will actually get to read this rambling narrative in its entirety (should he so care to inflict such needless abuse upon his brain cells) is my old *âmistâdé* from the Berkeley 70s days, the *Alcalde Honorario de Ajijic, Señior Estéban de Linea Corazo (de Los Huevos Profundos con Espiritu Sancte de La Virgin des Muchas Coitus Interrupciones)*...otherwise known as Stephen Christian Hartline If you run across this small contextual aside, Estéban, bless you indeed, me boney boy, for you alone and among all sentient human beings on the planet in this particular time-space temporality will probably understand the least bit of the worldly angst and philosophical frustration underlying all of this massive missive of inconsequentially compiled effluvia. [That having been spat out, only partly digested, *en avant!*]

So how did I end up getting married, anyway (despite the fact that the Christian institution of 'marriage' is at best a mutually agreed upon and contingently convenient state of suspended warfare between the genders—no credit to James Thurber for this insight, either)? There are many variations, each dependent upon who is asking that question and how flagrant a lie I feel like spinning on that particular day. There is one version in which Suki and I meet in the supersonic Concorde's VERY small restroom, half way to Kennedy Airport, while undergoing initiation rites attendant to induction into the so-called *'11.4-mile-high Club'* at an altitude of 60,000 feet. Another version has it that we both appeared simultaneously and spontaneously at the outlet of a very dark and bottomless black hole, somewhere on the *Third Bardo*, at about the level of the 5th dimensional time/space interstice. Another milder variant has us being introduced to each other at the Wiccan wedding reception of a local white witch (Suki, as a good Christian, heartily eschews that one). There is a still milder and more impecunious version that finds us encountering each other through a local personals ad column in a local newspaper.

Finally, there is yet another version in which we have actually dreamed each other up and fictionally exist purely as motes of Brownian dust that have had accidental sex with each other while in simultaneous transit to a certain far off libidinous region of the human mind. Whatever the real explanation, I was at first undecided after one date if I wanted to continue going out (I was, after all, a lifelong and somewhat contented bachelor), but she called ME up the next day to see if I was still interested. We got together again and the rest is *herstory* (and that is all I am going to say about this, despite a certain barely constrained compulsion to say a LOT more on the subject). Besides, we have to of necessity keep this all blather on the main track, without too many tangential side-track excursions.

Interesting to note that this laptop that was formerly my wife's, has a couple of electronic games on it. One of them, I found, is a game called *'SpaceCadet 3-D Pinball'* and that certainly fits, given my tendencies to navigate the spaceways of life like some sort of *fershlugginer* (for definition of this word, see *Mad Magazine Reader* #4, 1959) space cadet! I don't mind admitting that there have been more than a few moments on this trip when such idiot amusements have held great attraction for me. Dude! *Excellent*, Dude!

April 30th, 2005 (Saturday)

THE STORY SO FAR: REALITY CHECK! 6 more days to go before my flight back to the mainland. I am starting to see the wisdom of Cicada's suggestion that I spend a month here to decide if I like the place first...before making any decisions about relocating. Unfortunately, we have just closed on our property and NOW I am having lots of second thoughts about the wisdom of my decision. Although the property is 'only' $84,000, its assessed value at last Maui County property review was officially listed as $63,000. By selling it at $84,000, this gave the seller a $10,000 profit, paid the broker (Cheryl Apaia) her $8,000 fee and took care of a few other costs associated with the sale. Talk about fucking over the haoles!

Second thought #1: Suki may not like it here at all, since there's nothing to do, once you've taken the grand tour and seen everything. There are only a few Chinese people on the island, thanks to racial bias directed against the Chinese years ago (for being too hard working and inexpensive hired help—made everyone else look bad). The only Chinese I am aware of are the Chaos and the Lees (these latter folks are Cicada's family, and from what I have heard, her Hong Kong born sister-in-law is a real dragon lady and her gun-shop operating brother is apparently a pain, also). Haven't seen or met the Chaos, but they apparently own the large strip of *Kaloko'eli fish-pond* fronting property that lies directly behind our property (makai). Aside from them, I know of no other Chinese families here and the last census showed only a handful of Chinese surnames among the locals. Unless Suki were to take a deep interest in the locals, there probably wouldn't be much in the way of community affairs she could do (a la *'The Casa'* Children's Home she serves as a volunteer in, back at Sacramento). Further point to consider: her family all live back on the mainland and Chinese families always prefer to be close.

Second thought #2: There's no intellectual life here as far as I can discern, unless you count Sturgess of *'Sturgess' Coffee Shop & Gallery'* and the local artists (few of whom I've met). There are no book stores (which I feel is basic & necessary asset, no matter where you are), unless you include Jim's books at *'The Great Wind Kite Factory'*, up at Maunaloa Town. In addition to the difficulties of blending smoothly into a small community (as an outsider) that exist anywhere, here there is a distinct visual line of demarcation that further separates the *kama'aina* (long-time residents) from the *malihinis* (newcomers), and even within that tight milieu there are further in-groups based on skin-color (people of darker complexion are socially superior to those who are white, since native blood titer is the prime status qualifier). Hawaiian blooded locals doubtless view ultra-empathetic haole newcomers to the island with all the warmth and sympathy with which most blacks welcome white leftist liberals (eh!). Successfully breaking into the 'comfortably accepted' category here is achieved in one of only three ways: 1) you are a long-time resident, or 2) you have lots of money (like John MacByte) and demonstrate a willingness to use some of it to help the local community, or 3) you marry a local. Otherwise, it's 'take a number and good luck!'

Since we are basically very middle-middle class folks who had to go to some great lengths to fund this property purchase (I had to agree to sell both my Porsches and Suki cashed out some of her stocks—part of her PacBel retirement payout; further, we now have both the house mortgage payment and the property payment to make, which leaves us cash poor to a substantial extent for the next 5 years). The property purchase is just the tip of the iceberg (poor selection of words for this tropical area) and next phase is installation of a water line that will end up costing us at least an additional $10,000. THEN, and only then, will we be able to consider building something adequate to live in there. By the time we are ready to consider that, the cost will have gone up stiffly from what it is now, I would imagine (5 years or so hence).

Thus, the array of less-than-optimal considerations is daunting. If we had been able to purchase an already built-upon property (that is, with a home already on it), I would say the situation would be a lot rosier to contemplate. As it is, by the time 5 years goes by (assuming we live that long), we'll both be 64. That's a bit far along the life trail to undertake the sort of work required by this plan, as outlined. Of course, with current real estate rates being what they are, a property with an existing home would have cost us probably in the vicinity of at least $400,000, so that idea remained completely beyond any but the fantasy phase.

Of course, I'd love to be able to open up a book shop and coffeehouse in K'kai, but without any capital (or funding support) to do that, this idea also is still-born. Books stores and coffee houses are not big money makers (unless your name is *Barnes & Noble*), either, so lottsa luck there!

Perhaps I am just more susceptible to seeing the gloomy underside of things due to the fact that I am feeling somewhat 'isolated' here at the moment. Can't even belly up to the local bars and get a bit looser, since even a single glass of ETOH has a very bad effect on my GI system (for reasons unknown) and that's a great pity, as I used to really enjoy a little wine now and then as sort of creative catalyst. Moderate use of ETOH is always a useful 'temporary' means of overcoming the usual social inhibitions, but in my case, it's now off limits completely.

What I am starting to see is that Moloka'i may not be the answer I have been subconsciously seeking, after all. Perhaps what I really desire is a permanent orbit around Mars, or something like that. I am loathe to admit that, of course, since it was so easy to project my fantasies on this last vestige of 'old time Hawaii'. Even over here on isolated little Moloka'i, the basic signs of insidious mainland pop-culture (that I dislike so intensely) are evident: drug use by adolescents (crystal methamphetamine, or simply 'ice' as it's referred to); loud mega-bass thumper car audio systems; excessive 'car culture' (e.g. loud or noisy, 'jacked-up' pick-up trucks and SUVs); bias based on skin-color (i.e. white haoles versus dark-skinned locals); and last, but not least, evangelical Christians (there probably isn't another atheist or pantheist on the island, given the success the Christian missionaries had in routing out the ancient animistic religion of the original inhabitants). Ironically enough, Suki is also a good, God-fearing Christian, which is another consideration.

Some things to do today in town: Get a nail clipper (nails grow fast over here, seemingly, and my longish toe-nails really took a beating on the hike up the volcano a few days ago) at the drugstore. Look for some *Kukui* (the Kukui Tree is the official 'state tree' of Hawaii and its nuts have so many amazing uses that it is hard to recall them all) nut oil. Buy some cinnamon-apple bread at *Kanemitsu's Bakery*. Take Victor's beer over to him (if I can find him, this being a weekend). Drop by the (Saturday) arts &

crafts street market to check it out. Maybe get out in the sun a bit, since it seems illogical to spend a full month in 'paradisiacal' Hawaii without getting some sort of color on my skin (even if it is unhealthful). Drop by the local public library to check my email.

I am astounded to find that I have read through almost all of the 53 books I bought over here after arriving. May have to look for a few more, but the ones I'd really like to buy are long since out of print or currently unavailable (many published about Hawaiian culture by the University of Hawaii Press). *Hmmmm*. 'The summer of my discontent'. A great name for a book dealing with my momentary funk over how I feel on the subject of retiring on Moloka'i, at this precise moment. Can't mention any of this to Suki, of course, since she has gone along with my grand scheme despite some very strong reservations that perhaps I should have listened to. I should know myself better by now: a dreamer, not very well grounded in reality; a romantic, but not very skilled in literary expression; a very poor head for financial affairs or money management of any significant scale. OK, better stop there before I start getting slightly depressed. Need to shower before I start on the morning's tasks and it's already 8:30. Maybe I'll feel a bit better about everything after I get back. The big bumble bee I noted earlier seems to like hanging around my window, here. He's been blundering about the screen all morning, making a big, bizzy-buzzy deal out of it. Fortunately, the sound of his inept, droning flight maneuvers has a somewhat soothing effect on my mood.

Just got back from the arts & crafts market. Bought a couple of (Hawaiian children's books and some loaves of Kanemitsu's bread. There's an outrigger canoe race on tomorrow out Kaluakoi way. A number of the entrants are in town for it. This is an annual two-man and one-man race, from Moloka'i to Hilo, and several deeply tanned individuals from other islands are present. Number of women, too, all dark and buffed: *da kine dat look dey eat ums foh pupus, ho ya betcha!* Everyone comes to Hanemitsu's to buy bread before the small supply of the day's freshly baked goodies run out. I got 4 of their cake doughnuts along with the two loaves, since their doughnuts are also excellent (but just as bad for you as any other doughnut would be).

Had a chat with a number of interesting people at the arts/craft market (as usual) and found that one of the people (artists) selling things is an ex-CIA analyst (so I was told) who is collecting disability pay from *'the Agency'*. Further checking around revealed no one who was willing to admit this, so perhaps it was a spoof (although the chap who told me this I know from having seen & talked with him before). Lovely dark-skinned, long-limbed Locinda was there again (as she is every week); love to get into her tight jeans, of course. Eat your heart out, K2. Had one of the guys I talked with say some very complimentary things about our 'architect', Victor Montero. That's very reassuring, despite the sour innuendo that Cheryl Apaia seemed to cast his way, with aspersions about his 'beer-drinking buddies' (as she put it).

Funny how men seem to be ruled by the wisdom of their crotch. I guess I can take some small comfort from that, always thinking of sex first and all other things after. One of the children's books I bought was illustrated by a local artist—a woman who paints new-agey island dreamscapes, complete with fairies, mermaids, and such stuff. The fairies are all sans chi-chis and I couldn't help but think how characteristically gender-specific this sort of imagery is. Breasts are just as necessary on female fairies as *ule* would be on a satyr, I feel. Funny, but someone I knew in Saudi Arabia (a lovely slender nurse from South Africa I was half in love with) referred to such things as an *ule* as 'those dangly bits', which I thought was a deliciously droll way to put it.

One of the fellows I chatted with at the art market was a former customs & narcotics inspector at Heathrow before retiring to Moloka'i. Several people from the UK here, apparently. Suki's brother-in-law (Harold) would probably love that. Outside the window, sounds of the roosters rogering their flocks throughout the day (excited hen cackles, dust flying, etc.) and even wild birds getting it on in the overhanging boughs nearby. Spring is definitely here and at such a time a man's thoughts turn to...love? Nope, getting up a horrifically stiff whanger...alas, at some moments, such as this one, with no place to make a satisfying deposit! There were a few good looking young women at the arts mart, but most were either the *'eat you for breakfast and spit you out again'* type (outrigger canoe paddlers), or *'en famile'*. Very little middle ground here, it would seem.

Several people I talked to, who have been here a few years, confirmed that it takes some time to fit in on Moloka'i. The only thing that seems to work is 'time on station', to use the old military term; there's no effective substitute for years, apparently. One of the young artists is a good looking young guy (20s) who had some of his paintings out for sale. While I am not gifted in the area of painting, I am enough of an artist in other areas to be able to recognise and separate out truly talented painters from mediocre dabblers in the medium (he's a talented dabbler). The fact that this fellow is a painter, combined with his obvious good looks (he surfs), drew a particularly nice looking young woman over to chat with him (one of the buff lady paddlers, already mentioned).

I had a flash of envy for his ability to draw them out like that. Unfortunately, subtlety never worked well for anyone, to the best of my knowledge (at least not in the USA—might still work in Europe, where they are a bit more sophisticated and discerning). Painters can always sell (or try to sell) paintings; too bad us word-crafters can't as easily pass off our creations to make a few $$!

Definitely not inspired at the moment. Another doughnut and then some reading is in order. I'll take this up later. One local woman whom I was chatting with at the art mart said that you can over-dose on *Noni*; this I hadn't heard before. Most interesting and worthwhile information.

Library only open on weekdays (& Monday from noon to 5 PM). Drove by our property to find that the property owner on our right (*mauka*), parcel #23, has started to clear away the weeds. The weeds are huge (at least 4 feet high and very healthy ones, at that). This makes me wonder how we're going to be able to keep our lot clear once we are back on the mainland, unless either through Cicada's assistance in finding someone to do it or scouting for a local contractor who will hire out on it. The parcel #23 neighbor has a big unfriendly *'Posted: No Trespassing'* sign out already and the work looks recent. He must be in town, staying somewhere (or perhaps from an adjacent island). It will be interesting to see how he goes about developing his lot—have to rely on Cicada for some help with this, I guess. I hope she will be willing to provide a much-needed extra set of eyes peeled for us, in our absence. (It would make sense that she will, since we are directly next to her property...she has #21).

I see our subsequent steps as going like this, but God only knows where the money is going to come from to complete the plan (as below):

1. *Clear lot of weeds and spray with herbicide;*
2. *Install water line and water meter;*
3. *Hire dozer to finish off and clear ground level;*
4. *Hire contractor to install concrete pilings 8 feet off ground level, with concrete pad below house;*
5. *Build elevated rectangular ground floor on the pilings above the pad.*

6.Build house on the elevated ground floor deck (either from scratch or with prefab home brought over from mainland in cargo container—geodesic dome?).

Cars are parked under house; house has a double roof (air space) for thermal insulation from sun. Basic plan is for 1000 ft/sq, with one story. Solar heating. Water conserving toilets and pre-wired house for cable or satellite dish computer system. Two BR, kitchen, bath & a half, family room, and spare room—total of 5 rooms.

Overcast outside right now; lots of clouds over the island. Seems to be a spring pattern here. Fair night with gentle breezes. Rising trades at about 10AM. Clouds building in afternoon. Dissipate at night. Days can be warm (high 70s/low 80s), but regular daily breezes keep things cooled off.

Hope Cicada is up for a 'regular' dinner this evening (she's dropping by at 8PM), since I've had enough rice with something over too long. Could REALLY use a hamburger or something with some tasty & well-seasoned meat in it (but come to think of it, if Cicada is dropping by at 8PM, that means she will probably have already eaten—hmmm, better not count on a dinner out somewhere). Not in much of a writing mood today. I think that's because my adopted daily writing schedule was disrupted/thrown off by need to get up and out to the art mart at 10, this AM. I normally start writing shortly after I get up and continue till I either run out of creative juice or poop out. Afternoons are more humid and that makes it a bit less suitable for inspiration and 'freshness'. Among things I've done while here is an article for the Sacramento Bee about Moloka'i; we'll see if they think it may be suitable for the travel section, or whatever. Newspapers are always individualistic and quite quirky, from my experience. They'd probably reject a submission from GB Shaw, if the moon phase was wrong.

Lots of what I call 'amateur artists' in Moloka'i appear to have modest talent and few seem really gifted. A number of paintings by 'talented dabblers' being sold for way too much, but I guess that's because people with even the smallest amount of talent have an extremely low opinion of haole malihinis (tourists') art-discerning abilities. The artists hung upstairs at Sturgess' are even more expensive, but some of them are actually quite superb. The artwork on display at Kamakana Gallery is uniformly extremely expensive, but much of it is an order of magnitude above the Saturday morning art mart offerings, in terms of ability and skill.

Carlo continues to have some nice hand-carved deer horn items and other similar crafts. The other venders also have a nice selection of typical Hawaiian art (necklaces, bracelets, and shell-art). Richard Eloka (100% Hawaiian local) has some nice, basic pahus and fishhooks, etc. Never did connect with pahu master Bill Pekuni. Probably just as well, considering the cost of his traditional 'hula pahu' ($1250 for that large-ish shark-skin covered beauty of his I saw earlier in my stay). Guess I'm going to have to start playing the lottery to raise some money to finish this grand Moloka'i home idea of mine! I am reminded of comic Billy Connolly's famed song about 'Wellies' *("If it weren't for your Wellies, what would ya do? Work in your garden and step in the poo!")*. That's me Mabel…stepping in poo!

Started reading Queen Lilioukelani's book about the Hawaiian kingdom that she lost when the US annexed Hawaii as a territory in 1898. It was a sad moment in the history of the islands, without doubt, and a shameful one for the United States, given that the annexation was carried out through the concerted efforts of American business interests that simply wanted to be able to continue making money from their island investments (Dole, Spreckels, the 'Big Five', at al). At the time this annexation took place, Hawaii's native population had been paired down from about 400,000 to about 40,000, mostly through the effects of disease and illnesses brought in from other nations that they had no natural immunities to. Another tragedy involved the Chinese, who had originally been brought in for their excellent and hard work and paid practically nothing in return. The long existing US mainland bias against the Chinese greatly influenced this long-term prejudice against the Chinese in Hawaii, with the last blow being the infamous US Alien Exclusion Acts of the early 1900s. This concentrated effort to oust the Chinese has resulted in the fact that today the percentage of Chinese in the Hawaiian population is extremely low. Ironically, despite the war fought against Japan in the 40s, with all of its attending anti-Japanese sentiment, the Japanese population in Hawaii was and continues to be proportionately quite high.

Queen Liliuokelani had married a Scot immigrant (A. Cleghorn), which accounts for the rare beauty that their offspring was graced with (Princess Kaiulani). While Kaiulani's mother, the last Hawaiian Queen, was fairly typical for older Hawaiian women (large boned and very heavy), her consort Cleghorn is shown as a fairly tall and skinny fellow with a thick and bushy beard. The combination apparently was favorable for the princess, who is shown to be quite a beautiful young woman in all of the pictures taken of her, prior to her untimely demise.

After seeing all the possible permutations of cross-cultural pairing to be found over here, it seems likely that some of the most handsome people here have parents who are a well-blended mix of Hawaiian, Chinese, Japanese, and Filipino races. Gregor Mendel was absolutely correct about his genetic theories, if some of the lovelies on the main islands are any indication. Some of these strikingly beautiful island women are a strong argument in favor of deliberate genetic experimentation (eugenics),

I think. Can't even imagine what a world would be like in which everyone was equally handsome and beautiful. No more fat, ugly people discussing each insipidly dull moment of their lives with equally fat, ugly friends on cellphones in public. No more moronic individuals with marginal social awareness making the 6 o'clock evening news with their stupid acts. No more morbidly unhappy individuals whose grief is a result of having been born with homely features, weak chins, protruding ears, buck-teeth, flat chests, narrow shoulders, big butts, retarded children, et bloody cetera. Damn! Sounds great to me! Bring on the clones, Jones!

May 1st, 2005 (Sunday)

First thing to greet me this morning on *International Workers' Day* (all hail the Great Worker Proletariat!) was a big, squat cockroach that was perched soporifically on the ceiling, near the window. (We talkin da island kine, brah...*lahk B-52 boomer*). The kind that is larger than a silver dollar and twice as well armored. No teeny little hard-carapaced bit of scuttling activity here; these guys can make a good 30 knots when their boilers are fully stoked and they have a full head of steam up. Unusually, however, this guy just sat up there, hanging upside down and not moving, as if he was daring me to read him the rules of accepted human hygiene standards the hard way (*whack!*). Instant flashback to the old TV show *'Fantasy Island'* occurs, as *Poo-poo* (Hector Villanueva), standing next to Ricardo Montalban, points to the ceiling and yells *"Look Boss! Da bug, da bug, da bug...!"*

With all the gleeful anticipation of an Adolph Eichmann, I rousted myself out of the rack and grabbed the nearby handy aerosolized bug-bomb; after climbing up on a chair to bring the grotesque alien life form into full range of my deadly weapons, I let him have a full blast with the entire complement of my starboard phaser banks (just for good measure, I launched a few photon torpedoes at him, as well, and also ordered beautacious Borg-babe *Seven of Nine* to expose her high-tech killer chi-chis briefly to it on the stellar hyperspace communication screen). No response, unbelievable to this malihini as that fact may seem. He simply sat there without twitching an antenna and staring balefully out of his composite optical viewing components. Picture the sorely perplexed look on Adolph Eichman's face as he stares through the glass of his gas chamber at an erstwhile intended victim, who has miraculously produced a gas mask from out of nowhere and is making rude faces at him. Close...

Bemused, I watched this superbug for a few minutes as I made a cup of my special 310 octane coffee. After what seemed like an eternity (and probably was, in some other dimension), he fell off the ceiling and landed on one of my shirts. With this aerial high-dive act having been completed, he started scuttling off. The bug spray seemed to have slowed him down a teensy bit (he wasn't yet in warp drive), so I grabbed a nearby *slippah* (this is island talk for what we in Saudi Arabia used to call 'flip-flops', but what elsewhere is also known as a *Zorri*, a sandal, a *huarache*, and many other terms) and administered what I expected to be a *coop de grassie*. My massive slippah smash seems to have slowed him down even further, but after a few minutes this M1-A1 *Abrahms* main battle bug of the insect world started to crawl away again. Simply amazing, my dear Watson. No wonder it has often been said that these guys will outlast human beings on this earth (even more likely because they don't have fickle, nasty tempers and nuclear weapons with which to express their irritation, like we do). I finally decided to pick it up and deposit the little juggernaut on the nearest equivalent of a heiau *lele* (ancient Hawaiian sacrificial alter), an upturned plastic basin that lies outside in the back yard, thinking that perhaps he would at least make a tasty offering for the boids. So far, the special DDT salsa picante I sprayed him with seems to have deterred the small local winged life forms from swooping down on this otherwise tasty morsel. At least the birds have good survival sense around here!

Mentioned the fact that I am reading through the last reigning Hawaiian monarch's book, 'Hawaii's Story' (by Queen Liliuokalani). Since Cicada failed to show last evening (can't understand why, as I stayed up way past dark and waited expectantly), I whiled away some of the unaccustomed post-sunset spare moments by playing that electronic pinball game that I found in Suki's laptop. I also read a few more chapters in the Queen's book, as I sort of half-listened to Garrison Keiler's inspired humor on the Hawaiian PBS station (out of Honolulu).

One of the saddest aspects of Hawaii's last days as a sovereign nation (putting aside the matter of all the covert activity by American business interests dedicated towards encouraging the US to annex the islands), were the airs of pretentious and the slightly ridiculous regalness that characterised the Hawaiian 'royalty' in this final period. The Hawaiian Ali'i, upon having discovered how their European counterparts appeared and conducted themselves, immediately assumed all of the pompous trappings and pageantry of those royal courts. From my standpoint it was ridiculous to impose the conventional western (read: Christian) standards of dress and behavior of the Victorian era on the Hawaiians to begin with, but on that basis I suppose it was only natural that the Ali'i adopted counterparts of the elegant clothing, medals, orders, and military accoutrements of what they viewed as their culturally advanced, noble European peers.

The result of this was the Ali'i, acutely mindful of the fact that they were just a few years removed from being viewed as primitive savages by their western 'betters', tried all that much harder to adopt and affect the external signs, manners, and bearing of the European royalty. Reading through Liliuokalani's book, the high level of her native intelligence and successful absorption of a concentrated western education comes through quite clearly. She was a talented and intelligent woman, no doubt. However, the numerous superficial references to 'prince this' and 'princess that', ad infinitum, stand out awkwardly in her book.

From all evidences, the Hawaiian Ali'i were clearly obsessed with trying to continually demonstrate (to themselves as much as to the westerners) that they were every bit the respected and honored royalty their traditions and newly acquired knowledge of the western world told them they ought to be. The problem lay in trying to translate those feelings into the only comparative context available to them at that time, that of the monarchies of Western Europe (since America was a democratic nation).

Coming from a cultural background in which the ruler had absolute and unquestioned power over everything in the realm, it was undoubtedly extremely difficult (if not impossible) for them to conceptualise any other form of less absolute monarchical government (such as the modern enlightened monarchy that has evolved in the UK...but that process didn't come into being until long after Liliuokalani's time, of course), and a purely democratic form of government was especially alien to their traditional perspectives on social order. As a result, you had all these dark skinned 'royal' people traipsing about, wearing gorgeous gowns, costly jewels, and bemedaled uniforms, addressing each other as 'Your Royal Highness this' and 'Your Royal Highness that' while the mainland Yankees stood about taking it all in with a roll of the eyes. It must have been quite a droll and whimsical spectacle for many of the sharper, leaner, and more rapaciously astute *capitalistas*, as they circled on the fringes of the scene like hungry vultures.

With a 'Royal Navy' consisting of some dozen outriggers, a few rowboats, a couple of surfboards, and perhaps a motor launch or two, the bestowing of such ranks as *'Admiral of the Royal Hawaiian Navy'* (and so many other similarly grandiose parody titles proudly borne by the Ali'i) could only have been viewed as a true indication of their innocent and child-like (and therefore frightfully vulnerable) nature. It is of course highly regrettable that this perception came to be, but I have no doubt that their 'playing the role' so earnestly simply made it that much clearer to the capitalist plotters that these savage 'children', so caught up in their fantasy of playing regal kings and queens, were totally and completely ripe for the ruthless exploitation that followed.

If the Ali'i had been able to achieve a far more enlightened and appropriately egalitarian outlook, they might not have appeared to be so whimsical and pathetic from either the earlier or the contemporary historical viewpoint. I have no doubt myself that such a change in contextual circumstance would not, undoubtedly, have had much actual influence on the final outcome (e.g. annexation). My wish would have been merely that this might have at least spared the last of the Hawaiian rulers the indignity of appearing somewhat naïve and ludicrous as their fragile, natural world came falling down about them.

Perhaps the most important and lasting value of Liliuokalani's book, despite its being heavily artificed due to the Queen's desire to appear as 'westernised' as possible in its pages, is the insight it gives into contemporary Hawaiian culture of that final era of the Hawaiian monarchy. For that reason alone, I continue to plough through it, for, seen against the backdrop of American economic and political treachery that characterised her period, and all royal 'play-acting' aside, she and all of her cohorts are vastly deserving of our sympathetic understanding.

Interestingly, the matter of the last Hawaiian 'royals' aping western customs and protocols described above brings to mind another cultural parallel to be found in the Saudis, who back in the early 30s were still nothing more than a bunch of dirty, ignorant Bedouin nomads, scrabbling for a living in the desert wastes (although I am not really knocking that noble culture, since in many ways their harsh requisite austerities were aesthetically preferable to the hyper-synthetic and immensely frustrating complexities of our modern, high-tech western world). I have the same healthy and high regard for the ancient Hawaiian culture, of course, but both societies were faced with the immediate and perplexing problem of advancing rapidly into the 'modern' western world that threatened to subsume and overwhelm them. The Saudis were successful in retaining their sovereign autonomy, of course, because they had vast amounts of money at their disposal and were able to either pay-off their enemies or buy them out, whereas the Hawaiians merely had their beautifully arranged and furnished chunks of volcanic rock to live on and little else (no inherent economic resources at all, to speak of).

One of the observations that Liliuokalani makes in her book, for it is as much a revealing declaration of the Machiavellian infamy that lead to her deposal as it is an autobiographical sketch of her times, is that while the Christian missionaries ostensibly came with the original intent to save heathen souls for the Christian God, they ended up as the investment brokers of all the subsequent economic exploitations that resulted in Hawaii's loss of independence. Specifically mentioned (among many such individuals) are several of the original Christian missionaries, who after having established their missions sufficiently on Hawaiian soil, completely severed their ties with the religious organization that had sent them and plunged into full-time secular business activities that quickly saw them achieving a high degree of political influence and economic control over Hawaiian affairs. This was a pattern that became strongly established and continued, as offspring of the original missionaries were lured away from the more spiritual tenets of their religion to worship at the highly lucrative *Temple of Mammon*. Most students of history would probably shrug here and say *"What else is new?"*

Oops. Time for a big healthy dump. The combined effects of this morning's breakfast of battery-acid coffee, a banana (kapu food for wahines, gals...*neener-neener-neener!*), and half a loaf of Kanemitsu's strawberry bread, are conspiring to urge me to go pinch a loaf meself. It never fails to amaze me how this trash food diet I am on here recurrently results in these perfectly symmetrical little linear brown submarines. While back on the mainland, a typical dump would produce effluent varying from lumpy-dumpy dark brown pebbles to easily-squeezably light tan river sludge, here each a dump seems to produce only what I would imagine to be perfect paragons of text-book perfect human scats. For years I have been tempted to take a series of pictures of these little packages of metabolically processed and digestively reduced organic fuel, in order to highlight their uniquely distinct and varied characteristic appearances, but to date I haven't done so. About the closest I ever came to carrying out this plan was a short series of pictures taken after dumps in the toilet at home (this was in pre-digital image days) and three pictures of Adolph Hitler's personal toilet-bowl in his Berchtesgaden 'Eagle's Nest' playhouse (The *Kellsteinhaus*).

The former are now buried and lost somewhere in my thousands of pre-digital image photo files, although the photos of Hitler's W/C appliance did inspire several chapters in my great unpublished narrative of life in the Kingdom of Saudi Arabia, titled '*Wahoo Backdoor: A Thousand and One Arabian Days*'). At any rate, these perfectly formed little brown submarines all crash-dive without leaving skid-marks on the toilet bowl and amazingly enough, they also do not leave messy butt hairs to worry about, either. Simply amazing! Just another marvelous aspect of clean living in the islands, I expect.

[Note: I am always bemused when a post-defecation inspection of the bowl reveals a turd that is perfectly shaped in a question mark form. Is this God's way of sardonically and cruelly toying with us human beans (sic), I wonder? I suspect it is and that God is mocking us in His (or Her) infinitely mysterious (and doubtless cosmically humorous) style (in so doing) by giving us in this manner that single ultimate answer that the human race has been vainly seeking to the *Ultimate Question*, lo all these many centuries (viz. *"What the f**k is it all about?"*). That heavenly answer translates, I fear, to: *"It's all a bunch of shit!"* In that last sense, both Schopenhauer and Nietzsche were dead-on target!

As long as we've switched so blithely from ethnology to scatology, I don't mind wondering aloud about such things as follows: What does a gorgeous, beautiful, sexually alluring woman look like squeezing out a huge brown turd? Personally speaking, I am so much a product of our erstwhile civilisation that I can't even imagine this, due to its protective symbolic rapping of challenging taboos. We as a 'refined' and highly cultivated western civilization not only prefer to pretend that babies aren't casually created by a mindlessly horny man self-gratifyingly obsessed with fucking the hell out of some poor woman's cunt (in an act of passing and highly instinctual passion). We also pretend that human beings are not inherently sexual and sensual animals by insisting that they cover up all aspects of these natural reproductive parts (with clothing). In this last context, I agree fully with the nudists that there's nothing less sexy (and therefore more natural and well adjusted) than the display of the entire human body bereft of artful, titillating concealment of certain of its parts.

A trip to any nudist beach would quickly instill this awareness (e.g. the average human body is not intrinsically sexually alluring in the least, without at least some associated symbolic imagery and fetish-like psychological enhancement). Example drawn from personal inventory: 1) appearance of average young woman, not too beautiful, but also not too homely, in the nekked flesh: *some* interest. 2) appearance of same young woman in a tightly clinging black nylon tank suit that hugs her form like a banana's skin: *YOW!* Q.E.D. and the defense rests, yer Honner.

While I find myself somewhat involuntarily repulsed by such profoundly graphic illustrators of this principle as (for example) Robert Maplethorp, with his highly controversial (and admittedly somewhat disturbing) images of the 80s gay scene, the basic nature of the argument is no better expressed than therein. But (no pun intended), enough about such things as whip handles stuck up people's asses…it's another beautiful day in paradise and I'm still sitting here pounding away (on the laptop keys, you *dummies!*).

It strikes me that one of the problems we men have with such things as love and sex is the fact that men as a generalized gender are physiologically and psychically constructed to want physical self-gratification with very little prompting (often the product only of a mere thought or a random visual image). For the same reasons, once that gratification has been achieved, the moment is completely passed and over with. That preface having been expressed, another of God's cute little tricks seems to be that he has equipped the female of the species to respond the other way around (i.e. it takes a monumental amount of stimulation to even get her to think about such things and then only after LOTS of preparatory effort has been expended advancing the 'cause'). Finally, after WAY too much work by the male (that must go on and on and on, seemingly), she finally gets warmed up enough to give it some serious thought. By that time the average guy is always wandering around on the 16th hole (in the shadowy corners of his brain), club in hand, and wondering how to clear that looming water hazard ahead.

I suppose a man's idea of love isn't far from that oft-repeated joke about what constitutes a sailor's perfect woman: A retarded nymphomaniac who magically turns into a six-pack of beer at midnight. For this reason (and in view of the fact that such myth-ical creatures don't really exist), it is often monumentally complicated attempting to have one's needs attended to without suddenly finding that the cost for those few moments of pleasing pressure-relief (in the western world, under the 'Christian ideal') includes the permanent fitting of one's finger with a small metal band that is shackled to the (domestic) wall. I guess that's what God intended when he came up with the opposed-thumb feature of the highest primates: it does serve as an intermediate relief valve, short of the *Real Deal* (if it's any comfort, our little furry-brown Simian friends also relieve themselves this way, when there's no female handy—of course monkeys are far more fortu-nate than human beings in that they can just 'grab and go', whereas it ain't quite that simple with us more highly evolved hu-man monkeys).

Thoughts like this make me realise how truly enlightened the ancient Hawaiians actually were. Marriage was not a formal or ritualistically important deal to them. They simply decided to stay together, have sex when the urge hit, and remain with each other as long as it was mutually convenient. If someone else came along who was more attractive, nature took its course without any real protestations or physical fireworks. As a result of this VERY casual attitude towards mating, Christianity had a very hard sell, in its institution of marriage, to make to the ancient Hawaiians. I can just see all those stressed-out and embarrassed looks on the faces of the early Christian missionaries as they tried to get THAT point across and get it to take root (no allegorical pun intended) among these new-found children of God.

It's interesting how odd threads of random recollection tend to stray through one's mind as the ingested contents of a *penisbutter* (whoops! Make that 'peanut' butter) and jelly sandwich wind their tortuous way through the gut. I was just reminded of an old Filipino fellow (must have been thinking about 90 year old Selix, Inocencia's husband, who spends much of his time dozing on an old couch set up under the cool shade of the carport) I had as a patient once, many years ago. He was trying to give me his medical history and kept saying *"I had a pip in my peeni"*. I finally managed to grasp that the *"pip in his peeni"* was a reference to the fact that he had once had an indwelling urinary catheter. The "P" sound in most Filipinos dialects has a particularly strong recurrence (unlike "F"); same is true for the "B" sound. In Saudi Arabia we used to refer to Tagalog as *'Bukka-bukka speak'*, because the P/B sounds are frequently blended together labially in excited Filipino conversation.

Any old way, had a few other interesting moments yesterday at the art mart and afterwards that I neglected to mention. Aside from the alleged CIA disability retiree (whom I never found), one island guy walked by and lovely Locinda introduced him as having been a former drummer (bongos and conga drum) with Elvis Presley's band, when he played here on the islands. Yessir, old *Pelvis* hisseff. Apparently the effects of substance abuse had had a permanent effect on his brain, as Locinda told me he 'wasn't quite the same anymore', due to this former association. Everyone has heard stories about how Elvis was abusing 'stuff' big time in his last years; here's another curious little bit of correlative evidence, dug up where you'd least expect to find it...on sleepy little old Moloka'i.

After the mart closed up (noonish), I drove out to our property for a look-see, then drove a few hundred yards further east to the *Moloka'i Hotel*, where Suki and I had stayed on our last trip (October 04). The tide was out and I was able to talk along the Makai side of the ancient *Kaloco'eli Fishpond* and examine the volcanic rock wall that formed the eastern Makai-projecting arm of it. The beach was riddled with small burrow crabs, all snugly ensconced in their hidey-holes, the full length of it to the fishpond wall. All along the top of the wall are the sun-bleached remains of thousands of coconuts that have been washed up out of the ocean during storms and deposited there. About 200 yards along the perimeter from the short I suddenly stopped and found myself staring at what appeared to be nothing less than a baby's head projecting out of a woman's vulva.

Now you probably think I'm making this up, but there it was right in front of me. It was truly eerie to see! What had appeared to be a baby's head emerging from a womb was actually a huge old coconut, still partly wreathed in its fibrous outer husk. About half of the outer layers of the husk had been worn away and the inner coconut, polished smooth like the skull of a small infant, was still wedged in place. The three 'eyes' that every coconut has on the distal end of its inner shell were so perfectly aligned with the worn away outer husk that they looked like two empty eye-sockets and a small gaping mouth staring out of a baby's head. As I said, it was too perfect to be normal and unremarkable and the effect of suddenly seeing this was quite arresting, to say the least. Even someone possessed of a less than average imagination than I would not have failed to see clearly have this same impression in that specific light.

Oooogh! Boogety-boogety-boogety! I carefully placed it back where I found it, with a slight and involuntary shudder, but on second thought should have brought it back with me, since no one would ever believe the truly startling appearance it presented. Of course if it had contained the enchanted soul of some island *aumakua* (familiar spirit ancestor)...um, don't want to think about that possibility, really.

I ended up finding another, less scary coconut shell that appeared to have been sliced into two perfect halves. Since I am in the habit of carving the name 'Moloka'i' into a coconut each time we come out here, I took one half back with me for this purpose. This time I brought my super-gee-whiz $125 *gen-u-wine* North Woods whittling knife with me...the kind that has 7 traditional wood carver's chisel tips built into it. Always wanted to work with wood, but have never taken the trouble to do any serious study. Somehow, I feel that suitably unscarred and nice-looking coconuts carved with 'Moloka'i' on them (or perhaps "The Friendly Isle"?) would be hot tourist sellers. It's just tacky enough to have a certain appeal to the casual tourist-visitor who doesn't want to shell (sic) out $300 for some 'talented dabbler's' masterpiece. Hey, it appeals to me and I have a strong and remarkably well-defined sense of 'tacky' (QED: this book).

Sitting here a little while ago reading some collected 'gothic tales of the Polynesian region and ran across my old friend Somerset Maugham. It was just a short tale, but it made me want to revisit two of his more famous stories *('Red'* and *'Rain')*. Another respected Hawaiian named Glen Grant (PhD) has collected hundreds of stories of the uncanny and occult in Hawaii over past decades of residence and has published them in a series of books. One of these (his first such collection) is titled *'The Obake Files'*, 'Obake' being the Japanese term for spook, spirit, or ghost. These stories are all personally collected by Grant and are presented un-gussied up and bereft of embellishments; just the facts as reported to him by others who experienced these situations. What comes through strongly is the sense that all these people, coming from all ethnic backgrounds in the Islands, can't ALL be goofy. It's interesting reading at the least and compelling evidence at best to suggest there're a great many strange things we don't understand out there, that just because we haven't personally encountered any of them doesn't mean they don't exist. Excellent stuff to read by candlelight, I'd expect, and a sure-fire producer of what in the islands is called 'chicken-flesh'.

This reminds me of a place very close to work, back in Sacramento, where there is a resident spirit in the basement. The place in reference is a sort of 'no-name' music store on J Street, about a block from the Downtown Mall; it has a single sign hanging up out front that say simply 'Records'. In order to understand some important background information bearing on this subject, one has to realise that the original downtown Sacramento area was built on ground that was so low that every time the river flow surged up above its banks (which was frequently, a hundred years ago) the downtown area would quickly become flooded. Owing to this, after some years the level of the streets was built up so that what was originally the ground floor then became the basement area. Thus, the basement of this old building had originally been its street level floor.

Something shocking must have happened long ago, either in that basement area or immediately in front of it (now below the street level), for a ghostly presence has been recurrently seen in its farthest corner, way back at the end furthest away from the stairwell. This basement room is now used only to store old books and records, so it isn't often accessed by the public. However, from time to time strange things have happened to the people who work in that store. One of the most common is for the light bulbs to unscrew themselves, causing the stairwell and basement to suddenly go pitch dark. This most commonly happens when an employee goes down there to search for something. The employee will typically flip on the light switch before heading down the stairs and be somewhere in the basement when the lights all go off together. An examination of the switch when the lights fail shows that it is always in the 'on' position, but strangely enough, each of the light bulbs has become unscrewed just enough to cause a loss of current.

The most startling manifestation that is occasionally seen (in the far corner of the basement area) is the dimly visible and misty figure of an old man, who is reported to scowl deeply and wail *"GET...OUT...OF...HERE!"* in a low, but deeply unsettling tone. Or so goes the story I have had repeated to me by several people—two of whom normally work on the store's ground level floor.

I'm tempted (again) to say I'm 'dying' to go and witness these strange events first-hand, but so far, despite the fact that the place is located just four blocks from my Treasury Building office, I haven't availed myself.

Ooogh. Suddenly I'm dying for a good juicy hamburger. Haven't had anything like that since I arrived here and paid a stiff price for one (about $20), when Cicada and I visited the *'Paddler's Inn'*. I'm almost tempted to go down there again and have another one, but dining alone seems kind of awkward, so I will hold off. There are definitely times when being out alone and 'unfettered' is not a positive thing. Just having the physical presence of another known person at hand (like a drinking buddy wingman, if I engaged in such things) is very reassuring, but no such luck here. Wonder if Hemingway ever had such moments (*swordfish steak*)? Or Maugham (*breast of protestant missionary chicken*)? Or Alfred E. Newman (*knishes wit ferschlugginer sauce*)? Or Kamehameha I (*fresh, parboiled English sea captain, delicately spiced with tiny Noni garnishes*), but I do the Hawaiians a grave disservice with that sort of disingenuously aspersive innuendo.

Today they are staging that famous annual single and double outrigger canoe race (Moloka'i to Oahu) up at Kaluakoi, sponsored by the Bank of Honolulu, or *Bank'OH*. As I sit here writing like a listless slacker, those lovely, buff amazons I alluded to yesterday are by now half-way to Hilo. It looks like a good day out in the channel, with only moderate breezes and chop, to be Paddlin' Madaline home! Sure wish I were young and crazy again, so that I didn't mind spending another day roasting out there in the baking sun. Unfortunately, I'm all too aware of what the sun can do you your skin, as I alluded earlier. In fact, when I was talking to one of the older artists out there at the art mart, he suggested I get a hat and wear it. Then he showed me his face where he recently had to have some major plastic surgery done. They cut deep into his lower lip and left cheek and scooped out much of the tissue there—didn't say so, but it was obviously melanoma. I am well aware of at least two areas on my face where there are some pre-cancerous (so-called '*Actinic* changes') skin areas (on either side of my eyes) and I'm sure they aren't the only areas I damaged while getting my pale and pasty Celtic skin and fair complexion righteously bronzed. There's that irony again, about how haoles can never completely blend in with the locals without paying a stiff price in terms of skin damage.

It's a warm afternoon and despite the cooling breezes, I am sitting here getting humidly dank and more so with each passing moment. Didn't take a shower this AM and you can't get away with that sort of oversight in this place. Last night was a reasonably good one, sleep-wise. I managed to snooze comfortably through all the night-long dog & rooster choruses, thanks to the fact that my earplugs remained firmly planted in my ears throughout. I guess part of it was attributable to staying up later than usual (waiting for Cicada, who never showed). At home I usually go to bed at 9PM and get up at 5AM each day, but here I find I get up with the sun and go to bed when it goes down. It seems a very relaxed and natural way to work things. Wish I could do this back home.

Since it's now about 3:30 PM, I think I'll take a shower and then drop down to the K'kai wharf to see what's happening down there. Should be a nice time of the day to catch those cooling afternoon sea breezes that whip up the *Kalohi Channel* (the strait between Lanai & Moloka'i). The K'kai wharf is the only access through the formidable barrier of south coast reefs that ring this coastal area. They had to excavate the reef and dredge through the coral to make a ship channel, but once the concrete pier was laid-in about 20 years ago, it made a really nice, protected anchorage for passing yachts and other boats.

Carlo's old yawl, the *'Vanda'*, is tied up there. It has a pronounced list to port, so I wonder what's up with it; it's been that way since we were here last October. It doesn't seem to bother him, however.

Freshened up, combed some lemon-juice through my hair (excellent new substitute for hair spray, put on my 'stepping-out' slippahs (*dey look jus like muh reglah kine, y'know*), pocketed my cell-phone (that I don't need), adjusted my attitude (*wave shaka an make da kine smile*), and set forth on a voyage of discovery into sleepy Sunday post-meridian K'kai. As expected, all the locals were asleep or sitting in the shade wondering what the tourist in his bright yellow Chevy Cavalier was doing out there sweating in the heat, anyway?! Filled up the car's gas tank (low grade was $2.85 a gal, medium grade $2.96 *an'da regla wuz only tree-ohtoo*, which pretty much matches mainland California prices at the moment), then looped by the wharf, where I spotted Carlo on the starboard side, sitting in the sun on his sloop rigged sailboat, the Vanda. Didn't stop to think that I had a spare 6-pack of Tahitian beer in the trunk (which I would have shared with him for some *talk story* idle conversation), so I drove on by and back out to the Moloka'i Hotel. Some of the paddlers who hadn't gone out in the race had returned to the wharf and they were putting their outriggers up in the canoe barn, near the historic Kamehameha V beach residence site (now a state monument of sorts). Not much else going on anywhere, not that I expected much different.

When I reached the Moloka'i Hotel, I parked again near the beach and got out to retrace my steps on the eastern end of the Kaloko'eli Fishpond wall. Tide was out, but slowly coming back in, so I walked back out to yesterday's spot, looking for that eerie coconut I mentioned earlier. Didn't see it at first, but finally spotted it and brought it back to Ranch Camp to get some pictures of it. Now, we'll see how brave I feel about tempting the local *aumakua* by bringing it back to California with me. It definitely is a bizarre bit of natural strangeness. And somewhat more than a little creepy. Suki would have a double shit-fit if she knew I had brought it home with me; she is extremely superstitious about such things as portents, omens, spirits, ghosts, and other Chinese supernatural *boogety-boogety* things.

Thought about dropping by the *Paddlers' Inn* for a beer, but I know from experience that this would only bring on the usual flood of strange physical symptoms that no doctor seems to be able to understand. What a bummer to be out here in the middle of paradise, unable to get serenely blasted, and no lovely local girls to hang with! Moloka'i is definitely a place to send your husband if you don't want him to veer off the path of fidelity and indulge in a little fun trouble. More hens screaming in the background...those blasted horny little roosters again, no doubt! Local chopper passing overhead; must be the local *Life-Flight* returning from taking some critically ill patient over to a hospital on Oahu. And so ends another exciting, adventure-packed Sunday on this lovely little off-the-beaten-path isle. [More sounds of hens getting screwed—man! Do those roosters ever give it a rest?!]

Happy Mayday to each and every oppressed worker, no matter where you are! *This booze's for youse!*

May 2nd, 2005 (Monday)

Awoke to the sweet cacophony of more happy dumb-cluckers being screwed. The earplugs worked fairly well last evening. I dozed off reading some of Joseph Conrad's ripping south-seas tales. Last conscious thoughts were focused on what the tropical disease *'Yaws'* must have looked like, since every white adventurer in the South Pacific seems to have had it at some time or another. Conrad's stories of his voyages on the *'Snark'*, aside from being entertaining reading, are useful for highlighting a few of the salient differences between the ancient Hawaiians and some of the less equanimous peoples of the Polynesian region (head-hunters, cannibals, etc.). This was important knowledge to possess if any of the locals, for example, invited you 'to dinner'...or REALLY admired your hairdo... His writing reminds me that people always love rip-snorter stories that include a healthy element of self-deprecating humor. Conrad was famous for that and even now such a style is enjoyed by those whose idea of a good novel is somewhat above the usual Harlequin Romance bodice-ripper standard. This reminds me that in Germany, such stories are called 'Romans', which I suppose is short for 'romantic' and not the *Biggus Gluteus Maximus* type. I can only wonder what Conrad's companion/wife Charmian was like, to be able to share his adventures on the Snark with such admirable *savoir faire*. Back in the days when I had no really good idea as to what the medical condition referred to as the 'Yaws' was all about, I wrote a poem entitled *'Judy got the Yaws'*. I don't recall more than few lines of it, but that's probably all to the better, since it was not of *Nobel Prize for Literature* quality (close, but no *seegar*) and the person I wrote it for (who was a nuclear medicine tech named 'Judy') wouldn't have understand it anyway.

My favored *Moloka'i Coffee Plantation* beans are almost depleted and there will be no more available, once the few bags of them are gone off the shelf at 'The Friendly Market'. To recapitulate, the former owner of the island's Moloka'i Coffee Plantation, Inc., sold out to another inter-island coffee concern (*Island Coffees, Inc.*) and let the Moloka'i trees go to seed in their orchards (they are sun-grown Arabica trees). Therefore, once the reserves of the last crop are used up, there will be a lapse before the orchards can be made to bear regularly again. The last *'Grower Estate Reserve'* stocks of the old Moloka'i grown coffee beans are now gone, except for some local stocks remaining at the stores warehouse. I was told that most of their crop was sold in a bulk deal to the commissary at the Navy's Pearl Harbor base on Oahu, so bully for the Navy, which always has maintained fine coffee traditions. Reminds me that if I had to do the military thing all over again, I'd definitely have chosen the Naval Air over the US Air Farce. At the time I was poised on the horns of a dilemma over which service to join (when faced with a student deferment that was about to be yanked in 1966, thanks to President Johnson's escalation of the Vietnam War), my friends Mike B. and

Pete P. were entering Navy boot camp training at Treasure Island. I considered the Navy briefly, but the idea of having to wear those rinky-dinky sailor uniforms with the Donald Duck cap and looking like some grown-up version of a jumper-wearing early 1900s child just didn't do it for me. Instead, I ended up wearing the blue 'bus-driver' uniform of an enlisted member of the USAF, which involved a whole different set of experiences (mostly at a Strategic Air Command bomber base in North Dakota).

My references tell me that the first coffee was grown in Hawaii before 1817, since early botanical experimenter *Don Francisco de Richarda Marin* noted in his journal that on December 30th of that year he planted it in large gardens. The plants are reported to have died shortly thereafter, however. Eight years later, coffee was reintroduced by one *John Wilkerson*, who brought them from Rio de Janeiro and planted them on Governor Boki's estate in 1825 (5 years after the arrival of the first missionaries). Coffee has proven most successful on the drier *kona* side of the islands (in fact, the Hawaiian word 'Kona' means 'leeward') and today the 'Kona' coffees of The Big Island are considered among the finest found anywhere on the islands. Large scale planting of coffee as a commercial crop occurred in or around 1910, according to some sources. Due to a number of factors including pests, disease, shortage of labor, and not least of all the unpredictable ups and down of coffee prices, most coffee crops of the late 1800s failed, with only the Big Island plantations at Kona and Hamakua surviving. Coffee, as a luxury crop, was closely tied to the economies of Europe and America. As a result, when those economies were thriving, coffee prices soared; when the depression of the 30s hit, coffee plantations took the hit severely. Coffee as a sustaining industry in Hawaii only managed to survive due to a combination of Japanese field workers, subsidies from local corporate interests and the sugar magnates, but by the 1950s it was finally a stable part of the Hawaiian economy. Hawaii is today the only state in the nation to commercially produce quality coffees, with a total annual yield estimated at about 9.4 million pounds. Although the Big Island's 'Kona Coast' crop is most well-known, both *Arabica* and *Robusta* beans are grown at various places on Oahu, Moloka'i, Maui, *and* Kauai.

Going to have to clean up the room a bit before I leave this coming Saturday. I've tried to keep things reasonably tidy, but the room doesn't lend itself to proper housekeeping like a regular apartment would. Inevitably, small bits of food crumbs and such have fallen to the floor, making great prospects for the local bug population. Fortunately, aside from the Gecko mentioned earlier (they love bugs and insects), the in-room flora and fauna has to date consisted only of scores of teensy little (miniature or 'Menehune'?) ants, one die-hard cockroach, and a fuzzy little brown baby mouse (he doesn't actually count, since he was in the adjacent bathroom area). Other than that, I can thank my lucky stars that the room is equipped with excellent mosquito screens and so I have had no problems at all with those pesky pests. I can only hope that that small lump in my coffee cup that went down the hatch unseen (but felt) this morning was NOT some sort of insect and only a stray bit of oatmeal that got in there, hitch-hiking on a spoon.

Stacks of books in several places, all of which will have to be packed in my wheeled duffle-bag for the return trip to the mainland. Probably some food left over, which I'll leave for whomever follows me. Inocencia has someone else lined up to take the room for a long-term stay after I leave. It still amazes me to think that this room was once the residence of today's Governor of Hawaii, Linda Lingle.

It's always so cool and pleasant in the AM hours that I am tempted to remain and continue writing, but I need to get Victor's beer to him early, since he will probably be out and about later. Probably should also buy another loaf or two of Kanemitsu bread and see if the *Veterans of Moloka'i* office is open, so I can register as a member. They seem to be a good group of guys, but I'd almost expect that of people who have paid their dues dearly and largely without complaint, in order to satisfy Uncle Sam's imperialist tendencies of recent decades. *Mo'latah, brah.*

Went downtown and found Victor just leaving (it was good timing). He seemed to be surprised by the beer and I suspect that it was appreciated (although he told me he preferred wine!); he certainly spent some time checking on the waterline and meter, which he graciously did not accept any compensation for. Beer is the least I could do as a token 'mahalo'. Also bought some more bread at Kanemitsu's and was bringing back up the street when I ran into Cicada. She was trying to complete some tasks, so we agreed to meet at Sturgess' at 10:30.

When I got to Sturgess' I found Cicada and Ferdie, her husband. Ferdie seems to be of Filipino stock, rather than Chinese, so looks like either they aren't actually legally 'married', or Cicada kept her maiden name (Lee). We spent at least an hour talking things over, since I haven't had a chance to talk to her since my first day on the island. Cicada is retired from education, having last taught school about 10 years ago. She started teaching on Moloka'i back in the late 60s after graduation from college (on the mainland). When asked about the current situation (i.e. kids' uniformly poor attitude and the common disrespect teachers receive now from the HS age group), Cicada agreed that the situation has changed radically since she was actively teaching on Moloka'i (and she's quite glad to be out of it now, for that reason).

One of the things we talked about was how to keep the property clear of the local weeds (*Kiawe long-thorn* bushes). These things are tough as nails, grow about 5 feet tall, have tap roots that go WAY down, and have rather nasty spines you have to watch out for, as well. I guess the best thing we could do is arrange (perhaps through Victor) to contract someone to whack the weeds once a month (and spray herbicide) to keep them at bay. I should look into this before I leave on Saturday. I discussed the possibility of returning (perhaps in December) to supervise some further clean-up and also perhaps to have the land cleared a bit more (and built up with some land-fill). The next step would be to lay out the ground plan with Victor, then have the concrete pilings laid in (so as to elevate the main-floor 8 feet high, above ground level) and the basic main floor deck laid on top of them, followed by the septic tank installation and the concrete pad beneath the home. With those basic things in place, next would be the water line and meter installation. Then we could wait a bit before doing anything further. The final phase would be to decide on the house plan and build it on the elevated platform/deck.

Cicada's husband Ferdie fits the sort of casual impression I had formed of him during our only prior contact—a two-minute phone call. Friendly enough, but somewhat short on the genteel courtesies and a bit of mild (Filipino style) machismo in his make-up. He seems to be in his early 60s. That's a very cursory impression, of course, and how well can you get to know someone in a single hour of casual contact?

Went up to *Maunaloa Town* again on west end, mainly to visit the *Moloka'i Ranch Lodge* gift shop to see if I had missed any good books on the island. They didn't really have anything I hadn't already seen, but they did have a good selection of Hawaiian CDs, with an audio 'sampling' station where one could listen to the albums before deciding on one. Got about 6 CDs (each was about $24, whew!), but every one is a lovely one. Heavy on the traditional Hawaiian slack-key guitar, but also a few albums by really enchanting local women who have marvelously gifted singing abilities. There's a lot of island 'cross-over' music available, played by various local Moloka'i groups (example would be a mix of Hawaiian, rock, and Country/Western music stylizing) and much of that I don't really care for, so it was good being able to listen to each album before buying it. I prefer the traditional Hawaiian styles, early 'chant hula' style, and smooth 'new age' type interpretations of the traditional songs (such as the mixed-race group *HAPA*, some of these last being really rather beautiful and make excellent music for serene backgrounding or relaxation at dinnertime, etc.).

Finally, dropped by the Veterans of Moloka'i office (headquarters?) and signed up to join the group. The fellow in there wasn't very articulate (Caucasian, very much appearing of the mainland 'good ole boy' type, complete with baseball cap, scruffy beard, and shades). Probably well into a few beers by that time (noonish), but I finally filled out the card, paid my dues ($100), and presumably am now a 'street legal', card-carrying lifetime member in good (hic!) *sshtanding, yesshurree* Bob!

During my chat with Ferdie & Cicada, the question came up about whether or not Suki would enjoy living on the island. I had to defer that one for the time being, since it is a question I have also asked myself several different ways. It's a leap of faith assuming she would, but I'll just have to hope that she can 'get into it' without an inordinate amount of adjustment. As she would very likely say, *"We'll see, we'll see..."*; and so we shall, I hope. As regards the-wall-to-wall rooster population, Cicada says *"get used to it"*. Not only did the early Polynesians bring roosters and hens with them when they settled this island (originally back in 2000 BC and later in the 11th Century), domestic fowl have since become part of the everyday 'walking larder' of the islanders. I myself love chicken (cooked), but not so much alive and 'on the hoof', as it were, and I can do without roosters all together (unfortunately, the hens can't).

Tuned in to shortwave bands last evening, just before going to sleep. Reminded me of times spent tuning into short-wave bands while an expat in KSA, back in the 80s. I managed to dial up Radio Japan, Radio Australia, and several stations in other Asian language speaking nations (perhaps Singapore and Malaysia) before calling it quits. Rather lacking in literary inspiration this afternoon, so I'll let this trail off here for the moment.

May 3rd, 2005 (Tuesday)

Moloka'i's 'famous' Kanemitsu bread is generally overrated. It has acquired a local reputation of being *'onolicious'* (ono being the Hawaiian word meaning 'very tasty), but on the whole, it is merely *good* bread. Kanemitsu makes at least 6 or 7 varieties of bread with names like "Apricot-Pineapple", "Apple-Strawberry", etc., but in truth, they are all the same basic sweet-bread with some glazing on top and just the very tiniest bit of whatever fruit is supposed to be in them smeared along the top, mixed in with the glazing. As a result, they all taste pretty much the same. The one exception I have tried is their *"Tear-apart Cinnamon Bread"* that stands alone from the others simply due to the fact that there is more of the cinnamon flavoring mixed in with it. All of their breads make excellent and tasty toast, but the latter is indeed outstanding toasted. Kanemitsu started making their bread back in the plantation days of the 50s (so I am told) and served as the supplier of bread to the local plantations' work force. The standard Hawaiian bread that came into favor in that time was so-called sweet-bread, which is yellow in color (more eggs) and is noticeably sweeter than regular white bread. The nearest I can compare it to is certain types of Italian bread—probably one like old style Italian *'Panitone'*, but without the fruit bits that characterise that European bread. Half a loaf is a whole breakfast in itself.

When the major pineapple plantations went defunct (the last one on Moloka'i discontinuing operations in the early 80s), Kanemitsu was able to survive this unanticipated change in the local economy by continuing to offer its bread to the local community with a somewhat fancier image ('specialty bread'). Today, their baked breads are good and it's not hard to survive on their bread alone if one must, since it is appetising and filling. Kanemitsu bakes a range of breads and related pastries, including cookies, doughnuts, and breakfast Danish rolls, although their offerings change from day to day and not all of these are available on every day. One thing remains true, above all else, and that is that you must be there early in the morning to get loaves of their bread, since they usually sell out early (the 'Pull-apart Cinnamon' usually goes first). Still and all, despite the touristy hype about 'Kanemitsu's famous Moloka'i bread', it is something that no one visiting Moloka'i should miss, and the ramshackle-appearing bakery (located on 'main street'—*Ala Malama Avenue*) has over the years become something of a Moloka'i land-mark.

They also serve food there, breakfast being frequently enjoyed there by many of the locals. And of course, there are distinctive Kanemitsu's Bakery graphic-emblazoned, tank-top style T-shirts available that are quite colorful and probably worth taking home as a souvenir (the graphic shows a surfer shooting a tube at Papohaku Beach, one of the best surfing spots on the island--and there are many--with a loaf of Kanemitsu's bread in his hand; it's unique and interesting, and a notch above the usual touristy T-shirt offerings).

The 'Moloka'i look' is worth commenting on. As far as men are concerned, the darker-skinned locals, with their built-in intrinsic SPF solar-protective coloration, usually prefer shorts and a very loose tank-top. The shorts are usually either floral surfing style 'baggies', or the commercial spin-offs popularised by such firms as *Quicksilver*. Tank-tops are most often white (usual), with or without graphics. Youngish to early middle-age (but post adolescent) locals don't normally wear hats, but the younger ones (adolescents and high-school age) who have been sucked into the mainland commercial style vortices increasingly seem to favor that reversed ball-cap (gang-look) affectation I so despise. Older, fair-skinned haoles generally all wear a hat of some sort, with straw type 'Panama' style being favored by the most senior (who wish to eschew the stereotyped ball-cap look). These Caucasian types also seem to wear Aloha shirts much more than do the (darker-skinned) locals. Everyone wears the ubiquitous '*slippahs*', although a few more recently arrived from the mainland are seen wearing some of the newer, high-tech *Keen* sandal designs (expensive, too—try $100 a pair, or more) that now appear to be increasingly gaining market share over the 'traditional' German-made *Birkenstocks*.

Women's apparel varies considerably—much more so than men's—and again the styles seem to be defined by group and age. Local middle-aged women (usually wives, mothers, and such from the local community) tend to wear practical, comfortable things—loose casual pants, loose sleeveless cotton blouses, etc. The younger local women (school age) tend to wear tank-tops and that peculiarly popular type of low-cut, hip-hugger jeans that leaves the midriff bare (once again, probably due to the impact of mainland adolescent styles and trends), although shorts are also worn. Older haole women can be seen in all sorts of garish outfits, I guess thought by the wearers to reflect appropriate colorful vacation wear. Younger haole women are usually tricked out in far more body-conscious wear (and thank the gods for that, speaking as a typical red-blooded mainland male with the usual 'cheap' standards of female gender appreciation).

On the beach and by the pool, men wear standard baggy swim-shorts. This is probably partly due to the fact that most men these days simply don't have the physique to look convincing in *Speedos*, although I suspect there is also a healthy element of 'gay phobia' behind that preference, as well. The sort of regard for 'male beauty' that would prompt appreciation for Michelangelo's *David* (or classical Greek statuary) is anathema to most harry-chested, self-regarded 'real American' men, since rampant fear of homosexuality is so deeply ingrained in contemporary (white Christian) American culture. Therefore, even if a man had such a buff body, most American men would still insist on wearing the sort of 'Joe-boxer' progeny of this old-timey conservative look. Men who wear Speedos these days are generally regarded either as stupid (for failing to notice that an overhanging beer belly just looks grotesque, so garbed), or suspected as being overtly gay.

This has always been a subject of more than a little curiosity to me, since I have up until recently worn abbreviated racing suit briefs exclusively. I was on the swim-team back in school days and before a problem with foot cramps kept me from continuing to enjoy swimming, I felt that nothing was better suited for moving through a fluid medium than attire of this sort (the only thing possibly better would be to go without a suit at all, except that the drag induced by those 'dangly bits' might be something of a problem, both physically and aesthetically). I wore suits like this myself at the pool in Saudi Arabia without giving it a second thought, although observations there suggested to me that most western (read: American) expat women seemed to prefer guys wearing the usual knee-length baggies (probably a reflection of their narrow, Christian American conservatism, since none of them ever struck me as being too liberal or unconventional in their outlooks and/or behavior).

Contrast this strongly ingrained American suspicion of Speedo-wearing guys being 'gay' to the sort of health-oriented attitudes of Europeans (most especially the Eastern Europeans and Slavic peoples) wherein wear of such abbreviated swim-wear (more often than not even more abbreviated attire, such as male bikinis and thongs) is the norm, rather than a stringently avoided aberrant exception. I have no doubt that the mere insinuation to one such muscle-bound and thong-clad Slav that he might be 'gay' would result in immediate and forcefully physical redress (of the issue and the person), on the spot.

I guess our American fear of recognizing inherent beauty in the male form arises from our inexorable Puritanistic/Calvinist Christian traditions, that have in more recent years (probably thanks to the burgeoning gay pride movement of the 80s) considerably strengthened the already substantial American male's latent fear of being seen by his peers as homosexual. This sort of perceptional bias has the same sort of severely damaging effects on social behavior that ethnic and racial bias has (and this fact appears to be officially acknowledged through legislation of laws prohibiting bias against homosexuals on an equal basis with prejudice against people of other racial identities, religious beliefs, et al).

But, the logic of this awareness notwithstanding, the lasting conservative American bias against such things (e.g. homosexuality and/or an aesthetic appreciation for male as well as female 'beauty') appears firmly established and will probably never fully dissipate. This seems especially the case, given the fact that

American commercial advertising consistently seizes upon the 'gay fear' that characterises the stereotypical 'All-American macho man' image so often seen in the media (rough, tough, 4WD pick-up driving, smoking, beer-drinking 'blue-collar' construction worker, or alternately perhaps, the 'cowboy image', or any one of dozens more of these 'gay phobic' representations of American male machismo), to sell stuff.

Back in my mid-to-late 20s, I was going with a woman who had an absolute fixation about things like this. I was in the habit of wearing brief underwear and she found that scandalous, making it clear that from her viewpoint, real men wore boxer-shorts and not 'Jockey-shorts'. I merely found it more convenient to keep 'the boys' out of harm's way, whereas wearing boxer shorts created somewhat of a problem in a certain physical sense (with all that dangling, etc.). At any rate, this remained a problem for her. She either preferred no shorts or boxer-shorts. She was a strongly socialized good little Catholic ex-parochial school girl, of course, despite being quite intelligent; I always found this aspect of her curious inability to let intelligent reflection be the primary influence on her behavioral precepts (as opposed to deferring to the acquired biases inherent in her religious up-bringing) most inexplicable, to my way of viewing her.

Of course, when in Saudi Arabia (and not at the beach), I developed a preference for wearing nothing under my clothes. It was a decision based purely and simply upon expedience, since going about like that helps to keep one cooler in the sort of extreme heat that the desert regions feature. At the beach or pool, briefs (Speedos) were the order of the day for me. Of course, I didn't have a beer gut or overhanging belly and up until my 59th birthday really had no real fat to speak of, having always been a slender sort (the common German-language term is *Schlank*, interestingly, translating to 'tall and lean/slender').

One of the few really positive things about my wife, having come from China where such biases are completely unknown, is that she doesn't regard me as somehow odd for preferring the freedom and utility that briefs offer. Being a bicyclist and runner, I also wear Lycra tights, which is another type of clothing which tends to give traditional American males the cold shivers (or at least strong suspicions). They tend to think men wearing such apparel appear somehow effeminate, but of course there's nothing inherently effeminate about briefs or tights. Bias again exists only in the eyes and minds of the beholders. Of course, a further evidence of this uniquely American attitude is seen in the typical American male response to ballet. From the standpoint of most American men, ALL male ballet dancers are gay; it doesn't help that a good number of them ARE, of course, but these facts don't constitute grounds for the formulation of a *Masculine Unified Field Theory*, by any means. Again, we are dealing principally with cultural biases that have no discrete, inherent substance other than the fact that they are purely relative byproducts of acquired understanding, learning, partisan social/cultural perceptions, and contrived marketing schemes, etc.

This same ultra-conservative outlook is one of the most formidable motivations that spurred on the early Christian Protestant missionaries in their efforts to get those 'heathen savages' (read: healthy natives; well-adjusted, unaffected by unnaturally imposed artificial constraints of modesty, and comfortably attuned to nature and their environment) to cover their 'shame' with clothes.

Speaking of gays and homosexuality, it is interesting to note that the ancient Hawaiians had a far more liberal outlook on such things than their post-missionary 'betters'. Although there is no evidence available to suggest that female-to-female homosexuality existed (or the term: lesbianism) in the ancient Hawaiian culture, it is well-established that male homosexuality was a common and unremarkable fact of life in those days. There are a number of references available that refer to exclusively male relationships and even 'male societies' in which men preferred the company of each other to females. To my knowledge, there is no information on what exactly such activities or companionships consisted of at a more intimate level, but presumably they took the same form these 'same-sex' liaisons have taken since men first found they had 'dangly bits' that could inserted into various empty nooks and crannies. The absence of any reference to female homosexuality in ancient Hawaiian culture is probably more the result of the strictly male influenced *kapus* that structured all forms of normative behavior under the Ali'i rulers, rather than any possible interest of one woman for another, somewhere along the line.

Speaking of this subject, it was a great and considerably shocking discovery to find that a gorgeous creature I was strongly attracted to in Saudi Arabia was in fact gay (what I understand is termed a *'lipstick lesbian'*, or one who is extremely beautiful in the fullest, most traditionally feminine sense of the word, yet is attracted exclusively to other women, rather than to men). I certainly would never have guessed this unaided and if I hadn't had it broken to me by someone else whose opinion I respected (and who was also, incidentally a male gay himself), I would never have known it. Needless to say, it was an abrupt and unhappy awareness, although curiously enough, I suspect she may have been bi-sexual, since she gave evidence of also being quite interested in me (and it's quite hard to ignore those much ballyhooed *'dangly bits'*, of course). Later came to find out that there were many expats of gay persuasion in Saudi Arabia. This was partly due to the fact that Islamic religious dogma made it a serious crime for a single man and single woman to be caught together anywhere, at any time, whereas it was the common practice (for the austere Saudis, at least) to turn an unquestioning blind eye to any such pairings of two men or two women. This made it almost a paradise for gay expat men, since for this reason there pre-existed a large number of Saudi 'sidiyks' who were 'into men', rather than women.

I had the interesting (curious?) experience of being housed with a Canadian gay fellow named Gary, along with a straight (like me) Australian bloke named Bill. Gary was what many would call a 'screaming fag' in that he manifested a very definite and unmistakable (obvious) homosexual affect, complete with the stereotyped mannerisms, voice, and outrageous behaviorisms. Gary was from Canada and greatly seemed to take devilish delight in the fact that he had attended *Queen's College* in Quebec, which is a greatly respected and established liberal arts university. We got used to the fact that he was in the regular habit of having his Saudi *'Sidiyk'* male friends *sleep over* (ever since the 2005 Michael Jackson child molestation trial, I have abhorred that phrase), and it was also no secret that he enjoyed S&M (saw a number of pictures he showed us from his days spent enjoying the rather wild extremes of the 'Castro Gulch' San Francisco gay scene) and many of the FAR kinkier forms of voluntary physical abuse that some gays engage in (I could go on in great detail on this subject, having once worked at Highland Hospital in Oakland, where many of these unfortunates came in to have their serious 'private' injuries treated in the ER, but I'll leave it to your imagination).

Gary was a flagrantly out-going character to say the least (so far 'out of the closet' that he couldn't find his way back in, if his life had depended upon it), and he varied considerably from the sort of innocuous or unsuspected gay that one may find at the opposite end of the homosexual spectrum, the sort who appears perfectly 'normal' and gives absolutely no evidence of the fact that he sexually prefers his own gender. Since I was a native Californian, born in San Francisco, and a resident of Berkeley during those years when the gay pride thing started (70s), I bore no inherent bias against Gary of any sort and in fact actually found Gary quite a witty, intelligent fellow (if he could just lay off the recurrently heavy sexual innuendo for a moment) who was usually amusing, upbeat, and at the very least entertaining. I even got used to finding his Saudi boy-friends around the flat from time to time, and the proximity of this association did give me insights into his sort of 'gay culture' that would not otherwise be afforded. Too bad most other men are denied this sort of experience so they can see for themselves that 'gays' do not pose any sort of aspersive threat to their clearly fragile sense of masculinity. I am uncertain as to what happened to Gary, although I seem to recall hearing that he had taken a subsequent contract at a hospital in Qatar (he was a Registered Nurse), after our Riyadh SANG contracts ended.

Reading through some more of the tales of tropical life by famous authors, I was prompted to remember how wonderful my own place was in Santa Cruz, when I worked for the Santa Cruz Heart Institute (88-89). I had this absolutely idyllic little beach cabin that was perched up on top of a large sand dune in what is now *Sunset State Park*, just west of the artichoke and Brussels Sprouts fields of Watsonville and slightly north of the coast development called *'Pajaro Dunes'*. I had been immensely lucky to find it, having first and briefly been living in that fish-fry sum & bordello redolent place already described earlier. The place was rectangular, probably about 800 square feet total, and divided into 4 rooms (plus shower/toilet). It was made of clapboard, and a weathered rust-red in color, with white trim and a porch supported by two anachronistic appearing, neo-classic white pillars that faced the sea. The place had been built back in the 20s as a simple vacation getaway, along with a handful of others on the crest of this elongated mound of earth and sand that loomed about 200 feet above the wonderfully empty and limitless northern end of Monterey Bay beach near Watsonville. Over the years, and much later (50s) it had assumed such a special and unique flavor that the area of the large dune and its surroundings was made a State Park. Thus, the few existing cottages on top were surrounded and protected by the park boundaries, my cottage included.

I had been working in the heart institute cath lab and found out from a friend that he and his wife were being forced to relocate from this picturesque little place to a larger accommodation, due to a pending new child. I went out to take a look at it and fell instantly in love with it. It was perfect for me and all my many books! It didn't take me long to move in, leaving the ex-Navy guy and his fish-frying Filipina lover/wife/whatever to noisily reexamine their relationship each day, sans the benefit of my involuntarily voyeuristic proximity.

Thus, I enjoyed about a year and a half of perfect natural bliss in this culturally insulated and scenically splendid location. I will never forget my initial keen disappointment, the first couple of nights I spent in it (only about a hundred yards from the road of the ocean breakers, and two hundred feet above them), that despite being so far removed (about 3 miles) from Coast Route 1, I could still hear the traffic noise coming from that highway. There was a steady rumble in the background that I couldn't ignore, try as I might, and it kept me awake thinking about the irony of being here in such a wildly beautiful location and still being subject to dreadful highway noises! Of course, it didn't dawn on me until a day or two later that the 'bothersome' rumble wasn't highway traffic at all, but the wonderful, steady, and rhythmic roar of the restless sea, as it repeatedly broke on the shore below! That cosmic insight, when it finally hit me, was both endlessly funny AND somewhat of a sad comment on just how ineffably cosmopolitan my years of city living had made me! Overnight, that 'dreadful highway rumble' became bucolic, serenely beautiful white noise to fall asleep to, each night.

Sadly, in all too short a time, I left Santa Cruz (when the Santa Cruz Heart Institute was forced out by the ruthlessly aggressive competition—and dirty tricks--of nearby *Dominican Hospital*) and returned to our home in Sacramento, where I thereafter began two years of work at *Saint Joseph's Hospital* in Stockton. Still, when I reflect back on those marvelously halcyon days spent living on the edge of the Pacific Ocean, I feel fortunate to have been permitted that experience, as spiritually at one with nature as one could be in that otherwise well-peopled coastal paradise that is the greater Santa Cruz area. It remains one of the highlights of my life, in terms of the quality of life-experience savored there.

Note: Herein follows a special advisory to any of the female persuasion who may come across these words. What men *really* want in a relationship (isn't this what every woman is secretly curious to know? I know us men would sure as hell like to know what *women* really want!).

1) A woman who is intelligent enough to know that no matter how smart she is, needless intellectual sparing with a man is usually about as effective an aphrodisiac as a piece of ice dropped down his pants.

2) A woman who can stop thinking about the as-yet unachieved ultimate orgasm long enough to let a man gratify his immediate urges with her in any manner his fancy chooses, when and where (and not just in bed).

3) A woman who has enough sense to know that the best way to get a man to regard her with about as much dispassionate interest as he would subject the kitchen table to is to constantly chatter on about trivial things from dawn to dusk.

4) A woman who can turn from best friend and supportive partner into an alluring object of sexual lust with all the effort it takes to flick on a light switch.

5) A woman who can dress comfortably and sensibly most of the time, but doesn't feel uncomfortable about keeping a sleek black nylon tanksuit or two and a half-drawer full of 'special toys' handy for those moments when a sudden kinky feeling may hit her man unawares (and knows how to wear/use them).

6) A woman who understands that frilly, lacy feminine undergarments *DO NOT* turn-on most men, but that tight, black, and stretchy nylon things DO.

7) A woman who always makes an effort to remain hygienically 'fresh' and receptive, no matter what the time of day or night.

8) A woman who knows the difference between 'cheap sexiness' and 'sophisticated sensuality' and knows how to put that knowledge into use (as needed).

9) A woman who, although perhaps slightly conservative and modest by nature, understands the occasional need to let her caveman flaunt her in public, like the symbolic trophy he figures she figuratively is.

10) A woman who keeps the KY Jelly supply fresh and always within reach by the bedside.

11) A woman who understands fully and completely that all men are easily turned on by the slightest, most casual, most inconsequential sexual innuendo...and accepts that as just another of nature's unavoidably ironic (but immutable) tricks.

12) A woman with the heart of a saint, the mental clarity of an Emily Dickenson, the nurturing compassions of a Mother Theresa, the religious convictions of Karl Marx, the daring of a Faust, the spiritual courage of Joan of arc, the body of an exceptionally endowed Miss China, and the coital habits of a nymphomanical rabbit.

13) A woman who is so self-possessed that she can afford to let her male counterpart have all the glory, all the recognition and whatever else is required in the course of their interactions to keep his teeny, tiny little, fragile vestige of a manly self-image fully afloat and erect (ahem). OK, that's it, but you can quote me on all of it unreservedly…

I don't think that's asking for much, is it guys? Good luck finding one like this, though! Wow. All I can think of at the moment is how fortunate I am that my wife will never read this journal! Talk about instant *Lorena Bobbitt Syndrome…whack-whack-whack!* [Explanatory note for following generations: Lorena Bobbitt is a sort of modern day (late 1990s) counterpart of the 1890s' Lizzy Borden, except that instead of a hatchet, she used a knife, and instead of killing someone, she just whacked off her unfaithful husband's *ule* and tossed it out the window. Her husband, whose name was (no kidding!) *"John Wayne Bobbitt"*, was able to scamper outside, find his discarded *willie* and take his poor detached member to the local hospital where they made a brave effort to reattach it (they were only party successful, regrettably, although their whole surgical 'staff' made a 'firm' & 'outstanding' effort).] One of the wonderful things about journals like this is that they are kept only for the amusement (bemusement?) of the writer and are not intended for wide-spread disclosure. My wife makes no bones about the fact that she thinks I am incredibly selfish, and upon some reflection on that concept, I guess I am, but I also think that that is man's natural state (e.g. *'All for me, and all for me!'*). Women think men are absolutely obsessed with their *ules*, so I am informed from my reading. Naw, *couldn't be* (quickly and unconsciously checks pants to make sure it's still there)! Shades of *Bloom County*!

It's hot, muggy, and slightly overcast. The sea is choppy and the wind arrives and departs with small, unenthusiastic gasps. I'm reduced to my last Diet Coke with Lime as I forlornly scan the blazingly hot horizon for a friendly sail. If they don't find us before tomorrow on this lonely, desolate spit of land, were goners. Oops. Wrong journal, wrong scenario (takes another slug of Diet Coke, notes ripe smell rising from unwashed shorts, and finds the OTHER journal to continue narrative in...).

Left 90-year-old old Selix to enjoy the cool breezes that drift through the covered walkway that separates Inocencia's home from the semi-detached room I stay in and took the car out to the east end of the island this afternoon. Had the strangest experience out there. Having told Carlo I missed seeing the old *Ilio'iliopae Heiau* at about Mile Marker 15.5, I acted on his advice that there was another old and much more easily found ancient stone heiau (a fish heiau, dedicated to a minor god, Kulua) out on the east end, near Mile Marker 20 (close by Murphy's Beach).

Once there, it was as he said, relatively simple to find the old site, which lies on the *makai* side of the road between the roadway and the shore. There seems to have been an old hut built on the spot at some point in the recent past, covered in palm fronds after the ancient manner and it had a few conventional picnic benches outside to indicate people may use it for occasional gatherings. Although it is simple to locate, it can't be seen from the road either, so one must park and get out, lock the car (why bother? Old city habit, I guess) and hike up a couple hundred yards to where it perches unseen just over the downward side of a protruding spit of hillside that overlooks a beautiful greenish-blue lagoon.

When I finally found it, it was late in the afternoon, but there was a nice trade blowing to cool things off and chase away some of the afternoon's mugginess. I was sitting there on one of the benches, enjoying the freshness of the breeze and gazing at the stones that must have formed the base of the old heiau when I noticed a brief movement behind me, just out of the corner of my eye. The sun was now behind the hillside and long shadows were being cast by the trees; thinking it had been a bird, I paid no more attention. A few moments later, I again saw some movement from the same corner of my eye, so this time I swiveled around on the bench in time to catch just the faintest glimpse of a slender woman who was gone behind some trees before I could see much of her. There was no mistaking her gender, since she had had long dark hair with some curious gray in it and seemed to be wearing a white and green fabric skirt, wrapped around her hips in the style of a Tahitian *Pareo*. I didn't actually see her face then, which had been turned away from me, but she had a dark complexion—clearly a local. There is a native Hawaiian settlement close by.

The sun was getting lower yet, so I thought about getting back, but suddenly this same woman appeared behind me on the *other* side of the hut. This time I saw her face distinctly and she appeared to be young, about 20 or so, but there was that strange silver-gray highlight scattered about in her dark hair. I said hello, but she simply smiled—the flash of her teeth suddenly catching a few odd rays of the departing sun that still skipped through the trees—and then turned around to disappear again into the trees.

Her face was quite pretty in an austere sort of way and she had a look that was at the same time maidenly, but also strangely mature. When she had smiled, I couldn't help but notice how her

eyes seemed to glow for the briefest instant...or was it my imagination and the odd angle of the departing sun? She had no
flower on either side of her hair, but there was a green leafy
bracelet around her left wrist. I couldn't help but notice that she
had what looked like a purple bikini top on. Her hair looked as if
she had been swimming. She was pretty and she was nicely
'built'. Then she was gone and that's all I remember.

Odd, but oh well. I've never been a chick-magnet by any con-
ceivable stretch of the imagination, so I mentally shrugged and
felt as I always do at such time...a bit lonely and somehow once
again cheated out of a few simple minutes of pleasant contact
with a lovely young female creature. A little wave of chagrin
swept over me; always the same thing...a repeating theme of my
life. I am not, sad to say, a Brad Pitt. Not even his younger or
duller brother.

I stayed out there a bit longer, almost hoping that whoever that
had been would return and stick around for a few minutes. There
certainly had not been any guy with her. She did not return, however, and so after a few last looks about I headed back to the car
in the dimming light. Looking back, I didn't see anyone, but then
what had I been expecting, anyway? A lovely mythical *Lorelei*
right here on this single person's null zone of an island?

The drive back was uneventful and it finally occurred to me
that I had not had a chance to look over the old heiau site, so
preoccupied had I been with the appearance of this girl
(woman?). Funny how she had been so graceful, making no
noise at all on the stones or through the trees. Thinking about
her, I felt a little pang of most ungentlemanly lust rise up suddenly
within me.

After I returned from the drive, it was already getting quite
dark, but I looped by the Kaunakakai wharf and managed to find
Carlo sitting on his boat, the 'Vanda', opposite the side that lists

and cooking on a small hibachi. I pulled a few of the *Papeete* beers from the back floorboard of the rental car (having finally remembered they were in there), where they had managed to get very warm and we shared a brew. The boat was rocking a bit lopsided in the water...like a drunken sailor, I thought, to my mild amusement.

"Well," Carlo said in his thick German accent, *"So soon back. Did you find the heiau?"*

When I told him I had, I also mentioned the girl I had seen, giving him most of the details and not hiding the fact that I had found her more than a bit attractive, despite her brief appearance. As I spoke, he was gazing out at the water boundary where the Kaunakakai reef juts out into *Kailohi Channel* currents.

"Oh, you saw her then, eh? Was she wearing a purple top? Congratulations! She doesn't show herself for everyone."

I hadn't mentioned the purple swim-suit top. In answer to my puzzled look, he took a long draw on the warm beer and glanced over at me, beaming a shark-like smile as he continued:

'She' is a local woman that everyone swears is a ghost. According to the locals, she died some 13 years ago just off that point the old heiau sits on, while diving for Ahi. Accident of some kind. Her name is Corinne Popolohua...um, Hu'elani; they tell me her family lives just north of Kawelo way. I think she's buried there in the local cemetery. They say she only shows herself when she is not frightened by strangers who show up at the old fish heiau. I think she must like you, yes? Have you ever had a dead woman for a friend before?"

He took another draw on the beer and soberly gazed seaward in the direction of twinkling lights on Maui's north shore. He was not smiling when he had finished telling me this. Nor was he was smiling when I took my leave, a short while later, to drive back to

Ranch Camp. Across the channel, the setting sun was glinting off some buildings on Maui.

I am, of course, going to return to the Kawelo cemetery tomorrow and see if I can find a headstone that will convince me this is only another of Carlo's frequent expressions of dark German humor, but the fact that I have been searching so eagerly for my *white crow experience* makes me less than pleased to have this pleasant mystery laid to rest as a prank. Just for curiosity, I looked up the meaning of the name *'Hu'elani'*. The direct Hawaiian translation is 'Opening up to Heaven'. *'Popolohua* means 'Purplish blue, as in sea or clouds'. *Brrrr.* We shall see what tomorrow's trip to the Kawelo cemetery brings. A strange experience. A strange experience, indeed, for someone who does not believe in ghosts…either that or Carlo's sense of humor is darker than I thought.

May 4th, 2005 (Wednesday)

If I had to take one single impression home with me of Moloka'i, it would have to be of endlessly barking dogs and run-amok rooster noise at night. Of course, this is Ranch Camp I'm in and may not be characteristic of other less 'urbanised' parts of Moloka'i. Oh, how I wish we were able to afford a place on the more remote east end, rather than a compromise on the *makai* side of Kam 5 highway where we are. The good news is that we know our left side neighbor (Cicada) and our right-side neighbor I come to find is the nephew of a local fellow (nephew lives on Maui at the moment).

The big task that confronts me is to secure the services of someone reliable whom we can contract to finish clearing our property and then make monthly return visits to keep it cleared. I guess I'll head for the *Moloka'i Vistors' Bureau* tomorrow and see what I can find. The classified ads in the Moloka'i Island Times were no help. First call to what was advertised as 'CJ's 'Ohana ('Family') Yard Service' seemed to be some neighborhood school kid with big aspirations (lawn mowing yes, property clearing no).

Second call to 'Tropical Inspirations Landscaping' turned out to be a wrong number. Hmmmm. Back to square one. Maybe tomorrow will be more promising. In this search for just the right combination of capabilities, I am reminded of something our broker Cheryl Apaia told us: *"All Hawaiians are congenital, if entirely innocent liars."* [Makes mental note: not good, since we've heard many times that local Hawaiians are also lazy. I feel like a missionary must have felt, heading off into the unknown to save heathen souls for Jesus, difference being I am heading off into the unknown to find an honest, hard-working heathen to cut weeds.)

Just got a return call from CJ, who apparently used the phone 'trace caller number' feature on his phone to contact me, after I switched off. Turns out that CJ is the father and the school-kid is his son, 'CJ, Junior' (who had answered the phone and in response to my question *"Can I talk with CJ?"* replied with *"I'm CJ"*). At any rate, we meet tomorrow to take a look at the lot and 'Big CJ' will give me a quote for the job. 'CJ' is actually a fellow called 'Clyde'; I had called his home number, hence the confusion with his small son, and will use his cell number tomorrow. Ain't life interesting? Never a dull development, it seems.

Since I never have occasion to get any pictures of myself these days, I have fallen back to an old schtick I used to resort to in KSA—taking a few 'self-portraits' (now simply shortened to 'selfies' in our more modern social media age). Now while this may be considered an extreme expression of vanity by some, I look at it more as a sort of historical document recording changes in the old self. Besides, it's my life and I am interested in it much as an entomologist would be fascinated by a curious bug stuck to his collection board on a pin. Nothing really wrong with this, I think, since by so doing I only risk running afoul of my own disapprobations. The pictures are, on examination, fully as bad as I had feared: receding chin, barely kept in check with the Abraham Lincoln style goatee, gray hair gaining a noticeable foothold above ears, eyes reflecting a sort of uncertainty about them (have to remind myself to squint more often, like Clint Eastwood did; hey, it worked for him!). Other changes not so noticeable in the pictures: loss of skin elasticity all over, due to the savaging effects of the sun exposure in KSA (collagen destruction), some pre-cancerous skin changes on the cheeks (around the edges of the eyes--not good!) and perhaps even a bit of recently added adipose (too many chocolate toffee Macadamia nuts over the past week) around the midriff. The oval neck amulet is a small section of Tiger Shark skin, with a *Tiger Shark* tooth affixed to it (from Aussie friend, 'Dr. Shark' in Oz); the other item on silver chain is something Suki brought back for me from New Zealand, which I have always very much liked (it's a good-luck charm): a beautiful piece of jade-like stone carved into what the Maori aboriginals call the *'Path of Eternity'* (the stone is shaped in the form of a highly stylized *mobius* loop, without start or finish, and beautifully worked by hand—very unique item, actually). The hat, of course, is one I wore during the 1991 Gulf War in KSA; it's an old friend (lots of *mana*) that I take whenever I'm out somewhere 'adventuring'.

Breakfast was again library paste (Quaker Instant Oats) with the last of the dried cranberries, coffee (no bananas left), and the usual handful of vitamin and mineral supplements. Old Selix is out in the back yard, puttering about the grounds, raking up small leaves that have fallen from the Mango and Papaya trees. I guess this is what helps keep him going—90 years old! Tough old bird who obviously worked hard during his younger days, perhaps on the plantation.

Note on coconut carving: I managed to carve that coconut half mentioned earlier. I was reminded that carving coconut shells is much easier when the outer husk is still fresh and green; once the outer husk has become hard, they are a bitch to carve without screwing things up radically, through haste or impatience. This is good therapy and I find I enjoy it, although the small degree of dexterity I used to enjoy with my hands is greatly diminished from previous years (reason I don't attempt plastic model kits anymore). Wonder of I'd be any good at trying to make a hula pahu from a sectioned slice of coconut trunk? Just tried to reach Bill Pekuni, the pahu master, again. No joy. Maybe later. Only 4 days left to get this taken care of.

One thing about Moloka'i is the fact that fresh fish are commonly available every day. If not your own catch, someone else's. There are more highly edible species in the local waters than most can imagine. While I wouldn't want to tempt fate by doing any underwater spear-fishing, it's reportedly easy enough to drop a line in the water just about anywhere on the island and easily catch your limit within an hour. I've never been much of a fisherman (even trying to learn the knack of fly-fishing under Uncle Charlie's expert tutelage in Sun Valley, back in the late 50s/early 60s, but without much encouraging evidence of real piscatorial skill either then or now).

When living in Santa Cruz I even bought a surf casting rod & reel (still have it at home, in the garage), since I recall Dad formerly used to engage in that sport but never once caught anything with it. More proof of deficit talent in the Ichthyologic Department, I fear. Not much of a hunter/gatherer or fisherman, and definitely not much good at the ancient Neanderthal sport of clubbing women over the head and dragging them home. Impression: would have made a lousy stone-ager (also known as an easy meal for a Saber-Toothed Tiger), I'm afraid.

If we ever end up retiring over here, I would probably look forward to kayaking around the reef and fishpond areas. Maybe then stop and drop a line over the side, earlier in the AM hours before the trades pick up and make the waters a bit choppy. I haven't the extreme motivation to take up serious out-rigger racing (like some of the buff women I mentioned I ran into, yesterday), but at least I am fairly adept at splashing innocently about in a sea-going (keeled) kayak (thanks to former youthful days spent as an expert canoer and sailing instructor).

"Arrr, matey. We be castin' off soon for fearsome adventures with our rubber ducky. Avast! Yessir, the scourge of the local duck pond, that's our Crusty Christian. Beat to quarters, Mr. Cuthbert! Arrrr-arrrr-arrrr!" (I think that's how blood-thirsty pirates are supposed to talk, anyway). "A man's got to do what a man's got to do, Jaimie me boy! Arrr, etc., etc."

Email from the other Aviation Museum board members informs me that our museum's Convair F-106A *Delta Dart* has now been successfully taken apart at AMARC (Aircraft Maintenance and Regeneration Center, located at Tucson, AZ) and is in the process of being loaded up for shipment to us in Sacramento (they said that there was still 30 gallons of overlooked JP-4 left in one of its wing-tanks, surprise!). Just my blasted luck to miss out on this once-in-a-lifetime adventure, retrieving a rare surviving specimen of my favorite aircraft from its hibernation out on the desert wastes for display resurrection at MAM. The process was delayed so many times, fraught with so many setbacks and broken deadlines (due to technical difficulties and political/bureaucratic hurdles at AMARC), that by the time the plan was finally cleared for take-off, I was over here on Moloka'i. I'll probably arrive back in Suckatomato at just about the same time it rolls in on the truck. At least I'll get to participate in helping put it back together.

Took a bit of time off to return to the Kawalo area just now, to check on that cemetery, as related yesterday. I searched the whole area over several times and found no such grave for a *Corinne Popolohu Hu'elani*, although there two *other* Hu'elani graves (both men). This is probably sufficient evidence to conclude that Carlo was having a bit of fun with me about the ghostly girl at the heiau, but he persists in maintaining a straight face when he assures me that this is in very real fact no joke! That also doesn't explain away the perplexing fact that I hadn't mentioned the purple color of the swim-suit top she was wearing!

I suppose I'll never really be sure, one way or another, but I know that what I saw was no day-dream. She appeared as solid and real as anyone can be. You just can't imagine visual details like that and others aren't able to routinely read minds, either; I also haven't had any *Awa* (intoxicating, mildly hallucinogenic ancient Hawaiian beverage) recently, either! At any rate, I guess I owe Carlo another 6-pack of Papeete Beer for at least giving me a most unusual experience (and unforgettable) that I cannot explain away with logic, reason, or any other conventional science-based process of rational understanding! I'm greatly tempted to return to the heiau and see if I can repeat the experience...

Thinking about that lovely vision of (spectral?) beauty, I am reminded of the way the ancient Hawaiians instituted what passed for marriage in their traditional (pre-missionary) culture. As I observed earlier in this rambling narrative, nothing approaching a conventional western 'sacrament of marriage' was carried out when a man & woman decided to mate. The only officiation of their status consisted of having them 'sleep with each other' (according to the references) in the presence of the local priests. Whether this 'sleeping together' consisted of simply falling asleep and sawing Zzzz next to each other under the same *kappa* (native paper-like fabric made from tree-bark), or whether it meant getting it on coitally under the approving gaze of the elders, is left to speculation. I can't personally imagine feeling comfortable enough to screw someone (no matter how beautiful or alluring) as the grandparents watched, approvingly (but on second thought, perhaps that's just my own hang-up, based on cultural socialization under western customs and practices), so I'll assume that the 'sleeping together' was actually that and not wild coital debauchery.

One of the unique characteristics of the ancient Hawaiian culture that continually had the Christian missionaries sorely vexed was the perfectly natural native custom of what they (the missionaries) called 'an extreme act of apostasy'. By this, I mean the 'incestuous' practice of brothers and sisters 'marrying' (or even fathers and daughters, and sons and mothers). Although from a western scientific (genetic) standpoint this sort of behavior can have some very untoward results in terms of recessive genes being passed along to any offspring produced by the pairing, the custom was resorted to when a woman or man was considered to be of such 'high birth' (among the high Ali'i, or Hawaiian royalty) that a suitable mate of equal status could not be found. In that event, it was considered that the mating of a man and woman of the same immediate family bloodline was preferable to the mating of social un-equals. Thus, a brother and sister could (and frequently did) screw each other without much to-do. The curious thing about this is that there appears to be little documentation on the practice that survives today, despite the fact that even by non-scientific (i.e. Christian) standards, such behavior was regarded as being extremely reprehensible by the missionaries.

I am guessing that due to the extremely 'delicate' nature of this practice, the morally conservative and easily scandalised Christian missionaries were more than a bit reticent to discuss the matter, except within the most objective and figurative (religious) context. This is in all likelihood the chief reason why there was not much information on this subject recorded by those worthies that has survived to be passed along in their otherwise fairly comprehensive chronicles of heathen life. Too bad, too, since the speculative symbolic imagery of a brother and sister enjoying each other's healthy natural sexuallity is an attractive one, as long as the scientific and religious proscriptions have been carefully excised and set aside (observing good aesthetic surgical technique, of course). [A note to any righteously anointed Christian readers, here, who may be reading this: Remember, folks, I'm no God-fearing Christian myself; life is boring enough without removing some of the fun that such possibilities offer. If I had an absolutely drop-dead beautiful sister and I lived on an island paradise, I'd probably waste no time exploring her up-thrust mountains and lush, moist valleys myself. *Genetics and recessive genes be damned*!] We humans are, pretenses of being 'civilised' aside, merely evolved animals of a slightly higher order of development (and not much more, at that!).

Another common ancient Hawaiian cultural practice that was NOT quite so pleasant to contemplate was that of infanticide. According to many sources I have accessed, unwanted infants (there being no absolutely reliable birth control, per se, available—although some Kahuna-prescribed herbal preparations were used for this purpose) were not uncommonly killed. Apparently, if a child was born with less than perfectly normal features (and due to incestual mating customs, this was likely fairly common), that infant would be disposed of at birth. This apparently was routinely done by burying the infant alive, from what I read.

That seems more than a little heartless, given the fact that even sacrificial victims were usually strangled first, before being offered up at the heiau. However, I am reminded that human life mattered very little in a greater, overall context to the Hawaiians since theirs was a culture in which the social needs of all came far ahead of the needs of an individual. As Americans, who have been brought up from earliest childhood to subscribe to and embrace the ascendancy of individual rights over those of the majority, such an attitude seems grossly wrong. From my own personal viewpoint, as a person who has always felt the needs of the group should properly outweigh the rights and privileges of any individual member of society (within reason, of course), the practice in reference is slightly less shocking. In the absence of an artificially formulated religious proscription against such a practice, it undoubtedly made perfect sense to the early Hawaiians to kill a baby born with congenital defects of any discernible kind. The manner they used for killing the infants is still somewhat disturbing, however. Hawaiian eugenics, eh! *Huh!*

There's not much on the record concerning how the ancient culture treated mental illness, except for a few references to various individuals who were apparently so inflicted (again, such references as exist had to be passed along via oral histories, since there was no written language with which to record incidents of any possible relevance here), and the existence of several Hawaiian words that translate to 'sick in the head'.

It is also a fact that it was not unusual for Hawaiians (at least during the later Ali'i period, after the arrival of the priest Pa'ao (who incidentally was supposed to have white skin, and thereby assumed to be 'Caucasian', curiously enough) to regard very elderly members of the family as useless and not worth taking the requisite trouble to sustain, in the event they were incapacitated or incapable of supporting themselves. While this information conflicts somewhat with oral history information passed along about pre-Ali'i family customs on Moloka'i, it may in fact have some bearing on changes in ancient Hawaiian society that were due to or brought about by changes in the religion that occurred after the arrival of Pa'ao in the 11th or 12th Century. At any rate, the mention is made in several places that this was the later custom.

Naturally, as a western-raised person, the practices of infanticide and geriatricide seem unfortunate and somewhat disturbing to me (Haole kapu?), but seen strictly within the cultural context of their own civilisation ('Primitive cultures basic rule #1', as the cultural anthropologists are always reminding us), such customs appear perfectly functional and pragmatically practical.

I can hear the solar-heating water system cycling on the roof overhead. Apparently small, individual solar heating systems are routinely used on Moloka'i to provide hot water. Seems almost every home has some sort of solar water heating array on the roof, and why not? Now if they could simply harness the wind to tap into that cheap power source (the trade winds are always blowing here), they'd have the perfect little home-based closed system. Mainline electrical power on Moloka'i is provided by petroleum-fuel powered generation, as might be expected. There have been a few attempts to harness wind power on the other islands, but the cost of mechanical maintenance for those early and less efficient systems were so high that they ultimately failed. I am advised that with today's available state-of-the-art technology, such wind driven power generation schemes are once more cost-effective, but there has been little development of individual (residentially appropriate) private systems done, to my knowledge; most of the research has been done in terms of larger area-wide generation systems.

My friend the bumble-bee has been absent for a day or two. He is now back at his usual habits of buzzing ponderously about the awning, just outside my window. It's a good thing I enjoy writing, as otherwise I'd be hard pressed to stay amused during my stay here. Reading & writing are two favorite pastimes, of course, but neither is very demanding physically. I'm glancing down at my waistline, something I've never paid much attention to owing to the fact that I've always been on the slender side. However, these past 28 days or so have not involved much physical activity (aside from the volcano climb already mentioned) and the cumulative effect of this lethargy and the delicious chocolate covered toffee macadamia nuts that are a particular failing of mine has been a noticeable bit of added padding around the gut. Not much, but enough to make me take notice.

Horrors! My worst nightmare is (and always has been) being fat and out of shape. I can't wait to get back to the daily bicycle ride and a muscle toning work out at home on the *OwFlex* torture rack. If we end up retiring over here, I'll have to devise some sort of daily exercise regime to help stave off these prospects that are so especially loathsome to me. Maybe running, but that's not good for the knees at this stage of life. Bicycling would be best, but given the traffic habits here and the routine DUI pattern that prevails among the locals, bike-riding is not without considerable risk on the island (from what I have seen and heard).

One awareness seems to be vaguely developing within me, thanks to the reflection pause this past few weeks has afforded me. That is, perhaps life in the islands is not as perfectly suited to me as I may have earlier thought. It may well be that what I need more is a life on the mainland in the northern part of the state, perhaps somewhere along the north coast of California. I've always enjoyed the mountains and cooler climates found along the coast, so perhaps what I would really like is that sort of a climate-suited venue. Moloka'i would be wonderful, if I weren't so concerned about exercise, getting old and fat, and suffering from the sort of indolent lifestyle that characterises life in the islands. Further, my far too idealistic and enthusiastic preconceived notions about a sense of 'community' here may also have been slightly premature, given the wide divergence that seems to exist between several different groups that one finds here.

An additional concern is the contamination of the island's adolescents by mainland pop-culture (and American mainstream attitudes) that is already noticeable may just be the tip of the iceberg. If this process continues to develop unchecked (and there's no reason to suspect it won't, given the immediate access of media and internet entertainment, with its unhappy and highly exploitative commercial effects accessed through electronic technology), Moloka'i won't be half as insular and/or remote from these progressively deleterious cultural disruptions are I would hope it would remain.

Whatever the final impact on my perceptions, after I fly back to the mainland, I feel I have definitely rushed into our purchase of a plot of land here a bit prematurely (that is, without giving this a lot of wise reflection beforehand) and we are now faced with this unavoidable and concrete reality to deal with in future as best we are able. If we are very, very lucky, the value of the land may rise significantly in the 4 years ahead of us, and in that event we should be able to sell it at a small profit (perhaps $20,000). Meanwhile, however, we have to gear down to some serious meeting of the added financial responsibility that this new drain on our income poses. Consequently, perhaps I should investigate going on a regimen of Prozac to help me adjust to the unhappy realities of life that I thought were pressing in on me too much back home. Hmmm…strokes graying goatee absentmindedly for a second (but checks the unconscious urge to reach for another chocolate covered toffee macadamia nut).

In any comprehensive assessment of Hawaiian civilisation, from earliest origins through the latest period, one cannot but literally collide with the view that the early Christian missionaries were more of a harmful element (in the broadest sense) than a helpful one, considering the radical changes that the new religion brought to the Hawaiian islanders. It seems to be equally popular to take either one or the polar opposite other of two attitudes in this matter. There are those who will opine without restraint that the missionaries had, in their earnest desire to save the heathens' souls for their Christian god, by far a positive effect. There is another equally outspoken sentiment that the Christian missionaries bore ultimate responsibility for the fall of the Hawaiian monarchy (and the resulting loss of Hawaiian autonomy).

Both seem to carry partial validity, in my consideration, since there are as many positive as there were negative aspects of the early Christian missionaries' work. Among the most positive were the efforts they made to study and record the ancient culture and history and the devising of a written language for the islanders— something that the Hawaiians lacked, prior to 1820. The worst impact they had would probably have to have been their immense efforts to suppress the ancient morality and expressions of traditional cultural interactions with nature (in their efforts to save what they perceived as primitive godless heathens by converting them to the Christian religion).

As a proudly non-Christian heathen soul myself, I can never forgive them (the Christian missionaries) for their one-sided, mindless conviction that they had an iron-bound franchise or absolute insight on understandings of the universe, but I can acknowledge that given the mean, ruthless, degenerate and largely amoral nature of the non-religious white people who came to the islands (traders, whalers, sailors, soldiers, and commercial businessmen), the Christian missionaries are probably most wisely regarded, retrospectively, as the slightly better of two evils. Robert L. Stevenson commented on the grossly exploitative nature of those non-Christian white settlers, remarking that it was that sort of 'white person' who made him regret being of the same ethnicity. This opinion frequently mirrors my own feeling about modern American society, although you don't have to be white to be common-minded and totally lacking in higher ethical awarenesses, certainly. God knows that no one culture, race, or creed has an exclusive lock on the baser aspects of human behavior. It's just a matter of the purest coincidence that I am white and the people responsible for Hawaii's ultimate downfall (as an ancient and proud people, possessed of a unique and distinctive culture unlike no other) were *also* (as anyone with intelligence would hasten to confirm). Nietzsche would argue that point, doubtlessly.

All other things being equal (my Ivy League, button-down collar, and Harris Tweed jacket wearing college political science instructor's favorite utterance), the missionaries probably did much more good than harm, in the final assessment. That doesn't mean that I am willing to completely absolve them of the many harmful effects of their religious fervor (since this has been a common theme with all religions since the dawn of recorded history, each of which believes its distinctive concept of 'God' is the one and only legitimate one), but I am at least willing to allow that for all their very human failings, the Christian missionaries felt they meant well. I suppose you could use that same sentiment to say that despite all of Adolph Hitler's many heinous outrages (or Mao's, or Pol Pot's, or Saddam Hussein's, et al), *he meant well.* However, I think my intended meaning stands sufficiently well qualified within the supportive context of these paragraphs to allow those words to be safely used here.

No religion has ever had, nor shall ever have (in my humble opinion), any more truly sagacious insight into the deeper, ultimate mysteries of human experience than that of your average frontally lobotomized individual. For that reason, any seeking after absolute 'truths', when it comes to the Biggest Questions (e.g. *"What's it all about, Alfie?"*) is destined to wither on the vines of intelligent human inquiry. By virtue of that belief, I regard anything and everything accomplished anywhere in 'the name of god' as being nothing more than the inspired application of latent human abilities that arise solely out of the sources of all biological life (and sheer coincidence) that are as sentient or non-sentient as logical possibilities allow for (and not from any party-line connection directly to a 'God').

Against that Kevlar®-like backdrop of my own doggedly maintained personal prejudices, I am very sad to find that the ancient Hawaiians lost so much of themselves not to one group or another, but to the fact that whenever a weaker group (i.e. possessed of a lesser quality of weapons technology) meets a more powerful group (i.e. possessed of weapons technology of a higher level or quality), the weaker group is categorically *doomed* to be subjugated.

That is ultimately what happened to ancient Hawaii. Western man with his advanced weapons (and only coincidentally, with his religion) came along, contact was made, and the more rapacious, overwhelming force came out on top. In that sense, the end was already foreseen the minute Cook pulled into the Hawaiian's parking lot, back in 1978 and the early Christian missionary provocateurs simply tossed a few low-yield theological hand grenades into the cultural battle here and there.

Drove into K'kai to take a break and pick up some things at Friendly Market. In the hottest part of the day you you'd expect things to be pretty slow and surprise...they were! On a whim, I dropped in at Kanemitsu's to check out their remaining goods and bought a couple of apple fritters. Didn't notice Wally at first, an older artist whom I had met at the art mart, last Saturday, sitting behind me at one of the tables. His wave caught my attention and after I bought the stuff I sat down to talk story for a while. Wally is the fellow whom I had mentioned earlier had had surgery for skin cancer on his face. As we chatted, it came out that he has also had abdominal surgery for more CA and was on dialysis for years before finally getting a kidney transplant. Some medical history, I reckoned. He's only 66, too. Makes me reflect anew on the importance of having good genes (and also perhaps a healthy lifestyle).

Wally is an artist and as we talked about this and that, Sturgess of 'Sturgess' Café and Gallery' came by. When I expressed some regret over the fact that Sturgess refused to sell any of his personal works on display in the gallery, this seemed to be a hot button for Wally, who told me a few things about Sturgess that I'd never have guessed. Apparently, Wally had offered to help Sturgess renovate his old building some time ago and (Sturgess) then had rather rudely expressed no appreciation for Wally's help whatsoever. I told Wally that although I hadn't met Sturgess personally, I had gathered from this and that that he was somewhat of an arrogant individual. This Wally confirmed and went on to say that he thought it was ironic that Sturgess won't sell any of his local art to interested parties, while on the internet he apparently had quite a trade (apparently with customers in the Far East) going in works that Wally expressed as 'pure pornography'.

Wally doesn't strike me as a blue-nose Christian conservative, so his opinion of what he termed 'pornography' is of interest. Sturgess advertises a lot in the island papers for models that he wants to paint 'fully clothed' portraits of. Given this new bit of information about Sturgess' apparent erotic art side-line, I can't help but wonder about the emphasis on 'fully Clothed' and how that may tie into his other interests. Just goes to show you that no matter what the appearances seem to indicate, there's never such thing as a fully *complete* understanding possible, no matter who you are dealing with (e.g. President Willie's notorious dalliance with Monika Lewinsky in the Oval Office).

Wally apparently needs some money, since he offered to paint a picture similar to one I had briefly admired last Saturday (of Mt. Fuji in Japan), that he had said he was holding for someone else. Now, Wally is one of those souls I would call a talented dabbler, despite the fact that he tells me he teaches art at the local community center. Anyone with even modest ability can, of course, teach anyone of lesser ability, so that's not saying much. The proof in art is in the viewing and not in the self-pronouncement of one's 'instructor' status. This doesn't change Wally's stature as a good fellow who it is fun to chat with, needless to say. (I finally found among his offerings a quite striking impression of the *I'ao Needle* on Maui, which I rather liked and bought.)

As we were talking, an exceptionally good looking young lady walked in, took a look at the baked goods and then walked out. She definitely caught my eye and I tracked her out of the corner of my eye as she walked down the street, thinking to myself: *"Holy shit, can it be that a lovely unattached young woman has somehow ended upon little old Moloka'i?"* I should have known better, as in the next 5 minutes she returned with a hunky, buffed out boyfriend. Alas, there's no justice in life! She had a great set of chi-chis, too, sticking out nicely against her T-shirt. [Note to self: What is it about women's breasts, anyway? Is it the latent infant still trapped in us grown-up men that they exite? Or the recollection of the last good lustful suck we had? Wonder what a psychologist would have to say about men and their fixation with firm, full female breasts, anyway? Ah, the marvels of blind sexual instinct.]

Since Wally knows Carlo, I decided to ask him if he knew anything about that old heiau out at Murphy's Beach that Carlo had steered me to.

"Oh yeah," he replied, *"Been there. It's a fish heiau, supposedly dedicated to Kuula (a minor fish aumakua). Did you know it's haunted?"* Ah! I told him that I did and that I had in fact seen what could only have been the ghost in reference. *"No shit...you saw her, huh? She's supposed to be nice looking, young, but hardly anyone ever sees her. How did you luck out?"*

I couldn't explain it any better than he could, of course, but asked him if the story about a haunting was really legit or whether this was more of Carlo's humor? I told him also about finding no grave, as Carlo has suggested I would at Kawelo.

"Nope, supposed to be at Pu'uko'o, not Kawelo, from what I've heard. The locals there could probably tell you more about it, since she seems to have had family there. You really saw her, or are you just pulling my leg? Story goes she doesn't show herself unless she isn't afraid of you. Never heard of anyone I know actually seeing her before...must be afraid of everyone...but from what you said, that was one pretty lady...um, at one time, of course."

At that he stopped and looked at me with a puzzled expression. *"Strange stuff, that! You say you really saw her, huh? Wow!"*

I assured him I at least saw *someone* there. Whether a ghost or a real person was beyond my ability to say, since there was no indication of any ghostly behavior (or at least what I think would be ghostly behavior), as far as I could tell from those brief glimpses. She simply looked like a really good-looking young local lady to me, I guessed perhaps just walking back up from the sea, since *her hair was wet...*

I left Wally shortly afterwards to take my things back up to the place in Ranch Camp. Judging from Wally's reaction, I'd say that either this is a larger joke than I thought, or I saw something I simply cannot explain (there's that bit about her purple top and the translation of her name; everything else can be rationalized but those two tantalizing details!). Amazing and here I am, back at square one, a non-believer who doesn't know what to make of this whole thing. [Makes mental note to buttonhole Carlo again and ask him for more information. Maybe with some more warm Papeete.] I did learn one interesting further thing: it was the custom for the family to put a small circlet made of Maile vine on the left wrist of a very recently deceased person. I recall that she was wearing something on her left wrist, but the encounter was too brief to know what, other than it was green in color and seemed to be made of leaves. *Brrrr.*

Sitting here, thinking about the above developments and feeling a strong need for one of those apple fritters I bought earlier in the day (dripping with saturated fat and fried, to boot—*death wish*?). Clyde (CJ's Gardening Service) tells me he has a conflict in that his daughter needs to be at the library at 6PM to pick up some sort of award she won for reading. We've agreed to reschedule our rendezvous to check out the property for a cost estimate tomorrow. That's the Moloka'i way; nothing ever written in stone and always subject to the needs of the 'ohana (which is as it ought to be, I guess).

The last couple of days have been quite warm and humid. Lots of moisture-laden clouds developing late in the day, without a lot of the usual wind to cool things off. Since my room faces the sun (away from the trades), it gets fairly warm by about 4PM.

Another of my books sheds an interesting perspective on the early missionaries I have been holding forth about. The book was apparently written as a sort of response to all the less-than-positive insinuations James Michener made about them in his fictionalized novel *'HAWAII'*. By Michener's reckoning, the missionaries were all a bunch of holier- than-thou, blue-nosed prudes who had a greater number of human failings that most people, religious or not. The thread of hypocrisy runs strongly and centrally through the book. Apparently, some of the more 'God-fearing' brethren among us have felt Michener slighted their evangelical forebears a bit too much, even though Michener's book is fiction that was 'supposedly' based only roughly on actual people. The book (*'Hawaii: Truth Stranger than Fiction'*, by LaRue Piercy) takes pains to delve into the actual history that Michener researched so diligently (in typical Michener style) and contrasts the fiction to the true events that took place, since the parallels are quite real (just names, places, and actual events changed to make them seem purely fictional).

It makes interesting reading, but one gets the feeling that the author is trying hard to vindicate the historic figures that Michener used to model his characters after. He makes a remark in the preface expressing his pleasure in having received so many compliments from readers who felt such a book was 'long overdue'; one gets the distinct feeling that the 'grateful readers' are not modern-day godless heathens, either. At the very least it makes for interesting reading, since Michener's books are so well-known and widely read. An amusing image comes to mind: Michener returns from the grave and decides to do a similarly expansive and terribly complicated book with a bit sharper focus: 'MOLOKA'I'.

I can see parts of it in my mind as I write this. One unforgettable chapter features a particularly strong-minded (but intuitively brilliant) heathen high chief named Kalika (Hawaiian for 'Chris'), who has a rep for being a stupendously well-hung lover (his 'ule' is legendary, and in fact it's the real-life model for the sacred *Ka Ule o Nanaha*), and 6 wives, each of whom is more gorgeous than the next. As I see it in my mind's eye, Kalika has just sacrificed a particularly arrogant missionary (who bears a striking resemblance to *George Dubya Bush*) for mouthing off at him, is about to lead his people up against the missionaries to overthrow them and successfully reclaim the islands for the Hawaiians. Oh yes, in this he is assisted by a couple of passing friendly alien UFOs, who decide to trade him some of their older (last lightyear's model, actually) proton cannons for a load of coconuts (which just happen to be made of the EXACT chemical ingredients from which their interstellar fuel is synthesized...what a coincidence!). It gets even better...

Of course, there's already a book (several, matter of fact) by that name, as well as a movie. The subject matter focuses on Father Damien's work with the lepers in the Kalaupapa Colony. I haven't mentioned much about that particular aspect of Moloka'i, since it is well known by most of the world and besides, the guy had a saint complex. Not my kind of *mensch*, really. Oh yes, while on the subject of *Hansen's Disease*, those insinuating rumors you may have heard about Father Damien, Mother Marienne, and Baby Ignatz are not true.... Father Damien is on the road towards R.C. *saintdom* (along with Mom Theresa) as I write this, which is great, because he really was a marvelous human being (somewhat STRANGE, but still a really wonderful, selfless guy).

Someone once remarked that the only genuine state of self-lessness is achieved *after* one dies. Think about it. *Hmmmmm.* That was an 'off-handed' (pun) remark, if I ever heard one. Then there's the leper who left the prostitute a tip… This of course, reminds me of many more tasteless jokes one hears about lepers, but I'll spare you. They were questionably amusing originally and probably would not be much improved in the retelling here.

It's getting later, my humor is getting more tasteless and cynical, and that apple fritter is still sitting there on the counter, staring at me as it continues to ooze saturated fat in the afternoon heat like some baleful dietary monster. Come back tomorrow: I promise it'll only get better in these truly inspired pages.

May 5th, 2005 (Thursday)

Absolutely wretched night last night. The earplugs kept loosening and falling out, and the rooster/dog chorus began earlier than usual and lasted the rest of the remaining time, until well past dawn (it is now 7:42 AM and they are still at it). Had to take Benadryl instead of Actifed for sleep before bed and that usually imparts a groggy sensation on arising. As if that weren't enough trouble for the start of a new day, I also woke with a headache. Made my usually strong *cuppa* and popped the standard handful of mineral pills, including some native Noni herb. Then, after the coffee took hold, the ASA went to work, the Noni kicked in and I had consumed one of those gooey, drippy death-wish apple fritters, I was finally in better shape and ready to rock & roll.

The small electric coffee grinder I have here is made by the Braun (correctly pronounced *"brown"* and not *"brawn"*, as most non-German speakers assume) Company (GmBH); I brought it with me and have used it continuously for more than 21 years now. Cylindrical and bright orange (my favorite color), it still grinds away perfectly, although the blade is doubtless far less sharp than it used to be, having sliced through God only knows how many thousands of pounds of coffee beans over the past two decades. This is a meaningful measure of how seriously I take my coffee habit, I suppose, but every person has items in which he invests sacred significance. Some folks have crucifixes, others have pagan totems; I have my sacred coffee grinder and it certainly is a 'wholly' relic in its own right (wholly my salvation each morning). Well worth worshipping the product it helps create, I think, at any rate, since coffee, after all, is *GOD!*

I went out early this morning, after scrubbing the accumulation of sweaty dreck off my body in the shower. Ever since talking to Wally about that strange happening at the old heiau, I had been meaning to go back there and do some further investigating into that place. Taking my camera, therefore, I drove east along Kam V Highway toward Murphy's Beach, traveling at the posted 35 mph speed limit and constantly having impatient locals zip up behind me at near twice the speed. Strikes me as more than slightly ironic on this *slow-mo* island, that the locals are the most blatant violators of their own languid *kapus* against being in a hurry. I suspect that these speeders in their jacked-up pickup trucks are not the long time native locals, but impatient *haole kama'aina* (long-time residents) and *malihini* (mainlanders) who have migrated to the east end within the past 10 years.

After a half hour or so I passed the *'Neighborhood Store & Counter'* and reached Po'oku'u. The graveyard was supposed to be there somewhere, but I had no idea exactly where, so I finally ended up asking an old Kanaka who was walking on the Makai side of the road where I might find it. Expecting pigeon patois, I was pleasantly surprised to find he spoke regular English (or close enough to it to be able to understand him without first straining the words through a #4 trans-literative filter).

He directed me to the site, which was on the *mauka* side of the road, and not far from where we stood. After a short while I found the exit off the roadway and turned down the dusty road cut from the crumbled volcanic earth. The crunch of my tyres was the only sound that broke the stillness in that otherwise silent repository of mortal remains and I parked under a large Koa tree at the distal end of the cemetery. Half expecting to feel some sort of strange sensation (due to an over-active anticipation, no doubt), I slowly walked down the rows of graves, taking care to not step on the mounds themselves (I have these funny little attitudes about this, that I can't really explain...respect for the dead?). There weren't too many of them. Most appeared to be very old, with melancholic withered floral arrays long since dried out in the sun; a good number had ancient wooden markers on which the names and dates had long since been weathered off. Large flies and bees droned here and there in the morning sun, plainly irritated by the nectar-less brittle plastic flowers on some graves.

The graves were not arranged in neat, orderly rows, but appeared to lay scattered about. One section had children's graves clustered together. I recall having read that this was an ancient practice that was done to allow the spirits of the dead children to play together and thereby be less lonely in death. Some of the children were newborns, more than a few less than a day or two old, according to the markers that could still be read.

A thorough search of the graves produced no grave identified as being that of a Corinne *Popolohu Hu'elani*, but the skeptic in me had half-expected this outcome. After taking a last look around, I walked the short distance back to the car. The sun was already getting noticeably hotter, despite the early hour (10 AM) and I found myself getting thirsty.

The old heiau was not far off, so I drove back to that point and parked. There was no one else about within eyesight as I walked up the slightly inclined slope to the crest of the mound and peered down at the heiau wall, with its nearby old and tattered hut, some 100 yards away. The volcanic rock (*a'a*, which is the crumbly, jagged type—as opposed to the rounded *paho'eho'e* type) under foot crunched satisfyingly as I walked over to the hut. The view to Maui across the *Pailolo Channel* was clear and beautiful, as always. On the east end of the reef, where the shallows ended and the deep lay nearer to shore, the waters varied from a lovely turquoise shade to the deepest cobalt-blue. The whiteness of the breaking surf was startling. I could see why this would be a favorite diving spot and it was conveniently close to the dazzlingly bright stretch of sandy beach that lay just at the foot of the old heiau.

Someone had been in the water already, as the light impressions of vaguely discernable footprints leading to and from the water suggested. As I neared the old heiau I looked carefully around; part of me, hoped, but didn't really expect to see the figure of the strange young woman I had seen before. There was no surprise in store for me (sadly) as I sat down on the same bench I had originally been seated on several days ago. The sun was by now shining fully on the spot and there was only the vague cacophony of the surf, breaking on the reef beyond the lagoon, to interrupt the silence.

Suddenly, my gaze was arrested by something breaking the surface of the water, out in the lagoon near the reef's edge. It was definitely the flash of a dorsal fin; probably one of the small black-tipped reef sharks that sometimes come in close to shore. A *Mano*, as the Hawaiians would term it. The fin was soon gone as quickly as it had appeared, however and the small dark shadow accompanying it quickly vanished. The stillness persisted. Clearly this was not a day for unusual sightings that couldn't be explained. After 15 minutes or so, hoping that I was wrong, I grudgingly admitted to myself that Carlo had been pulling my leg after all. Somehow, I was being exposed to this joke as perhaps all newcomers must, by informal local custom.

It was then that I spotted it. Out on the beach, along the track of those footprints from the heiau to the water and about halfway up from the edge of it, lay a shockingly purple flower of unusual size. It was quite large and I felt a little tingle of excitement as I walked over to it. The flower was still glistening with moisture. I picked it up and examined it more closely, all the while thinking somewhat perplexedly about how the color purple seemed to be a common thread running through all this. I turned the flower over, and registered the fact that it had veins of subtle, slivery-grey shading on the indigo under-surface of its velvety petals. That sent a slight shiver through me as I placed the flower back on the beach and gazed out at the lagoon. 'Another coincidence?' I thought, as I tried to dismiss the odds against this further strange turn of events.

Clearly, though, there was nothing more to be gained from lingering further, so I walked back to the car and drove slowly back west on Kam V Highway. Stopping *en route* at the 'Neighborhood Store and Counter', I walked in and picked up a chilled carbonated coffee drink from the cooler. The lady at the counter had been chatting in an animated fashion with a local as I waited to buy the item. The banter went on for an unusually long time, it seemed—probably trying to underscore a subtle point for the benefit of the haole tourist about what the local 'lay back' attitude concerning the flow of things is.

Finally, she waved goodbye to the local and turned to me, but the happy relaxed look was gone and replaced by an 'Oh, one a-

dem' look. I decided to take a chance on being treated like an unwelcomed haole and after paying for the drink, *asked "Do you know anything about an old fish heiau, back there, that supposedly has a ghost?"* Her look hardened immediately as she asked me why I wanted to know. She knew something; it was easy to see this, from the slight change apparent in her attitude, but she wasn't about to admit anything to a strange haole.

"Well, a friend in town told me about a young woman who apparently died out there in the lagoon while diving, some time ago. Some story about her ghost returning to that spot."

She looked hard at me again for a few seconds before replying *"Eh! Dat's jus one ole chicken-flesh story dey tell the keiki. Keep dem out of wattah dere. Not real."*

I briefly told her about the girl, the purple flower and what I had been told by others. She looked a little startled for just the briefest second, but said again. *"No wahine name a Corinne, no ghost. Jus one ole kine story, you know. We all Christians here; don believe any dat ole stuffs anymore; keiki chicken-flesh story, you know...das all."*

Someone had come in and there was no further time to continue our conversation, for she had handed my change back to me and wished me a good day before turning to greet the new customer (a dark-skinned, older local Kanaka). *"Hey Onkle Tom, wat stuffs you up to?"*

I drove back to K'kai, more bemused than ever and no further along the path towards any sort of resolution in my mind on the subject. After I got back, I ran into Carlo on his old bicycle (this is how he gets around, since he lives on his boat at the K'kai Marina) and told him what I had experienced earlier. He was on his way to the local community disadvantaged adult center, on the hill near Moloka'i General Hospital, where they operate a sort of continuous garage sale of old recycled items, and didn't stop very long.

"Well, I tell you that the woman was wrong. They don't want to admit these things to outsiders. She knows. And you say you saw a purple flower there today, didn't you? How do you explain that, eh? That woman at the neighborhood store may say she's 'Christian', but the old traditions out there on east end are not yet all dead. I introduce you sometime to a local guy who knows these things; doesn't allow himself to be called 'Kahuna 'Ike Kuhohonu' ('seer' with deep spiritual insights), but he knows about these things. Later."

Then Carlo was off, peddling up the street on the old bike and somehow managing to still look dignified, despite his trademark faded aloha shirt and dingy white ball cap he habitually wore.

No closer to any sort of understanding, I spent the following few hours reading through some more of my accumulation of books. In a very good collection of strange stories written by various authors about the Pacific islands, I ran across a quote by a very readable author (of the 30s and 40s) named Clifford Gessler. Gessler had been a journalist for the *Honolulu Star-Bulletin* back in the early 30s, before getting bored and running off to the South Pacific islands.

In one of his stories, called *'Phantoms and Physicians on Tepuka'*, he strikes a resonant chord with the following excerpt: *"Part of the celebrated lure of far-away and primitive places no doubt is a response to the boy in man; in such surroundings (as the Pacific islands), among child-like peoples, he regains the play-world of his childhood. Where the pursuits at which he played as a boy are the serious vocations of adults, he finds a satisfaction of some instinct as old as the childhood of his own race."*

The truth of this simple statement of fact comes across quite clearly to those of us possessed of a more vivid imagination than others. I have long joked with friends about the fact that you 'scratch the man and find the boy'. I think it is a lucky woman who recognises, accepts and is able to appreciate this inescapably latent quality in her husband, for aren't we all *child-men* (as opposed, say to *"child-ren"*?) in some manner or another, despite all our solemn self-regard?

I decided to skip the bi-weekly email answering session at the local library and in the hot middle of the day I again ran into Carlo (Moloka'i is really just a very small community, after all). This time he found the time to take me to the house of a local named Joe, who was a traditional herb master in the old Hawaiian manner (he would have been called a *'Kahuna La'au Lapa'au'*). Carlo assured me that Joe was also supposed to have additional gifts befitting one who is a *'Kahuna Ninau 'Uhune'*, or 'communicator of spirits', although that fact was not advertised widely, except in the local kanaka circles.

When we arrived at his simple, old style single-walled home, Joe was sitting out back in a tattered old plastic deck-chair, sipping a beer under the shade of his car-port. He was somewhat portly, with a grey beard and long slender fingers that seemed somewhat out of character with the rest of his ample girth. The well-worn white tank-top he wore said *HARD ROCK CAFÉ: SAIGON*, in faded script.

"Ho, Carlo! Wassup, eh?" He greeted us with the obligatory shaka, as he dispatched another dead soldier into the nearby waste can with the perfected aim of a sharpshooter. I decided that in addition to his ancient knowledge, he had also been *'in country'* at some time in the 70s ('Nam slang for a tour in that war).

Carlo introduced me and we both found cold beer cans thrust in our hands as we sat down on a battered old couch in the cool breeze-way.

"So, Carlo tell me you wen meet da kine wahine lapu (ghost woman) at Pu'kuo fish heiau, den wen gon' way on you, hm? You mind me aks you wat she look like?"

Joe listened very attentively as I gave him the full extent of my observations, the *Pareo*, the purple suit top, the floral bracelet, dark hair with silver-grey streaks and finally the large purple flower I had seen on the sand earlier in the morning. The mute testimony of several nearby empty beer cans seeming to have had absolutely no effect on his ability to concentrate, he listened carefully, observing me with a calm and steady gaze as I spoke. Joe certainly didn't look out of the ordinary to me...just another pot-bellied Kanaka...but the keen dark eyes under bushy eyebrows told a different story. For my part, I certainly must have looked exactly as a pale-skinned haole should, as I finished up my story. Joe took another slow draw on his beer before replying.

"I tell you now dis wahine you see, not many see her. Dis no jokey stuffs, here. Dat wahine genuine akua lapu (ghost) at dat fish heiau. Mebbe um Hanehane, but good stuffs no pakalaki (bad luck) fo you. Dis wahine lapu seem like you or she not let you not see um."

Joe shifted in his dilapidated old chair, took another draught, and thoughtfully scratched his *ma'i* (balls) for a minute with his other hand.

"Should not bodda you, brah. Dat wahine lapu gotta rep fo be 'olu'olu akua lapu (gentle, unharmful spirit), mebbe even auma-kua (ancestral or familiy spirit). Sum nani koki wahine lapu (beautiful ghost), eh? You aks me, I return dere, take La'i (Ti leaf) an put on beach, wheh befo you see flowa. Don take flowa if you

*see anudda dere alreddy, doh: dat be pomaika'i nui (*very un-
lucky*)!"*

Carlo had been listening quietly as he worked on his own beer.
There was no smile on his face and no indication that this was
simply another phase of what might still be a complex and well-
rehearsed joke. When Joe had finished, I asked him about the
missing grave.

*"Ho, brah! Dat simple enuff. Dey no foun body wen dis wahine
wen missing. She prolly join mano aumakua (*'shark ancestor',
protective family shark spirit) *who out dat way. Wen take La'i, not
hurt um say prayer lak 'Auhea 'oe, e ke kanaka o ke akua, eia ka
kāua wahi 'ai, ua loa'amaila mai ka pō mai; no laila nāu e 'aumakua mai i ka 'ai a kaua!' "*

There was little to be said after that. Joe confirmed the wahine
lapu existed and there's no reason to doubt that, since it all
seems to add up in a strange (but very Hawaiian) sort of way. We
downed another can and took our leave after a bit, leaving the
remainder of the Bud Lite six-pack for Joe to polish off. Joe
waved a parting shaka at us, but he was not smiling, either, I
noticed. He seemed to be staring out at the distant bulk of Maui,
across the channel's hazy mists.

The part about the purple top and the flower can't be explained away, but it is worthy of some reflective bemusement that
I seem to have a ghostly friend who took a fancy to me on that
lonely stretch of coast. I am not ashamed to admit I did in fact
take a *Ti-leaf* offering and place it on the beach, where I saw the
foot prints and purple flower. I had written down the prayer Joe
suggested and repeated it when I placed the Ti-leaf there; there's
that healthy streak of rebellious pagan heathen in me that really
wants to believe what I saw was actually inexplicable by any
means known to westerners; perhaps this experience is that
'white crow' I've always vaguely searched for.

Suki, of course, would be frightened to hear of any of this; she had warned me before I left the mainland specifically not to have anything to do with the old legends of the island, since she knows of my burning curiosity about such things. The woman I saw at the old fish heiau, whether real or not, was unquestionably beautiful and an interesting memory to take with me from Moloka'i. One final mystery also remains: according to Joe, who knows much about such things, there are no indigenous large purple flowers on Moloka'i such as that I saw there in front of the old heiau…go figure, eh?

It's late in the afternoon now and the humidity is not as noticeable as it has been over the past two days. There are a few clouds starting to gather, as usual, but the breeze is enough to keep the heat from being oppressive. I had another of my cheap & dirty peanut-butter & jelly sandwiches (a perfect 'Sandwich Island sandwich', it seems to me) and was able to successfully fend off the urge to eat that other certain death apple-fritter (saving it for Friday).

I was staring at all my books just a few minutes ago. That's a heavy load of stuff and I hope they won't hit me with a baggage surcharge, owing to it. I think about the fact that I only weigh about 160 pounds soaking wet and a number of other passengers (probably hefty local types) typically weigh twice that amount. Surely the combined weight of me and by books won't unduly exceed existing figures for the average passenger, in light of such a fact? Guess we won't know until the moment of truth at the Inter-Island ticket counter on Sunday.

Looking back over the past month or so, I am thinking that there isn't anything I couldn't have gained just as easily in two weeks here as I have in twice that amount of time. Except the lengthy bulk of this journal, which at this time is just about to exceed 110,000 words (exactly 98,889 words at this juncture). This will cost me about 160 hours of hard-earned vacation time, and since the water line didn't really require my presence over here to begin with, it may have been a bit of an extravagant excess on my part (not that I can't afford to spend those 160 hours of paid leave, what with a grand total accrued of over 450 vacation hours).

Aside from the strange experience at the old heiau, nothing I have seen or done here has really been too startling. It would have been more stimulating to have someone along with me with which to share the time. Perhaps a gorgeous & ravishingly sensual female to while away the hours with (but alas! I have to make do with the mere suggestion of one and you can't easily *get it on* with a ghost, can you?) would have helped a lot. Moloka'i remains, after all is said, read, and done, NOT a place high up on the list of *Sierra Hotel* (US Air Force slang for 'shit hot') singles watering holes (not that I normally or customarily play that game, as a soberly married person, of course). Of course. I didn't come here for that purpose, since my main intent was to have some long-overdue peace and quiet in which to read and write. Thanks a heap, roosters!

The wind is picking up a bit outside now and there is a lovely wind-chime that someone has hanging nearby. I keep thinking about all the hundreds of different kinds of flowers on the island...and the fact that among them all (a botanist's Fantasy Island—*"Look Boss: da flower, da flower, da flower!"* The scornful response in a deep Ricardo Montalban accent is unpredicted and unexpectedly Monty Pythonesque: "Oh shut up, Poo-poo, you disgusting little scum bag!"), *there are absolutely NO large, velvety purple blooms to be seen anywhere.*

I don't really want to start thinking about what I shall find back at the office, with all the petty 10 cent intrigues that characterise its irritations and frustrations so perfectly. As for that, I am going to take the wisdom of the ancient kahunas (and also that of psychologist Dwayne Dyer, which he appears to have borrowed for his own secular application of the concept) regarding the *'power of the word'* (Dyer actually calls it the 'power of intention', but it's clearly derived from the archetypal heathen source in reference) and make plans to get out of my present occupational *Black Hole* and into another hopefully adjacent department that isn't so damn constipated.

Have to buy some cheap trinkets to take back to the office natives, although they are mostly a sorry lot, without much ability to even appreciate such tokens. Returning to Enrico's watch will certainly not be a happy one, although it will be interesting to see how well he has mastered the areas of work he is supposedly supervising. It will also be of additional interest (although likely not much fun) to see whether I have been further cast up on the shoals of neglect and incompetence by any changes in staffing made in my absence. Since I am returning on Sunday and going to work Monday, it will be a truncated night for me. I will undoubtedly have a bit of a struggle getting plugged back in at the appropriate stress level required to survive there. Could have planned the reentry better, I guess.

One of the most famous cases of ethnic bias in the Hawaiian Islands in modern times has to be the infamous 'Massie Case' of 1931. At that time, the status quo obtaining in the Territory of Hawaii still strongly favored and reflected traditional mainland white majority bias against any and all 'people of color'. The case involved the alleged abduction and rape of the white wife of a US Navy submarine officer by 5 'locals' (two Japanese-Hawaiians, two native Hawaiians and one Chinese-Hawaiian). The alleged rape of the officer's wife took place late at night (between 12 midnight and 1 AM) after she had left the club at which they were drinking, and walked down a nearby street. In a different location, a car with the five locals had had a run-in with another party in a near collision. In the resulting chaos, given the extremely one-sided bias which existed between all whites and all 'people of local color' at the time, the 5 locals ended up being accused of being the rapists--even though they had not been near the area where Massie was supposedly raped and despite absolutely no evidence, either circumstantial or otherwise, to support the charges. The resulting trial was a sham, reflecting the extreme white bias that prevailed at the time, but despite this, the 5 men were released on their own recognizance.

Outraged over this perceived 'miscarriage' of justice, the plaintiff's mother, her son-in-law, and several others abducted one of the accused locals in an effort to 'force' a confession out of him. This effort failed and the abductee was shot dead in the process. Fortunately, thanks to a sequence of favorable circumstances, the conspirators were apprehended in the act of trying to dump the body of the local man in the ocean and were brought to trial for their act. After an equally chaotic trial (featuring Clarence Darrow as the defendants' attorney), the 4 conspirators were found guilty of second degree murder. They were sentenced to 10 years at hard labor, but this penalty was reduced immediately thereafter by the Territorial Governor to only 1 hour, served in his office.

My point in bringing this scandalous old case up is to highlight once again the effects ethnic bias has in any contention over legal matters. Of course, bias is not, as I said before, an exclusive preserve of the white race, any more than it is of any other. The Massie Case was only enabled by the existing racial biases that have plagued the islands ever since the second wave of Polynesian settlers followed High (& supposedly white) Priest Pa'ao from *Kahiki* (the ancient Hawaii term for 'any distant land beyond our shores', but often used to mean 'Tahiti') to Hawaii. The most flagrant post-missionary bias involved strong white condescension towards the native Hawaiians and continued after other Asian ethnic groups were introduced (Japanese, Chinese, Korean, and Filipino, mainly), extending equally and as strongly to them as to the native Hawaiians.

The United States of the 20s and 30s was strongly swept along in a lingering and irrational fear of the people from the Far East (the so-called 'Yellow Plague'), principally because the imported Asian peoples were hard-workers who required little pay and as such constituted a received economic threat to poor white workers. The blacks on the mainland, meanwhile, continued to suffer from the same racial bias they had always suffered under.

In the eyes of the wealthy haoles in Hawaii, all these 'inferior' peoples were equally looked down on. This state of extreme racial profiling existed even amongst the sub-groups of the 'people of color' themselves, with pecking orders, hierarchies based on nationality, racial origin and even neighborhood or family affiliations back in the nations of origin, as well as any number of further divisive criteria ordering their interactions towards each other.

Naturally enough, other nations had and maintained their own extreme biases, as well, for the Chinese felt all non-Chinese were grossly inferior, the Japanese felt similarly, etc., etc. In this matter, the whites were only engaging in the same stupid and narrow-minded acts people have committed against each other since the beginning of time.

The point here is that these same unconscious prejudices are still at work among us and even remain active on Moloka'i, where so my observations confirm, the dark-skinned 'locals' tend to consider themselves the unfairly persecuted minority, simultaneously as visiting haoles quite frequently tend to look slightly askance at them as those 'poor native people'. There are also divisions among the dark-skinned people, based on how much Hawaiian blood they can claim (a factor based on intermarriage with other groups over the years).

Even here on the so-called 'Friendly Isle' (public relations hype that it is), you can still see everyday occurrences of this. In this week's edition of the John MacByte funded 'Moloka'i Island Times', a local mother, describing herself in part as a 'common, ordinary woman with four small kids', wrote a letter to the paper detailing an encounter in the (this is further rife irony, to be sure!) 'Friendly Market' check-out line with someone she described as an arrogant, condescending haole (white) woman, who seized upon an innocuous situation involving her child to humiliate and embarrass her in front of every in the store. She noted that this most unfriendly and unsympathetic white woman had recently arrived, so she came to find out and was in fact scheduled to teach at one of the local schools. This local wahine's points were almost valid and salient, and it is a fact that many people from the mainland do in fact come to the islands abysmally ignorant of the local customs, attitudes, and/or outlooks on life.

This is just one of many such incidents that seem to be occurring more and more frequently. The result is that the native Moloka'iians, who are normally very relaxed, openly friendly and naturally (by virtue of their Hawaiian traditions and customs) hospitable, are starting to become 'infected' by the same sort of divisive disregard that has been a recurring problem everywhere on the mainland. Ominous indications of this feeling are cropping up here and there (such as the signs that are displayed in front of east end homes on Kam V Highway stating that '...visitors are always welcome, because visitors spend their money and go home again!', etc.) on the island.

The bottom line now maintained as the 'norm' by most locals is fast changing so that instead of the former condition of unqualified openness and warmth that obtained, any such unqualified gesture of welcome will be subsequently withheld until the visitor has indicated whether he is worthy of that regard or not (i.e. *"Do unto others as you would so unto yourself...or else!"*). As someone who has been very much aware of the rules by which appropriate cross-cultural interactions are properly engaged in, I find these acts of callous disregard and crude insensitivity by my white tourist brethren very unsettling and not a little disturbing. This does not bode well for the future of Moloka'i as these clashes resulting from increased interactions continue, and it is definitely something to reflect upon for anyone considering relocating to Moloka'i. More food for thought as the world turns (and burns).

Just got back from meeting Clyde of *CJ's 'Ohana Gardening Service*. Really enjoyed meeting him, too. Took him down to the parcel and explained what we needed (for someone to keep the lot clear of weeks, spray herbicide occasionally, and generally look in on things from month to month). Clyde brought his family to town and was picking up a prescription when my call rang through to him. He started the business as a method of teaching his kids practical lessons about money—how to earn it, value it, and take care of things with it. He also said that rather than let his kids cadge money from him as a sort of 'you owe me' allowance, he wanted his kids to learn like he did as a child, that nothing is free. His son is named "CJ" and thus he named the business after him, so that the son would grow into the responsibility. I was very impressed with Clyde and this philosophy. He struck me as a very nice guy, quite honest and sincere. Left my card with him and he said he'd give me a call with an estimate. I hope it works out, since a good working relationship with Clyde would prove to be another good link to have here on the island, I think. We shall see.

Went to bed last night listening to a Honolulu radio station (call sign KORL, at 670 AM). They have a nightly program called Radio Spirits that replays remastered old classic radio programs. Last night I was treated with episodes from *'Father Knows Best'*, *'Yours Truly, Johnny Dollar'*, and an old chestnut called *'Quiet, Please!'* by the producers of the famous *'Lights Out'* series.

Absolutely great stuff and it more than made up for the lack of cooperation from the local roosters and dogs. Used to love this old radio theatre and as a kid well recall catching the final years of such programs (late 50s) before TV totally forced the old radio classics off the air. I remember enjoying *Johnny Dollar* in particular, although the Radio Spirits narrator (Comedian *Stan Freeberg!*) mentioned that the program was so unsuccessful lining up sponsoring advertisers that it lacked a sponsor totally for its last few years (although it ran for over 14 years total; hard to believe).

The programs are all available on CD collections that may be ordered from a website (http://www.radiospirits.com). Can't wait to order a bunch of old favorite like *'X-Minus-1'* (science fiction), *'The Shadow'*, *'Green Hornet'* (both mysteries) and many others I enjoyed as a kid. Amazing what you find way out in the middle of the Pacific Ocean (which I probably don't have to iterate is the most remote site in the world, being over 2400 miles from the nearest land).

May 6th, 2005 (Friday)

Interesting dream(s) last night. Thanks to anti-rooster earplugs that actually worked, for a change, I even awoke recalling segments of it. The dream had balky computers in it, some lovely gals (one of who seems to be a special someone remembered from past), strangely gaunt and starkly gutted high-rise buildings (*a la* post nuclear war) outlined in black and fiery red against the night sky, a couple of odd Amazons who whirled over the city on a long steel cable (about a mile long), and some sort of store in which a local goody-good group was having serious second thoughts about sharing it with my group. People were wearing abbreviated attire, there were Aloha shirts, Rugby shirts and some nudity, and a couple of black pimps skulking around in the background. That's really all I can recall and the continuity of the story is already *way* slipped down stream, unfortunately. My dreams would probably be considered pretty bizarre by what I reckon would be ordinary standards, but they are always in color and never lacking for interesting juxtapositions, in any event.

Just now it sounded like one of the rooster screeched aloud *MISS AMERICA*....? Wonder if there was any *Awa* (a moderately hallucinogenic island plant, often used by the ancients in the form of a tea) in that Diet Coke I had before bed last evening. Either that or I am hornier than I realised. Trouble with me is that I've always been one of those *decent, honorable* types all my life who assume sex, love and marriage all come under the same heading. The idea of deliberately scheming to get an illicit quickie without having to assume any responsibility for the emotional consequences (baggage) just never seems to have been part of my personal *Weltanshaung* (sadly enough), although today casual, strings-free sex is a *given* for those under 30.

Friday today, and the last effective day to wrap any loose ends up before returning to mainland Sunday AM. That dog with the weird, unearthly howl is holding forth, backed up by the full resident rooster chorus. They must enjoy keeping visiting haoles bothered to distraction; probably the only major excitement for them in the past month in their layback island lives, poor clucks.

Read in the latest issue of the Moloka'i Island Times that a group of German nationals were in K'kai to shoot some documentary footage on the island; this after running into two of them in the 'Friendly Market' earlier in the day. They were shopping for some things and I was in the line behind them. Having an interest in German *kultur*, I noted an accent, but couldn't pick up on it well enough to place it. After asking them where they were from, we chatted a few minutes. The pair--a fellow and his wife--were slightly confused over the issue of 'Gold Savings Stamps' (similar in intent to 'Green Stamps', the original grocery store 'rewards' scheme of the 50s) to them with their receipt. Apparently, they don't have such advertising gimmicks in Dusseldorf. The fellow was nice enough, but his female partner was a bit distant. Perhaps she doesn't speak English as well as he did. I'm sure the more astute among the locals would probably feel positive about the prospect of tourists other than mainland American haoles might be aware of Moloka'i, although clearly Moloka'iians have no first-hand experience with the more common vacationing Germans (such as I ran into frequently in Thailand and the Austrian border regions of the *Oberbayern*). I distinctly recall having dinner in the ancient eatery that is *Otto's*, in Innsbruck, one evening and my encounter with a bunch of Bavarians.

I was wearing a *Trachten* suit (regional traditional dress made of Loden wool and unique to Austria and Germany), trying to look as 'local' as possible and couldn't help but notice the raucous and rowdy clamor coming from the adjacent room. When *Herr Ober* came back to pour me more of the delicious white Austrian wine, I commented to him that it was certainly a shame that the 'typical American tourists' were so rude and inconsiderate when dining in elegant old establishments like Otto's. He surprised me by assuring me that to the contrary, the Americans were usually fine and that it was the neighboring Bavarians who were typically the loudest and most objectionable bores.

This mirrored an experience I had in Bangkok once, on an R&R break years ago during the Vietnam War. I was sitting with a couple of American buddies at a table in a steamy bar on *Patpong Road* having a beer; since the floor show (local Thai girls doing amazing feats with their private parts, like opening coke bottles with their cunts and smoking cigarettes with their anal sphincters) had ended, we were pretty much the only westerners there, aside from a table with four other Caucasians, a few tables away.

They had already had far too much Thai beer, from appearances, and were holding forth obnoxiously in German. I caught a few phrases being uttered and learned that they were criticizing the Americans for their actions in Vietnam; the language being used was blunt and uncomplimentary, since I have no doubt they felt no one within earshot understood their German. Finally, passing by their table on my way over to the bar for more beer, I tossed out a remark in German that us Americans were certainly *all of that*...and more.

The fact that I was an American who understood German apparently penetrated through their drunken buzz sufficiently to either confuse them or shame them with awareness of my irony, for they did button it up noticeably after that. Rude or not, Germans are at least capable of perceiving the subtle nuances of *aspersive innuendo*—even when pretty far along in their cups;

the average American is not...especially true whenever strong drink is in evidence. At least, this is my experience.

One of the things that registers with me, concerning our property, is that it is (or at least soon will be) entirely nude and devoid of any growth (no shade trees, plants, or other domestic greenery...other than a health crop of *Kiawe Long-Thorn* bushes). Given the importance that green stuff has on the island for keeping things cool and pleasant appearing, we will have nothing around us to help enhance the aesthetics of the property when we finally build and move in (unless we plant things deliberately). Even if we plan trees, we'll likely be long gone before they are even large enough to make their presence felt. That's indeed a pity, since it would be nice to have a well landscaped and provided-for area surrounding the house. However, given the $150,000+ that building a house is likely to cost, we probably won't be able to afford any serious landscaping. Just another sad aspect to my great plan to retire in this tropical 'paradise'. As always, my plans are all typically a day late and a dollar short. Donald Trump may be a cheap, conniving garden-variety, sleeze of a commercial asshole, Bill Gates may be simply a grown-up if wealthy nerd and Mark Zuckerberg may be the world's wealthiest adolescent twit, but it certainly would be nice to have just a few of their $$$. I wouldn't require that much, really. Just a few hundred thousand. That's chump change to the likes of those paragons of capitalistic virtue.

Took care of a few last-minute tasks today. Got some of the luscious island bananas (they have 4 varieties here—in the ancient society, women were forbidden these articles of fruit for reasons already gone into) and a few cheap trinkets to buy off the natives back home. Checked out my mailbox at Ho'olehua, and acquired a couple of copies of '*100 Years of Medicine in the Islands*' (supposed to be an excellent history), one for cousin

Chuck in Oregon, who's a retired infectious diseases specialist (since infectious western diseases almost killed off the entire Hawaiian race). One last stop at Moloka'i Public Library to check email before returning (Suki's going to kill me when she gets my message that another surfboard is on its way to our house!).

Couldn't believe the haole lady next to me sitting at one of the library's computers. She carried on a lengthy cell-phone conversation for at least a half hour, right there at my elbow. It was so noticeable that the local guy on my left nudged me and we both rolled our eyebrows over this characteristically dumb haole woman and her mainlander lack of good sense. That's exactly the sort of insensitive, inconsiderate crap I thought I left at home and here I am experiencing it on Moloka'i! Of all the times when I wish I had my handy-dandy cell-phone jammer (good for jamming all cell transceivers within a 50 foot radius) with me, that's one! Unfortunately, CP jammers are still technically illegal, so I had to leave it at home (otherwise someone would have raised an alarm when they saw it at the passenger security check-through site and likely confiscated it; at $300 penalty a pop, you don't want to risk that possibility). People continue to amaze me! This lady could have been right off a plane from Manhattan, from the appearance and nature of the conversation she was broadcasting to everyone in the room (and this is a public library, too, where the usual rules about respecting noise restriction rules apply!).

Final stop of the day was to drop off a six-pack of Tahitian beer off at the *Vanda* for Carlo (as a little parting gesture). He wasn't at the boat when I arrived and his bike was gone, so he was obviously off somewhere else; I left the beer where he would find it, by the cabin door in the boat's cockpit. If it were me sitting on my boat in the marina and finding an unexpected 6-pack of Papeete brew, I'd really be tickled. What better way cap a perfect day than to sit on the up-slope side of a charmingly listing boat and down a few (warm or not!) *brewskis* as I admired the cool channel breezes blowing in from across Maui way. I hope he enjoyed several in this manner.

Hard to imagine that I'll be gone from Moloka'i very shortly. I was just starting to get to know a few people and meet some locals. One last visit was to the local surf shop (called *'Moloka'i Surf'*, appropriately enough). There were a couple of nice local women watching things for the owner (really pleasant older *'Tutu'I'*Auntie' types). I bought a few surf stickers for my boards back home and very, very late in my stay realised that I had finally found *the* place to connect with a few of the local young women. In the course of 30 minutes spent in there, no less than 6 exceptionally 'nice' young wahines dropped in. Of course, most were high school age, so I felt appropriately like the dirty old man I am, admiring these firm young bodies behind my shades, but...hey, any port in a storm and besides, back in pre-Christian times here, 15 year old brides were the norm! Fortunately, I know better than to transgress the bounds of propriety, but even if I weren't inclined to observe the niceties, modern legal statutory age regs are hard to ignore. (But I can still lust, can't I?)

Earlier this afternoon I drove back to the east side, along Kam V Highway and spent some time on the beach near Mile Marker 20. The beaches all throughout here are breathtakingly lovely and virtually uninhabited. There was one couple only taking the sun throughout the whole length of the 6 most beautiful miles of sandy beach along the end of the island! Otherwise the sandy shoreline was entirely empty and the weather was the same beautiful weather you find every day here. While I wouldn't recommend Moloka'i as a place for single hot young studs to come who are hunting *quail*, it most definitely is THE place to bring your lady if you want paradise entirely to yourselves. It stupefies me that this remains largely an unknown secret to the mainlanders, but I guess I should be grateful for it or paradise would quickly become the *haole hell* that the others islands have morphed into.

I stopped along the way, parked, and dropped down to the beach where I spent an hour or so, wishing I had someone special by my side. Interestingly enough, as I walked back a bit toward one of the ancient fishpond walls, I looked up into the thick tangle of trees a few yards away and spotted a sign in one of the trees that had the appearance of having been growing there for a century or more, right by the water's edge. The sign said simply: *'Burial: Stay Away'*.

Clearly, a site where the remains of an ancient Hawaiian had been buried and undoubtedly just one of thousands of such sites, scattered throughout this island and the others. There was no fence or other barrier in place, just the sign. Fortunately, all islanders (and most visitors) understand and respect this custom. One of the reasons these sites are scattered all over the place is that in the ancient days it was considered absolutely vital that none of your enemies knew precisely where your remains lay, since anything that came from you (personal possessions, excrement, sputum, fingernails, hair, etc., or even your bones) could be used by sorcerers to carry out spells against your spirit.

Considering the reputation of Moloka'i as *'Moloka'i of the Powerful Prayers'* and the reputed abilities of some of its 'prayer-killing' kahunas (the island was particularly renown for this type of sorcery), these precautions seem relatively reasonable. I sat by the tree for a while, but didn't disturb the site or poke around curiously (obviously). It was an interesting feeling to have this tangible link with a part of the past that had once been so powerful. I have no doubt there are many similar unidentified sites, although I have no idea who the individual was in this particular locale. It is likely that the deceased was one of the lesser local chiefs, given the proximity to the water's edge, and the carefully chosen setting, with its stunning outlook over the lagoon.

The *'Tutus'* at the surf shop were telling me that I am (unfortunately) missing one of the great annual events of Moloka'i by leaving this Sunday (there are several, but two of the best are the annual *Moloka'i to Oahu Outrigger Race* held annually in October and the annual Hula celebration in May). This last fascinating and widely attended event is a festival celebrating the birth of the hula, held every May in the latter two weeks. Hula, that internationally recognised and most characteristic cultural aspect of Hawaiian culture (past and present), actually originated on the island of Moloka'i (*Hula a'piko*, or literally 'the navel of Hula'). Each year this fact is acknowledged anew through a week-long series of cultural activities centered on or about the hula; as a profoundly and uniquely Hawaiian medium for expression of the culture's history, it is unsurpassed. Since hula and Hawaii go together much like Bavarians and beer, this is missing out on something of real value. Pity my timing is off in this respect, since the visual spectacle is reported to be quite something.

Today there are several types of Hula. Hula originated as an ancient Hawaiian ritual of religious expression (although related to traditional dance practices of Tahiti and other Polynesian areas) and when the missionaries arrived in 1820, Hula was looked upon by them as both immodest and pagan, therefore it was strongly censured and nearly became extinct. It wasn't until *King David Kalaukua's* reign that Hula enjoyed a redemption from its former state of neglect, and since that time it has been reembraced as perhaps the most traditional of all Hawaiian cultural practices. The most authentic and pure of the Hawaiian Hula schools is that of 'chanting Hula', which is highly ritualised and consists of a dancer (or dancers) going through very stylized motions while accompanied by duo-tonic chanting and calabash drumming.

Other instruments such as the *Pu-niu* (leg drum made from half a coconut shell and worn tied to the thigh) and the *Pahu Hula* (a large drum made from the sectioned trunk of a coconut tree with a drumhead made from sharkskin) were also used. Several other types of Hula dance are also practiced, with the melodic version that most people perceived as a stereotype of all Hula dance being the most common. In the latter form, the movements are smooth, undulating and graceful flowing, while in the older and more ancient forms, the movements may range from more disconnected to even sharply discrete. One type of the ancient dance is actually extremely vigorous and highly energized; in this, it appears more closely related to the very energy-charged Tahitian dances.

The Tutus at the surf shop were telling me (and my reading confirms this) that the most serious practitioners of the ancient forms of Hula are extremely dedicated to its study and 'culture'. A certain amount of asceticism is expected in its adherents and the comment that a truly skillful dancer is 'married to the dance' is apparently not as far from the truth as one might assume. When girls are accepted into the various schools of this traditional and most ancient style of the dance, they are expected to remain free of encumbering distractions…and this includes boys, after puberty exerts its inevitable influence on the growth & maturity processes.

Most commonly, casual tourists to the islands who have no deeper knowledge of ancient Hawaiian customs and culture leave with the standard *'Tourist Lu'au'* Hula stereotype fixed in their minds and this is usually further reduced in most male fantasies to images of scantily clad brown maidens swiveling their

333

hips suggestively to guitar music (hence the popular admonition to '...watch the Hula hands, not the lovely Hula hips'). Interestingly enough, the earliest traditional Hula was performed by dancers clad only in Ti-leaf skirts (the stereotypical 'grass skirt' is NOT indigenous to the Hawaiian Islands and has never been worn by anyone on them, dancing or not) and floral leis, with head and wrist wreaths of Maile leaves. Women were always bare-breasted, until the missionaries came along and banned the dance, being erotic, barbaric, and 'wicked'. When the Hula was much later resurrected by King David Kalaulua, dancers wore the hideously inappropriate full-flowing dresses that the blue-nosed Christians considered appropriate for them. Only much later (1940s) was the costume modified somewhat to include a halter top, although Ti-leaf skirts were reintroduced and remain the custom today (as they were in ancient times). As for today's frequently seen 'coconut bra', well...it's about as traditional as prohibition was in Bavaria.

While I have never had the pleasure of watching 'serious' Hula being performed (on the islands), I have seen enough mainland hula groups perform to keenly appreciate the sharp distinctions that differentiate formal hula from the far more casual 'tourist Hula' that most visitors to the islands take home with them in their recollections of island experiences. My interest in the traditional Hawaiian drum, the pahu, sparked this interest initially, but as with all things in Hawaii, even the most casual aspect of the culture leads inexorably onwards to other aspects of ancient Hawaii. One cannot be interested in the traditional Hawaiian drum without being forced to recognise and appreciate the religious motivations which preceded and accompanied its use.

In this latter context, there were 3 main types of indigenous Hawaiian drum instrument. These were the Pahu, a large drum made from the trunk of a tree (either breadfruit or Koa could be used, although coconut was by far more commonly employed), the *Pu-niu* (a small drum made from half a coconut shell and played while worn strapped to the thigh), and the *Double-Calabash* (the most traditional of the Hawaiian drums, made from a large figure-eight shaped gourd).

There were two types of Pahu drum used in the ancient times, the *'Pahu-Heiau'* or temple drum, that was considered sacred and was used exclusively by the priests at the heiau temples, and the *'Pahu-Hula'*, that was slightly smaller and was used to accompany the traditional chanting Hula dances. Today there are traditional Hawaiian craftsmen who continue to make these beautiful and unique instruments and I am always keen to seek them out wherever I can (they are always expensive, however!). Originally, sharkskin was used to cover the drum-head, but since most sharks are now considered semi-endangered (due to overfishing) and owing as well to the fact that they are regarded as one of the more sacred traditional Hawaiian marine creatures, calfskin is most commonly used for this purpose at present. Thus, sharkskin covered pahu are somewhat rare these days. There was that beauty I saw briefly, made by local Bill Pekuni, at the Moloka'i Coffee Plantation. It was quite large (about 20 inches in diameter and about three feet high) and was covered in sharkskin; the price was (gulp!) $1250. I am told (and my experiences confirm this) that that is not an unusually steep price for the genuine article (and that really was).

My efforts to meet with Bill and perhaps buy a pahu from him were frustrated by the usual difficulties involving cell-phones and his schedule, which keeps him out and away most of the day). Of course, with the possibility strongly evident of my wallet being substantially lightened by about twelve hundred and fifty small portraits of George Washington, it is undoubtedly best that our paths did not after all meet. I have several pahu at home, most of them really exceptional, although there is one being made for me on Kauai by a former Tahitian émigré on Kauai named *Tikrit* (I even sent him a 3x4 foot section of Tiger Shark belly to make the drum-head from, for my drum). Originally, the pahu was actually brought to Hawaii in its archetypal form from Tahiti (supposedly it accompanied the priest *Pa'ao* on his journey to the Hawaiian Islands in the 11th Century), so there are many similarities between drums made in French Polynesia and on Hawaii.

May 7th, 2005, (Saturday)

Spent some time this morning at the weekly Saturday art mart, browsing for some last-minute things and talking with some of the artists (Wally, Carlo, Sally, Richard, and luscious, lovely dark-skinned Locinda, from whom I bought another aloha shirt). Bought a small carved ironwood owl and shark from a local woman, who admitted that they had been carved in Arizona; I was impressed with her candor and that as much as anything else prompted me to acquire them. The owl, which is one of the important *amaukua* (family spirits), along with the Mano (shark), carries great significance in ancient Hawaiian culture. Thought to be the spirit of departed ancestors, it is regarded as having especially great *mana*.

As we talked, she shared two stories from her own family with me. One concerns her actual experience and another was that of an unusual uncle. She is presently building a home in the Hawaiian Homestead area of the island, near Ho'olehua, and told me that next to her is a lot that is vacant, but which has a large old Koa tree growing on it. When they were excavating the area, the construction crews disturbed an old burial place that seems to have contained the remains of 5 ancient islanders. The site was immediately recovered and left permanently vacant, out of respect for those whose remains are located there. At any rate, she said that despite the fact that there are many other trees in that area, there are no less than 5 owls that prefer that particular tree to perch in. She said it is very unusual in almost every consideration and the local surmise is that these owls are ancient aumakua that have some sort of a tie to those 5 ancient departed souls. This is a small indication of the symbolism that owls have for the Hawaiian peoples. It is curious to note that the owl is held in similarly high regard by a great many other ancient civilisations we would casually dismiss as being 'primitive'.

The other incident she told me about involved her uncle, who apparently was frequently in trouble with the law. This uncle, who was in and out of prison on various minor charges almost continually, once escaped from the county jail on Maui (this was back in the 50s, apparently) and swam across the Pailolo Channel to Moloka'i. She said he arrived safely on Moloka'i's shores after that prodigious swim to find the sheriff's men waiting for him and was promptly put back in jail. More amazing than the fact that he was able to swim this distance (without the aid of a flotation device) was the accompaniment of two sharks, one on either side of him without changing position, all the way from Maui to Moloka'i. The inference is that they were _mano aumakua_ (shark ancestral spirits), since for her family the shark has traditionally been regarded as a familiar protective spirit. She tells me that this is absolutely true and as such it falls into a category of similar occurrences that have been recorded over at least two centuries (mostly by oral history, before the development of a written Hawaiian language in 1835). I have no reason to disbelieve her and she struck me as a very fine, honest woman.

Just another of the many such stories that one encounters here as one gets to know more about the locals and the lives of their family members.

While at Sturgess' Cafe & Gallery earlier (trying to check in with Hawaiian Airlines for tomorrow's AM flight), I found that my timing was off, requiring a return after 1PM today (24 hours or less). The counter person, who is nice enough, is a bit ditzy (she's haole). She saw my coffee cup and saucer sitting on the table next to the computer's keyboard and asked me to move it away, cautioning me about the possible consequences of a spill near the computer. Of course, the coffee had long since been emptied from the cup and I never leave any left, anyway! Still the request. This suggests to me that many people are far more ritualistically motivated than situationally motivated in their actions. She must have clearly seen that there was no coffee in the cup, hence no possible hazard resulting from the spill of an empty cup. Funny, though.

Bought a beautiful little scene painted by Wally—the 'talented dabbler' (& art instructor at nearby Senior Center) I mentioned some while earlier. It's a volcanic pinnacle (*I'ao*) of some repute found on nearby Maui and although the style is still a bit on the naïve side, it is better than many of his things and I like it quite a lot. Very phallic in appearance, not that that has anything to do with my preference for it.

Just loaded up my huge duffle with the books and other stuff. My god but it weighs a ton. Must be a good 100 pounds if its 10, since I all but bought out the bookstores on the island. I sincerely hope this is not going to cause problems with the flight tomorrow, since I likely exceed max allowable weight limits by a goodly margin. We'll see when it comes 'weigh-in time' on the morrow. Might as well tie a rope to them, attach the other end to my leg and throw myself into the ocean. It's that kind of heavy-duty sea-anchor. Ah, books, *books*. They'll probably eventually bury me with a couple hundred of them.

More perfect long brown submarines...*ah.* Mother Nature must find Moloka'i extremely gratifying, although I do have a major complaint over the lack of apparent basic ergonometric understanding so many designers of human 'convenience fixtures' seem to demonstrate in designing those ceramic *wunderapparat.* Specifically annoying and aggravating is the failure many exhibit in the shape of the front part of the bowl. While women's needs are simple and straightforward (a simple circular opening and seat suffices admirably), men need an elongated bowl with sufficient depth in front to prevent what I must delicately term the *'dork dangle'* factor. That is, the tendency for the male 'member' to hang down in front while seated on that throne.

Now nothing...NOTHING...can be quite as annoying as having one's member dangle down into the bowl so that it contacts the fluid level therein—worse yet if it drops into a recently deposited brown item of excretory nature, as happened just a few moments ago. Is it asking too much, toiler designing engineers, to look down and check out the maximum possible extension capability of your own *whanger* if need be, so as to remember to allow for this critical factor?!

While I was in Sturgess' a while ago, confirming my flight out for tomorrow AM, Carlo dropped in and we had another little conversation while I was on the computer. Turns out Carlo was working in Arabian Gulf off-shore oilrigs back in the 60s, cleaning marine growths off the pilings. He apparently is familiar with *Basra* of that period and that was indeed the 'bad old days' there in terms of religious austerity. His recollections make my own encounters with the *Mutawa'an* (religious police) sound positively playful. Carlo mentioned that Locinda's pet name is 'Luc' (with a hard 'c', in the French manner) and that before she met the fellow she's presently married to, she 'led another life'. He mentioned some line of work like an exotic dancer and it doesn't take much imagination to see how, since she has a killer body *still* at the age of 54. Many Filipinas tend to be on the thin side anyway, but Luc is slender and tall, but well-built as well. *Woof.* Some combination of resources, since she's sharp and thoughtful also. Husband can be considered a lucky guy, I guess. Her 16 year old daughter is also nice looking but seems to have developed a healthy share of that adolescent 'attitude' pose that today's kids think is so cool.

This is just about the end of the log to date and I have to admit that my super-heavy luggage is quite worrisome (so much so that I am leaving about 20 books behind at Inocencia's place. I checked on the *Aloha Air* max baggage allowance and it states clearly 'No bags over 70 pounds accepted'; it's a no-brainer that *Hawaiian Air* has the same limit).

At this point it's entirely uncertain as to what the future holds in terms of us ever getting this wild idea of mine grounded in the reality of a living structure on our property. Late this afternoon I heard from Clyde (CJ's Ohana Gardening Svcs) with an estimate for the initial clean-up and thorough spraying with herbicide. He estimated $500 for the whole thing, including any follow-up that may be needed on a PRN basis, from month to month. We'll see how it goes. I gave his wife a cheque for the amount and will advise Cicada of the arrangement, so that she can keep her eyes on things for us to see that it all happens as promised. I have good feelings about Clyde, though. They are church-goers and apparently good Christians, so my rather off-the- chart feelings about religion notwithstanding, I'd rather deal with a Christian ka-naka than a haole missionary any day!

The sub total expenses for this wild 30-day sojourn on Mo-loka'i breaks down as follows:

1. Cost of 30 days rent in Inocencial's spare room, $300.

2. Cost of Budget car rental (Chevy Cavalier) for same period, $950.

3. Cost of RT airfare on Hawaiian Air (exclusive of any luggage penalties accrued), $695.00

4. Food (groceries) for same period, $400.

5. Miscellaneous expenses, $300.

6. Books, about $1000.

7. Gas for car, about $80.

8. Slop factor of whatever additional I've forgotten to include, probably $200.

9. Cost of gardening fees for lot clearance, $500.

Woof! I don't really want to add that all up, but I don't have to pretend that it's a chunk of change! This has been an expensive trip and a half. Fortunately, we have been able to defer the additional anticipated cost of about $9,000 for the water line & meter until a future date, but that's a load of money anyway. I'll have to work that total out per word, to see what this 400-page, 110,000+ word journal has really cost me, *hee-hee*.

Tomorrow at 0930 I fly off island for Honolulu. Probably won't get any sleep tonight, due to all the usual factors. As Suki would say, *"We'll see, we'll see..."* And speaking of my wife, lest anyone think that I do not appreciate all that she is and has done for me, I must say that she has to be a pretty special lady in order to have agreed to follow me down the jagged and irregular path of life I seem to have followed. Not many would do the same, I think, if they knew everything in advance that that formidable and thankless task has included over the 18 years of our marriage. On that note, this massive missive finally comes to an end (aren't you glad of that!?).

May 8th, 2005 (Sunday)

Jig-a-jig-jig and it's home again. Let's hope for good news on the baggage limit!

ADDENDA:

The luggage allowance limit for transpacific flights on all major carriers is 80 pounds. My luggage weighed 140 pounds. A substantial number of books were left behind at the Aloha Airlines counter, almost all dealing with Hawaiian culture, history, and ancient society. Needless to say, the counter persons at the Moloka'i terminal (Ho'olehua Airport) are now probably among the most well versed of their fellow islanders on all aspects of these subjects.]

POSTSCRIPT:

In 2015 we finally managed to sell our property on Moloka'i, after trying vainly to find a new owner on the island for many years. It was our incredibly bad luck to have purchased it just before the 2007 recession dropped the bottom out of all US real estate (including that on the HI). The selling price? About *half* what we originally paid for it. This remains perhaps the worst financial adventure I've ever engaged in and marked the total crash and burn of my last vestige of youthful, romantic idealism, but the experience was priceless as writing grist for the mill!

[I sense a sequel in the offing, but that will have to wait for a bit. Don't hold your breath!]

Other books by Kalikiano Kalei

'Santa Cruz Sargasso, Berkeley Fog' (poems), 2017, ISBN 978-0-692-93137-0

'Falling Off the Mountain' (poems), 2017, ISBN 978-0-692-83819-5

'Saunas and War Toys', 2017, ISBN 978-0-692-94059-4

'US Chemical and Biological Defense Respirators', 1998, ISBN 0-7643-0387-2

Contact: *AEOLIAN FLIGHTS PRESS*
5960 S. Land Park Drive, #256
Sacramento CA 95822-3313 USA

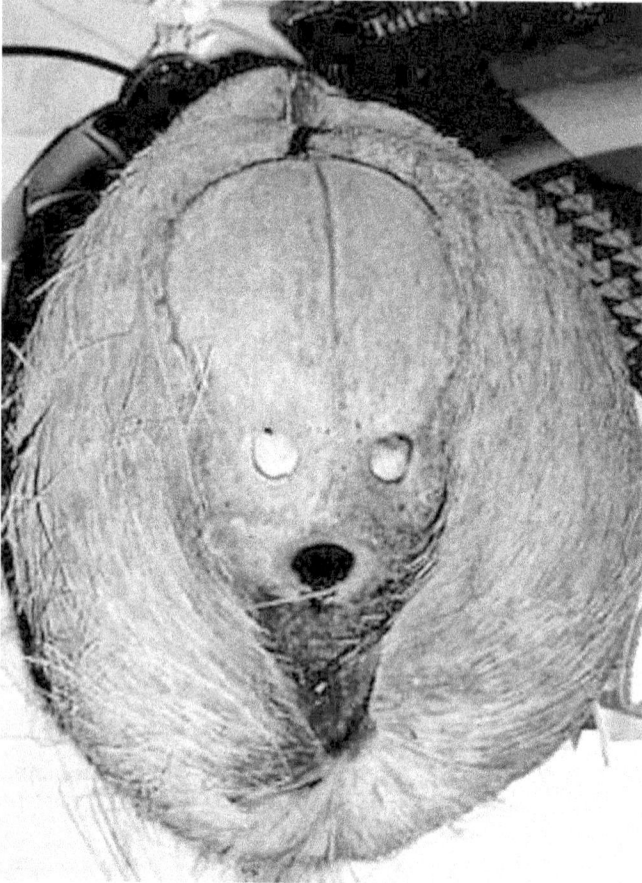

Ecce parvulum hominum

'Death is implicit in birth.'

-A.F. Schoenderheim

ABOUT THE AUTHOR

Kalikiano Kalei, who formerly possessed property on the island of Moloka'i, and who was partly brought up on Oahu, now resigns himself to being regarded as just another wild-eyed *haole malihini*, whose dreams (like those of so many other *haoles*) were dashed to bits on the island's great south coast reef. *Li'dat, eh!* He has written several other books, including *'Santa Cruz Sargasso, Berkeley Fog'* (poetry), *'Saunas and War Toys'*, and *'Falling Off the Mountain'* (also poetry).